Analogy for Middle Schools

© Okyere Bonna, MBA, MSEd

This book was printed in the United States of America.
To order additional copies of this book, contact:
OKAB
P.O. BOX 79029
Charlotte, NC 28271
Website: www.okyerebonna.com
Email: okab.publishing@gmail.com
Book id #: AFMS2 WB

ANALOGY

Analogy is an inference or an argument from one particular to another particular, where at least one of the premises or the conclusion is general. E.g.

1. Analogue or source	**The target**
Boy : gentleman.	*Girl : lady*
2. Analogue or source	**The target**
Instrument : orchestra	*Voice : choir*
3. Analogue or source	**The target**
Throw : baseball	*Kick : soccer ball*
4. Analogue or source	**The target**
Swimming pool : concrete	*Ocean : sand*
5. Analogue or source	**The target**
Taste : mouth	*Smell : nose*

In a narrower sense, analogy is the process of drawing a conclusion by applying rules of logic, statistics etc. The word analogy can also refer to the relation between the source and the target themselves, which is often, though not necessarily, a similarity, as in the biological notion of analogy. Two structures are said to be analogous if they perform the same or similar function by a similar mechanism but evolved separately.

Analogy plays a significant role in problem solving, decision making, perception, memory, creativity, emotion, explanation and communication. It has been argued that analogy is "the core of cognition" because it plays a significant role in communication, to wit: problem solving, decision making, cognitive process, perception, memory, creativity, emotion, and explanation. It expresses basic tasks such as the identification of places, objects and people. E.g.,

I. Holland : tulip ::	Mexico : **dahlia**
2. Barnacles : animals ::	Algae : **plants**
3. Galaxy : Milky Way ::	Planet : **Earth**

4. Ghana : Accra   USA : Washington D.C

The concepts of association, comparison, correspondence, mathematical and morphological homology, homomorphism, iconicity, isomorphism, metaphor, resemblance, and similarity are closely related to analogy. In cognitive linguistics, the notion of conceptual metaphor may be equivalent to that of analogy.

Analogy is important in ordinary language and common sense. Proverbs and idioms give many examples of its application. Analogy is also important in science, philosophy and the humanities.

ANALOGY PRACTICE EXERCISES

Study the relationship between the first set of words. Pick the word that completes the second pair with this same relationship.

1. _____ : yellow :: eyes : bloodshot

   Ⓐ pet   Ⓑ silver   Ⓒ girls   Ⓓ teeth

2. abdomen : _____ :: fuselage : wings

   Ⓐ jacket   Ⓑ mouth   Ⓒ eyes   Ⓓ arms

3. eagle : fly :: penguin : _____

   Ⓐ see   Ⓑ swim   Ⓒ crawl   Ⓓ walk

4. wings : _____ :: mandible : head

   Ⓐ abdomen   Ⓑ wings   Ⓒ thorax   Ⓓ exoskeleton

5. small : _____ :: large : tuba

   Ⓐ guitar   Ⓑ flute   Ⓒ foghorn   Ⓓ instrument

6. fish : fins :: bird : _____

   Ⓐ paddle   Ⓑ fly   Ⓒ beak   Ⓓ wings

7. red : purple :: yellow : _____

   Ⓐ black   Ⓑ green   Ⓒ ground   Ⓓ cut

8. apple : red :: pumpkin : _____

   Ⓐ orange   Ⓑ purple   Ⓒ knife   Ⓓ blue

9. termite : wood :: mosquito : _____

   Ⓐ honey   Ⓑ blood   Ⓒ aphids   Ⓓ water

10. adorable : _____ :: teensy : small

    Ⓐ friendly   Ⓑ helpful   Ⓒ funny   Ⓓ cute

11. Caucasian : white :: _____ : black

    Ⓐ Chinese   Ⓑ Spanish   Ⓒ Italian   Ⓓ African-American

12. orange : naranja :: yellow : _____

    Ⓐ rojo   Ⓑ gris   Ⓒ azul   Ⓓ amarillo

Study the relationship between the first set of words. Pick the word that completes the second pair with this same relationship.

1. Halloween : orange :: _____ : red

    (A) February   (B) Labor Day   (C) St. Patrick's Day   (D) Valentine's Day

2. skin : melanin :: _____ : chlorophyll

    (A) butterflies   (B) plants   (C) patients   (D) sand

3. termite : wood :: mosquito : _____

    (A) honey   (B) water   (C) aphids   (D) blood

4. entomology : insects :: botany : _____

    (A) mammals   (B) birds   (C) trees   (D) plants

5. wings : _____ :: mandible : head

    (A) abdomen   (B) thorax   (C) exoskeleton   (D) wings

6. _____ : yellow :: eyes : bloodshot

    (A) girls   (B) silver   (C) pet   (D) teeth

7. whippoorwill : bird :: wisteria : _____

    (A) insect   (B) mushroom   (C) snake   (D) plant

8. _____ : whale :: insect : fly

    (A) wings   (B) marsupial   (C) mammal   (D) frog

9. black : _____ :: color : crayon

    (A) pastels   (B) pencil   (C) clay   (D) school

10. legs : walk :: wings : _____

    (A) sing   (B) eat   (C) fly   (D) jump

11. termite : wood :: mosquito : _____

    (A) honey   (B) blood   (C) water   (D) aphids

12. produce : gardening :: honey : _____

    (A) pollen   (B) sugar   (C) nectar   (D) beekeeping

Study the relationship between the first set of words. Pick the word that completes the second pair with this same relationship.

1. Caucasian : white :: _____ : black

   Ⓐ Italian   Ⓑ Spanish   Ⓒ African-American   Ⓓ Chinese

2. abdomen : _____ :: fuselage : wings

   Ⓐ eyes   Ⓑ arms   Ⓒ jacket   Ⓓ mouth

3. cherries : red :: _____ : yellow

   Ⓐ yellow   Ⓑ bean   Ⓒ green   Ⓓ banana

4. wasp : fly :: cricket : _____

   Ⓐ jump   Ⓑ glide   Ⓒ write   Ⓓ speak

5. _____ : whale :: insect : fly

   Ⓐ mammal   Ⓑ marsupial   Ⓒ frog   Ⓓ wings

6. _____ : yellow :: eyes : bloodshot

   Ⓐ girls   Ⓑ silver   Ⓒ pet   Ⓓ teeth

7. legs : walk :: wings : _____

   Ⓐ sing   Ⓑ fly   Ⓒ jump   Ⓓ eat

8. Halloween : orange :: _____ : red

   Ⓐ Labor Day   Ⓑ St. Patrick's Day   Ⓒ February   Ⓓ Valentine's Day

9. termite : wood :: mosquito : _____

   Ⓐ aphids   Ⓑ blood   Ⓒ water   Ⓓ honey

10. skin : melanin :: _____ : chlorophyll

    Ⓐ butterflies   Ⓑ patients   Ⓒ plants   Ⓓ sand

11. yield : yellow :: stop : _____

    Ⓐ red   Ⓑ white   Ⓒ blue   Ⓓ green

12. produce : gardening :: honey : _____

    Ⓐ beekeeping   Ⓑ sugar   Ⓒ nectar   Ⓓ pollen

Study the relationship between the first set of words. Pick the word that completes the second pair with this same relationship.

1. sow : plant :: _____ : harvest

   (A) transplant   (B) scythe   (C) tend   (D) reap

2. good luck : red :: bad luck : _____

   (A) green   (B) yellow   (C) blue   (D) black

3. orange : naranja :: yellow : _____

   (A) amarillo   (B) gris   (C) azul   (D) rojo

4. fly : spider :: aphid : _____

   (A) cockroach   (B) bird   (C) dog   (D) lady bug

5. termite : white :: cricket : _____

   (A) red   (B) black   (C) yellow   (D) green

6. bird : _____ :: rabbit : hop

   (A) fly   (B) sing   (C) roll   (D) jump

7. _____ : slice :: orange : peel

   (A) book   (B) cake   (C) tool   (D) guard

8. elephant : large :: mouse : _____

   (A) goblin   (B) home   (C) small   (D) dirty

9. people : oxygen :: plants : _____

   (A) carbon dioxide   (B) food   (C) air   (D) green

10. librarian : _____ :: gardener : plants

    (A) shelves   (B) books   (C) quiet   (D) librarian

11. car : drive :: airplane : _____

    (A) wings   (B) pilot   (C) fly   (D) crash

12. _____ : fins :: birds : wings

    (A) rice   (B) turkey   (C) fish   (D) slug

Study the relationship between the first set of words. Pick the word that completes the second pair with this same relationship.

1. _____ : fly :: squirrels : climb

   (A) bats   (B) birds   (C) bees   (D) plants

2. _____ : horns :: pterodactyl : wings

   (A) giganotosaurus (B) velociraptor (C) triceratops (D) allosaurus

3. tapestry : fabric :: topiary : _____

   (A) doom   (B) mold   (C) plant   (D) mushroom

4. fish : _____ :: bird : wings

   (A) gills   (B) swim   (C) scales   (D) fins

5. bee : yellow :: ladybug : _____

   (A) red   (B) purple   (C) blue   (D) green

6. elephant : large :: mouse : _____

   (A) dirty   (B) goblin   (C) small   (D) home

7. flea : bite :: bee : _____

   (A) sting   (B) queen   (C) honey   (D) ant

8. ant : colony :: bee : _____

   (A) honey   (B) hive   (C) drone   (D) queen

9. carrot : _____ :: corn : yellow

   (A) purple   (B) white   (C) orange   (D) yellow

10. people : oxygen :: plants : _____

    (A) air   (B) green   (C) food   (D) carbon dioxide

11. good luck : red :: bad luck : _____

    (A) yellow   (B) blue   (C) green   (D) black

12. calcium : _____ :: vitamin C : oranges

    (A) milk   (B) bananas   (C) cows   (D) blood

Study the relationship between the first set of words. Pick the word that completes the second pair with this same relationship.

1. sow : plant :: _____ : harvest

   Ⓐ reap   Ⓑ tend   Ⓒ transplant   Ⓓ scythe

2. _____ : fins :: birds : wings

   Ⓐ turkey   Ⓑ rice   Ⓒ slug   Ⓓ fish

3. wings : thorax :: mandible : _____

   Ⓐ compound eye   Ⓑ abdomen   Ⓒ jaw   Ⓓ head

4. ant : colony :: bee : _____

   Ⓐ hive   Ⓑ drone   Ⓒ honey   Ⓓ queen

5. dragon : _____ :: snake : slither

   Ⓐ wings   Ⓑ fly   Ⓒ crash   Ⓓ pilot

6. snack : small :: _____ : large

   Ⓐ feast   Ⓑ forage   Ⓒ reap   Ⓓ catastrophe

7. _____ : fire truck :: yellow : school bus

   Ⓐ green   Ⓑ sharp   Ⓒ red   Ⓓ clear

8. Halloween : orange :: _____ : red

   Ⓐ Columbus Day   Ⓑ St. Patrick's Day   Ⓒ Labor Day   Ⓓ Valentine's Day

9. car : drive :: airplane : _____

   Ⓐ pilot   Ⓑ wings   Ⓒ crash   Ⓓ fly

10. flea : bite :: bee : _____

    Ⓐ sting   Ⓑ honey   Ⓒ queen   Ⓓ ant

11. _____ : fly :: squirrels : climb

    Ⓐ plants   Ⓑ bats   Ⓒ birds   bees

12. calcium : _____ :: vitamin C : oranges

    Ⓐ milk   Ⓑ bananas   Ⓒ cows   Ⓓ blood

Study the relationship between the first set of words. Pick the word that completes the second pair with this same relationship.

1. endangered : safe :: dull : _____

   (A) cold   (B) admired   (C) soft   (D) bright

2. sky : _____ :: clouds : white

   (A) blue   (B) red   (C) white   (D) yellow

3. pitch a ball : throw :: pitch a tent : _____

   (A) sleep   (B) pack   (C) carry   (D) set up

4. _____ : scrape :: arrange : place

   (A) beat   (B) graze   (C) herd   (D) horn

5. bag : carry :: scale : _____

   (A) weigh   (B) move   (C) pay   (D) lift

6. catch : grab :: toss : _____

   (A) stand   (B) backpack   (C) pitch   (D) carry

7. woman : mare :: _____ : trot

   (A) jog   (B) rode   (C) running   (D) horse

8. telephone book : people :: map : _____

   (A) numbers   (B) weather   (C) time   (D) places

9. brazen : bold :: valiant : _____

   (A) lucky   (B) brave   (C) angry   (D) confident

10. stop : halt :: go away : _____

   (A) come   (B) hush   (C) scat   (D) freeze

11. gloomy : dreary :: bright : _____

   (A) daylight   (B) sunny   (C) light   (D) cheery

12. grizzly bear : brown :: polar bear : _____

   (A) black   (B) candy   (C) white   (D) gray

Study the relationship between the first set of words. Pick the word that completes the second pair with this same relationship.

1. bee : sting :: lice : _____

   Ⓐ bite   Ⓑ head   Ⓒ crush   Ⓓ carry

2. bright : cheery :: gloomy : _____

   Ⓐ sunny   Ⓑ dark   Ⓒ daylight   Ⓓ light

3. whole : complete :: segment : _____

   Ⓐ hole   Ⓑ line   Ⓒ piece   Ⓓ area

4. bright : _____ :: gloomy : dreary

   Ⓐ daylight   Ⓑ light   Ⓒ cheery   Ⓓ sunny

5. dim : _____ :: moist : dry

   Ⓐ admired   Ⓑ soft   Ⓒ bright   Ⓓ cold

6. never : always :: _____ : all

   Ⓐ none   Ⓑ many   Ⓒ ecosystem   Ⓓ poaching

7. when : time :: where : _____

   Ⓐ clue   Ⓑ weapon   Ⓒ victim   Ⓓ scene

8. _____ : scrape :: arrange : place

   Ⓐ beat   Ⓑ herd   Ⓒ graze   Ⓓ horn

9. brazen : bold :: valiant : _____

   Ⓐ confident   Ⓑ brave   Ⓒ lucky   Ⓓ angry

10. gloomy : dreary :: bright : _____

    Ⓐ cheery   Ⓑ light   Ⓒ daylight   Ⓓ sunny

11. baseball : throw :: tennis ball : _____

    Ⓐ bounce   Ⓑ toss   Ⓒ roll   Ⓓ carry

12. compass rose : cardinal directions :: scale : _____

    Ⓐ location   Ⓑ streets   Ⓒ city center   Ⓓ distance

Study the relationship between the first set of words. Pick the word that completes the second pair with this same relationship.

1. bike : ride :: _____ : throw

    (A) triangle   (B) golf   (C) rectangle   (D) ball

2. when : time :: where : _____

    (A) victim   (B) clue   (C) scene   (D) weapon

3. prod : poke :: douse : _____

    (A) cradle   (B) carry   (C) perch   (D) drench

4. ride : bicycle :: drive : _____

    (A) car   (B) scooter   (C) tricycle   (D) skateboard

5. compass rose : cardinal directions :: scale : _____

    (A) city center   (B) distance   (C) streets   (D) location

6. Santa Claus' beard : white :: Rudolph's nose : _____

    (A) green   (B) yellow   (C) red   (D) black

7. woman : mare :: _____ : trot

    (A) rode   (B) running   (C) jog   (D) horse

8. bag : carry :: scale : _____

    (A) move   (B) weigh   (C) pay   (D) lift

9. whole : complete :: segment : _____

    (A) area   (B) piece   (C) hole   (D) line

10. bright : cheery :: gloomy : _____

    (A) daylight   (B) sunny   (C) light   (D) dark

11. bright : _____ :: gloomy : dreary

    (A) light   (B) daylight   (C) sunny   (D) cheery

12. rode : ride :: _____ : hide

    (A) hidden   (B) hode   (C) hid   (D) lied

Name _____   **LESSON 10**   Date _____

Study the relationship between the first set of words. Pick the word that completes the second pair with this same relationship.

1. bag : carry :: scale : _____

    Ⓐ weigh   Ⓑ lift   Ⓒ move   Ⓓ pay

2. baseball : throw :: tennis ball : _____

    Ⓐ roll   Ⓑ carry   Ⓒ bounce   Ⓓ toss

3. bike : ride :: ball : _____

    Ⓐ camp   Ⓑ kick   Ⓒ throw   Ⓓ hike

4. heroic : brave :: confident : _____

    Ⓐ powerless   Ⓑ sure   Ⓒ authority   Ⓓ friendly

5. never : always :: _____ : all

    Ⓐ poaching   Ⓑ many   Ⓒ none   Ⓓ ecosystem

6. telephone book : people :: _____ : places

    Ⓐ spaceship   Ⓑ boat   Ⓒ captain   Ⓓ map

7. russet : red :: albino : _____

    Ⓐ yellow   Ⓑ white   Ⓒ green   Ⓓ gray

8. car : seat :: horse : _____

    Ⓐ ride   Ⓑ saddle   Ⓒ cowboy   Ⓓ wagon

9. graze : scrape :: arrange : _____

    Ⓐ jab   Ⓑ place   Ⓒ cover   Ⓓ stare

10. light : white :: dark : _____

    Ⓐ green   Ⓑ yellow   Ⓒ black   Ⓓ red

11. prod : poke :: douse : _____

    Ⓐ cradle   Ⓑ perch   Ⓒ carry   Ⓓ drench

12. rode : ride :: hid : _____

    Ⓐ fire   Ⓑ hide   Ⓒ track   Ⓓ carry

Name _____   **LESSON 11**   Date _____

Study the relationship between the first set of words. Pick the word that completes the second pair with this same relationship.

1. catch : grab :: toss : _____

    Ⓐ carry   Ⓑ pitch   Ⓒ backpack   Ⓓ stand

2. prod : poke :: douse : _____

    Ⓐ drench   Ⓑ cradle   Ⓒ carry   Ⓓ perch

3. quake : shake :: hunker : _____

    Ⓐ retreat   Ⓑ squat   Ⓒ swim   Ⓓ carry

4. heroic : brave :: confident : _____

    Ⓐ powerless   Ⓑ authority   Ⓒ sure   Ⓓ friendly

5. woman : mare :: _____ : trot

    Ⓐ rode   Ⓑ running   Ⓒ jog   Ⓓ horse

6. negro : black :: blanco : _____

    Ⓐ candy   Ⓑ purple   Ⓒ black   Ⓓ white

7. pitch a ball : throw :: pitch a tent : _____

    Ⓐ sleep   Ⓑ set up   Ⓒ carry   Ⓓ pack

8. bag : carry :: scale : _____

    Ⓐ lift   Ⓑ move   Ⓒ weigh   Ⓓ pay

9. stop : halt :: go away : _____

    Ⓐ freeze   Ⓑ come   Ⓒ scat   Ⓓ hush

10. termite : _____ :: cricket : black

    Ⓐ yellow   Ⓑ white   Ⓒ brown   Ⓓ gray

11. graze : scrape :: arrange : _____

    Ⓐ jab   Ⓑ place   Ⓒ cover   Ⓓ stare

12. never : always :: _____ : all

    Ⓐ ecosystem   Ⓑ none   Ⓒ poaching   Ⓓ many

Name _____ **LESSON 12** Date _____

Study the relationship between the first set of words. Pick the word that completes the second pair with this same relationship.

1. russet : red :: albino : _____

   Ⓐ yellow   Ⓑ white   Ⓒ gray   Ⓓ green

2. rode : ride :: hid : _____

   Ⓐ track   Ⓑ hide   Ⓒ fire   Ⓓ carry

3. ride : bicycle :: _____ : car

   Ⓐ saddle   Ⓑ Distance   Ⓒ Direction   Ⓓ drive

4. car : seat :: horse : _____

   Ⓐ cowboy   Ⓑ saddle   Ⓒ ride   Ⓓ wagon

5. quake : shake :: hunker : _____

   Ⓐ carry   Ⓑ squat   Ⓒ swim   Ⓓ retreat

6. baseball : throw :: tennis ball : _____

   Ⓐ roll   Ⓑ toss   Ⓒ carry   Ⓓ bounce

7. intelligent : knowledgeable :: courageous : _____

   Ⓐ scared   Ⓑ brave   Ⓒ angry   Ⓓ lucky

8. catch : grab :: toss : _____

   Ⓐ pitch   Ⓑ stand   Ⓒ carry   Ⓓ backpack

9. light : white :: dark : _____

   Ⓐ black   Ⓑ red   Ⓒ green   Ⓓ yellow

10. graze : scrape :: arrange : _____

    Ⓐ jab   Ⓑ place   Ⓒ stare   Ⓓ cover

11. pitch a ball : throw :: pitch a tent : _____

    Ⓐ pack   Ⓑ set up   Ⓒ sleep   Ⓓ carry

12. scared : frightened :: courageous : _____

    Ⓐ funny   Ⓑ brave   Ⓒ friendly   Ⓓ kind

Name _____ **LESSON 13**   Date _____

Study the relationship between the first set of words. Pick the word that completes the second pair with this same relationship.

1. large : pile :: small : _____

    A trunk   **B** pool   **C** racket   **D** speck

2. diamond : hard :: _____ : soft

    A gem   **B** talc   **C** emerald   **D** rock

3. _____ : grape :: large : watermelon

    A cat   **B** small   **C** ugly   **D** home

4. soft : hard :: nice : _____

    A ice cream   **B** mean   **C** friendly   **D** mice

5. mansion : large :: cottage : _____

    A cross   **B** small   **C** nice   **D** dirty

6. January : _____ :: April : spring

    A gloves   **B** winter   **C** night   **D** fall

7. _____ : soft :: rough : gentle

    A hard   **B** clear   **C** wet   **D** cold

8. eighth : August :: third : _____

    A March   **B** May   **C** December   **D** October

9. beginning of the week : _____ :: beginning of the year : January

    A Friday   **B** Monday   **C** Sunday   **D** Wednesday

10. January : winter :: April : _____

    A fall   **B** May   **C** spring   **D** summer

11. March : St. Patrick's Day :: May : _____

    A Mother's Day   **B** Good Friday   **C** Easter   **D** Father's Day

12. largest : whales :: smallest : _____

    A plankton   **B** sea turtles   **C** dolphins   **D** sea urchins

Name _____ **LESSON 14** Date _____

Study the relationship between the first set of words. Pick the word that completes the second pair with this same relationship.

1. March : St. Patrick's Day :: May : _____

    Ⓐ Good Friday   Ⓑ Father's Day   Ⓒ Easter   Ⓓ Mother's Day

2. hard : soft :: wealthy : _____

    Ⓐ rich   Ⓑ lonely   Ⓒ kind   Ⓓ poor

3. St. Valentine's Day : _____ :: St. Patrick's Day : March

    Ⓐ March   Ⓑ February   Ⓒ January   Ⓓ April

4. smallest : _____ :: largest : half-dollar

    Ⓐ 50 cent piece   Ⓑ nickel   Ⓒ dime   Ⓓ dollar

5. first : last :: beginning : _____

    Ⓐ stop   Ⓑ end   Ⓒ start   Ⓓ over

6. diamond : hard :: _____ : soft

    Ⓐ rock   Ⓑ gem   Ⓒ emerald   Ⓓ talc

7. large : pile :: small : _____

    Ⓐ trunk   Ⓑ pool   Ⓒ racket   Ⓓ speck

8. start : home :: finish : _____

    Ⓐ begin   Ⓑ caps lock   Ⓒ end   Ⓓ delete

9. _____ : grape :: large : watermelon

    Ⓐ ugly   Ⓑ home   Ⓒ cat   Ⓓ small

10. beginning : start :: end : _____

    Ⓐ closed   Ⓑ stop   Ⓒ exit   Ⓓ finish

11. mansion : large :: cottage : _____

    Ⓐ nice   Ⓑ dirty   Ⓒ cross   Ⓓ small

12. to walk in step with others : _____ :: to keep in one place : hold

    Ⓐ October   Ⓑ January   Ⓒ June   Ⓓ march

19

Name _____   **LESSON 15**   Date _____

Study the relationship between the first set of words. Pick the word that completes the second pair with this same relationship.

1. _____ : spring :: September : autumn

    Ⓐ December   Ⓑ April   Ⓒ March   Ⓓ June

2. hard : soft :: wealthy : _____

    Ⓐ kind   Ⓑ poor   Ⓒ lonely   Ⓓ rich

3. smallest : _____ :: largest : half-dollar

    Ⓐ dime   Ⓑ 50 cent piece   Ⓒ nickel   Ⓓ dollar

4. St. Valentine's Day : _____ :: St. Patrick's Day : March

    Ⓐ February   Ⓑ January   Ⓒ April   Ⓓ March

5. beginning : start :: end : _____

    Ⓐ exit   Ⓑ finish   Ⓒ closed   Ⓓ stop

6. largest : whales :: smallest : _____

    Ⓐ sea urchins   Ⓑ sea turtles   Ⓒ plankton   Ⓓ dolphins

7. mansion : large :: cottage : _____

    Ⓐ dirty   Ⓑ small   Ⓒ cross   Ⓓ nice

8. January : winter :: August : _____

    Ⓐ vacation   Ⓑ summer   Ⓒ scooter   Ⓓ fall

9. January : _____ :: April : spring

    Ⓐ night   Ⓑ winter   Ⓒ gloves   Ⓓ fall

10. to walk in step with others : _____ :: to keep in one place : hold

    Ⓐ march   Ⓑ January   Ⓒ June   Ⓓ October

11. start : home :: finish : _____

    Ⓐ caps lock   Ⓑ end   Ⓒ begin   Ⓓ delete

12. _____ : soft :: ice : hard

    Ⓐ snow   Ⓑ mud   Ⓒ wind   Ⓓ water

Name _____ **LESSON 16** Date _____

Study the relationship between the first set of words. Pick the word that completes the second pair with this same relationship.

1. eighth : August :: third : _____

   Ⓐ October   Ⓑ May   Ⓒ June   Ⓓ March

2. eighth : seventh :: second : _____

   Ⓐ third   Ⓑ first   Ⓒ last   Ⓓ two

3. cease : stop :: inquire : _____

   Ⓐ brood   Ⓑ ask   Ⓒ argue   Ⓓ release

4. bird : chirp :: lion : _____

   Ⓐ eat   Ⓑ cub   Ⓒ den   Ⓓ roar

5. exhausted : tired :: famished : _____

   Ⓐ alert   Ⓑ thirsty   Ⓒ hungry   Ⓓ lost

6. sand : sand crabs :: dirt : _____

   Ⓐ humans   Ⓑ bees   Ⓒ worms   Ⓓ fish

7. gnu : chiropractor :: knight : _____

   Ⓐ chasm   Ⓑ night   Ⓒ knew   Ⓓ chirp

8. man : shirt :: woman : _____

   Ⓐ shorts   Ⓑ blouse   Ⓒ cap   Ⓓ boots

9. third : Earth :: fifth : _____

   Ⓐ Saturn   Ⓑ Jupiter   Ⓒ Mars   Ⓓ Venus

10. pants : legs :: _____ : arms

   Ⓐ shirt   Ⓑ tools   Ⓒ paper   Ⓓ flowers

11. _____ : question :: define : explain

   Ⓐ mutter   Ⓑ assign   Ⓒ argue   Ⓓ ask

12. food : nourish :: water : _____

   Ⓐ thirsty   Ⓑ urine   Ⓒ kidneys   Ⓓ hydrate

Name _____ **LESSON 17** Date _____

Study the relationship between the first set of words. Pick the word that completes the second pair with this same relationship.

1. bird : chirp :: lion : _____

   ⒜ den   ⒝ cub   ⒞ roar   ⒟ eat

2. bamboo : wood :: clay : _____

   ⒜ dirt   ⒝ house   ⒞ stone   ⒟ spice

3. food : nourish :: water : _____

   ⒜ kidneys   ⒝ thirsty   ⒞ urine   ⒟ hydrate

4. _____ : "Please?" :: receive : "Thank you."

   ⒜ ask   ⒝ assign   ⒞ demand   ⒟ brood

5. gnu : chiropractor :: knight : _____

   ⒜ chirp   ⒝ knew   ⒞ chasm   ⒟ night

6. eat : hungry :: go to sleep : _____

   ⒜ angry   ⒝ tired   ⒞ thirsty   ⒟ dirty

7. sand : sand crabs :: dirt : _____

   ⒜ humans   ⒝ bees   ⒞ worms   ⒟ fish

8. eighth : August :: third : _____

   ⒜ June   ⒝ March   ⒞ May   ⒟ October

9. negotiate : deal :: solicit : _____

   ⒜ ask   ⒝ demand   ⒞ assign   ⒟ release

10. _____ : question :: define : explain

    ⒜ argue   ⒝ mutter   ⒞ ask   ⒟ assign

11. mound : dirt :: dune : _____

    ⒜ maple leaves ⒝ sand   ⒞ diving board ⒟ fish

12. worm : _____ :: bee : flower

    ⒜ stone   ⒝ spice   ⒞ air   ⒟ dirt

Study the relationship between the first set of words. Pick the word that completes the second pair with this same relationship.

1. bamboo : wood :: clay : _____

    Ⓐ spice   Ⓑ stone   Ⓒ dirt   Ⓓ house

2. eat : hungry :: go to sleep : _____

    Ⓐ tired   Ⓑ angry   Ⓒ dirty   Ⓓ thirsty

3. food : nourish :: water : _____

    Ⓐ hydrate   Ⓑ kidneys   Ⓒ thirsty   Ⓓ urine

4. shirt : clothing :: quilt : _____

    Ⓐ bedding   Ⓑ book   Ⓒ furniture   Ⓓ tool

5. sand : sand crabs :: dirt : _____

    Ⓐ bees   Ⓑ worms   Ⓒ fish   Ⓓ humans

6. worm : _____ :: bee : flower

    Ⓐ stone   Ⓑ dirt   Ⓒ spice   Ⓓ air

7. bird : chirp :: lion : _____

    Ⓐ roar   Ⓑ den   Ⓒ eat   Ⓓ cub

8. blouse : _____ :: loafers : shoes

    Ⓐ tools   Ⓑ flowers   Ⓒ paper   Ⓓ shirt

9. man : shirt :: woman : _____

    Ⓐ boots   Ⓑ shorts   Ⓒ blouse   Ⓓ cap

10. eighth : August :: third : _____

    Ⓐ October   Ⓑ May   Ⓒ March   Ⓓ June

11. cease : stop :: inquire : _____

    Ⓐ release   Ⓑ brood   Ⓒ argue   Ⓓ ask

12. negotiate : deal :: solicit : _____

    Ⓐ assign   Ⓑ demand   Ⓒ ask   Ⓓ release

Study the relationship between the first set of words. Pick the word that completes the second pair with this same relationship.

1. cynical : distrusting :: cryptic : _____

    Ⓐ trusting   Ⓑ puzzling   Ⓒ simple   Ⓓ controlling

2. literally : actually :: gingerly : _____

    Ⓐ cautiously   Ⓑ desperately   Ⓒ sweetly   Ⓓ sharply

3. a quickly spreading disease : epidemic :: a collection of objects : _____

    Ⓐ priority   Ⓑ trove   Ⓒ etude   Ⓓ barrage

4. amplify : intensify :: differentiate : _____

    Ⓐ encourage   Ⓑ lead   Ⓒ adapt   Ⓓ distinguish

5. always : never :: frequent : _____

    Ⓐ seldom   Ⓑ circumspectly   Ⓒ reliable   Ⓓ often

6. atrocious : dreadful :: intrepid : _____

    Ⓐ fearless   Ⓑ distinct   Ⓒ prominent   Ⓓ wonderful

7. book : read :: puzzle : _____

    Ⓐ run   Ⓑ hear   Ⓒ think   Ⓓ sing

8. ideal : inadequate :: ecstatic : _____

    Ⓐ obsessive   Ⓑ decent   Ⓒ woeful   Ⓓ happy

9. winding : meandering :: something that stands out : _____

    Ⓐ bizarre   Ⓑ prominent   Ⓒ demented   Ⓓ lurking

10. friendly and welcoming : hospitable :: scheming : _____

    Ⓐ conniving   Ⓑ condescending   Ⓒ prominent   Ⓓ salacious

11. to move in a circular pattern : circulate :: to work together : _____

    Ⓐ collaborate   Ⓑ justify   Ⓒ enthrall   Ⓓ bereave

12. to end : terminate :: to start : _____

    Ⓐ hesitate   Ⓑ ruminate   Ⓒ radiate   Ⓓ initiate

Study the relationship between the first set of words. Pick the word that completes the second pair with this same relationship.

1. to sparkle : glisten :: to hold steady : _____

   (A) focus   (B) generate   (C) stabilize   (D) initiate

2. teacher : instructor :: custodian : _____

   (A) principal   (B) librarian   (C) student   (D) janitor

3. certain : _____ :: prominent : imperceptible

   (A) determined   (B) nimble   (C) doubtful   (D) confident

4. cynical : distrusting :: cryptic : _____

   (A) controlling   (B) simple   (C) puzzling   (D) trusting

5. argue : debate :: bargain : _____

   (A) negotiate   (B) alleviate   (C) delegate   (D) initiate

6. to encourage : motivate :: to require : _____

   (A) distinguish   (B) demand   (C) request   (D) enlist

7. pathetic : pitiful :: barbaric : _____

   (A) angry   (B) uncivilized   (C) dirty   (D) intelligent

8. puzzled : confused :: astonished : _____

   (A) amazed   (B) relieved   (C) saddened   (D) surprised

9. a quickly spreading disease : epidemic :: a collection of objects : _____

   (A) trove   (B) barrage   (C) etude   (D) priority

10. literally : actually :: gingerly : _____

    (A) sweetly   (B) sharply   (C) desperately   (D) cautiously

11. winding : meandering :: something that stands out : _____

    (A) bizarre   (B) demented   (C) prominent   (D) lurking

12. illustrious : distinguished :: avid : _____

    (A) stubborn   (B) enthusiastic   (C) intentional   (D) condemned

Study the relationship between the first set of words. Pick the word that completes the second pair with this same relationship.

1. laborious : difficult :: phenomenal : _____

    Ⓐ amazing   Ⓑ ridiculous   Ⓒ disgusting   Ⓓ sad

2. tell a joke : laughter :: frighten : _____

    Ⓐ scream   Ⓑ whisper   Ⓒ sleep   Ⓓ ghost

3. extravagant : _____ :: preposterous : absurd

    Ⓐ luxurious   Ⓑ quiet   Ⓒ generous   Ⓓ famous

4. tell a joke : laughter :: frighten : _____

    Ⓐ peaceful   Ⓑ journey   Ⓒ Halloween   Ⓓ scream

5. conventional : typical :: _____ : creative

    Ⓐ conceptual   Ⓑ traditional   Ⓒ entrepreneurial   Ⓓ innovative

6. revelry : celebration :: crockery : _____

    Ⓐ embarrassment   Ⓑ trickery   Ⓒ dishes   Ⓓ relaxation

7. recent : new :: _____ : old

    Ⓐ broken   Ⓑ ancient   Ⓒ same   Ⓓ different

8. conventional : typical :: _____ : creative

    Ⓐ traditional   Ⓑ entrepreneurial   Ⓒ conceptual   Ⓓ innovative

9. pester : bother :: gloat : _____

    Ⓐ help   Ⓑ ignore   Ⓒ tease   Ⓓ brag

10. _____ : boast :: brood : mope

    Ⓐ ignore   Ⓑ tease   Ⓒ brag   Ⓓ help

11. earnest : _____ :: preposterous : absurd

    Ⓐ harmful   Ⓑ courageous   Ⓒ vague   Ⓓ serious

12. reassure : calm :: frighten : _____

    Ⓐ flatter   Ⓑ horrible   Ⓒ ghost   Ⓓ terrify

Name _____   **LESSON 22**   Date _____

Study the relationship between the first set of words. Pick the word that completes the second pair with this same relationship.

1. tell a joke : laughter :: frighten : _____

    A sleep   **B** whisper   **C** scream   **D** ghost

2. evade : escape :: topple : _____

    A punish   **B** shock   **C** talk   **D** fall

3. question : answer :: solution : _____

    A solution   **B** error   **C** clue   **D** thinking

4. ridiculous : absurd :: horrid : _____

    A ghastly   **B** putrid   **C** venerable   **D** brazen

5. vehicle : _____ :: pedestrian : person traveling on foot

    A road   **B** tire   **C** automobile   **D** boat

6. typical : conventional :: creative : _____

    A traditional   **B** innovative   **C** entrepreneurial   **D** conceptual

7. earnest : _____ :: preposterous : absurd

    A harmful   **B** vague   **C** courageous   **D** serious

8. ridiculous : absurd :: adorable : _____

    A helpful   **B** cute   **C** funny   **D** friendly

9. pester : bother :: gloat : _____

    A ignore   **B** help   **C** tease   **D** brag

10. modest : bragging :: uninterested : _____

    A ogle   **B** mesmerized   **C** modest   **D** reflective

11. street : driver :: sidewalk : _____

    A walking   **B** pedestrian   **C** traffic   **D** concrete

12. tell a joke : laughter :: frighten : _____

    A journey   **B** peaceful   **C** Halloween   **D** scream

27

Study the relationship between the first set of words. Pick the word that completes the second pair with this same relationship.

1. vehicle : _____ :: pedestrian : person traveling on foot

    A boat   **B** automobile   **C** tire   **D** road

2. approve : yes :: veto : _____

    A no   **B** review   **C** elect   **D** campaign

3. lead : govern :: promise : _____

    A campaign   **B** oath   **C** veto   **D** elect

4. duel : fight :: slay : _____

    A nick   **B** frighten   **C** kill   **D** truce

5. reassure : calm :: frighten : _____

    A flatter   **B** terrify   **C** ghost   **D** horrible

6. evade : escape :: topple : _____

    A shock   **B** punish   **C** fall   **D** talk

7. sentimental : emotional :: optimistic : _____

    A hopeful   **B** humorous   **C** ridiculous   **D** negative

8. endure : sustain :: overcome : _____

    A oppress   **B** dream   **C** equalize   **D** triumph

9. enlisted : signed up :: killed or wounded : _____

    A strategy   **B** casualty   **C** promoted   **D** discharged

10. rule : regulation :: advisory : _____

    A law   **B** apology   **C** request   **D** warning

11. impolite : brusque :: ridiculous : _____

    A deceitful   **B** boorish   **C** conniving   **D** absurd

12. brave : cowardly :: careful : _____

    A cautious   **B** bold   **C** reckless   **D** deliberate

Name _____   **LESSON 24**   Date _____

Study the relationship between the first set of words. Pick the word that completes the second pair with this same relationship.

1. factory : work :: tenement house : _____

    Ⓐ worship   Ⓑ live   Ⓒ learn   Ⓓ shop

2. letters : words :: _____ : music

    Ⓐ notes   Ⓑ sing   Ⓒ numbers   Ⓓ whistle

3. essential : _____ :: occupied : busy

    Ⓐ together   Ⓑ dangerous   Ⓒ indulgent   Ⓓ important

4. common : rare :: vague : _____

    Ⓐ distinct   Ⓑ phony   Ⓒ important   Ⓓ true

5. thirst : _____ :: appetite : eat

    Ⓐ napkin   Ⓑ quench   Ⓒ drink   Ⓓ table

6. endangered : few :: extinct : _____

    Ⓐ none   Ⓑ poaching   Ⓒ ecosystem   Ⓓ many

7. numerous : few :: gigantic : _____

    Ⓐ tiny   Ⓑ many   Ⓒ huge   Ⓓ giant

8. risk : _____ :: serious : important

    Ⓐ destiny   Ⓑ announcement   Ⓒ danger   Ⓓ storage

9. isolated : alone :: significant : _____

    Ⓐ together   Ⓑ indulgent   Ⓒ important   Ⓓ overcome

10. many : plentiful :: few : _____

    Ⓐ none   Ⓑ taunt   Ⓒ lazy   Ⓓ scarce

11. dolphin : swim :: bat : _____

    Ⓐ fly   Ⓑ walk   Ⓒ jump   Ⓓ run

12. _____ : west :: north : south

    Ⓐ east   Ⓑ city   Ⓒ north   Ⓓ Italy

Name _____   **LESSON 25**   Date _____

**Study the relationship between the first set of words. Pick the word that completes the
second pair with this same relationship.**

1. isolated : alone :: significant : _____

    (A) important   (B) together   (C) overcome   (D) indulgent

2. wasp : fly :: cricket : _____

    (A) write   (B) jump   (C) glide   (D) speak

3. letters : word :: sentence : _____

    (A) statement   (B) paragaph   (C) noun   (D) period

4. peculiar : odd :: unadulterated : _____

    (A) pure   (B) alone   (C) childish   (D) important

5. anxious : worried :: entitled : _____

    (A) hardworking   (B) deserving   (C) important   (D) eager

6. _____ : sip :: eat : nibble

    (A) parched   (B) napkin   (C) drink   (D) table

7. cross : annoyed :: pompous : _____

    (A) important   (B) sympathetic   (C) humble   (D) arrogant

8. increase : more :: decrease : _____

    (A) add   (B) crease   (C) decease   (D) less

9. letters : words :: _____ : music

    (A) whistle   (B) numbers   (C) notes   (D) sing

10. legible : _____ :: edible : eat

    (A) understood   (B) felt   (C) read   (D) seen

11. _____ : asset :: labor : work

    (A) state   (B) country   (C) capital   (D) mountain

12. factory : work :: tenement house : _____

    (A) learn   (B) shop   (C) worship   (D) live

Study the relationship between the first set of words. Pick the word that completes the second pair with this same relationship.

1. many : abundant :: none : _____

    (A) abundant   (B) extinct   (C) epoch   (D) fossils

2. eat : food :: recycle : _____

    (A) waste   (B) drink   (C) reuse   (D) meat

3. deafening : loud :: urgent : _____

    (A) mysterious   (B) dangerous   (C) important   (D) heavy

4. graze : eat :: stampede : _____

    (A) sleep   (B) fight   (C) gather   (D) run

5. letters : words :: _____ : music

    (A) notes   (B) sing   (C) numbers   (D) whistle

6. risk : _____ :: serious : important

    (A) danger   (B) storage   (C) destiny   (D) announcement

7. eagle : fly :: penguin : _____

    (A) swim   (B) dig   (C) crawl   (D) waves

8. thirst : _____ :: appetite : eat

    (A) quench   (B) table   (C) drink   (D) napkin

9. school : work :: vacation : _____

    (A) read   (B) eat   (C) summer   (D) play

10. letters : words :: pictures : _____

    (A) sign language   (B) papyrus   (C) hieroglyphics   (D) origami

11. many : plentiful :: few : _____

    (A) scarce   (B) lazy   (C) none   (D) taunt

12. sturdy : strong :: crucial : _____

    (A) important   (B) secret   (C) dangerous   (D) planned

Study the relationship between the first set of words. Pick the word that completes the second pair with this same relationship.

1. book : read :: puzzle : _____

   Ⓐ sing   Ⓑ run   Ⓒ hear   Ⓓ think

2. always : never :: frequent : _____

   Ⓐ seldom   Ⓑ reliable   Ⓒ circumspectly   Ⓓ often

3. illustrious : distinguished :: avid : _____

   Ⓐ enthusiastic   Ⓑ intentional   Ⓒ stubborn   Ⓓ condemned

4. regular : consistent :: occasional : _____

   Ⓐ frequent   Ⓑ seldom   Ⓒ intermittent   Ⓓ constant

5. literally : actually :: gingerly : _____

   Ⓐ cautiously   Ⓑ desperately   Ⓒ sharply   Ⓓ sweetly

6. brief : long :: rare : _____

   Ⓐ object   Ⓑ few   Ⓒ frequent   Ⓓ sanitation

7. cynical : distrusting :: cryptic : _____

   Ⓐ controlling   Ⓑ simple   Ⓒ puzzling   Ⓓ trusting

8. confused : puzzled :: aghast : _____

   Ⓐ happy   Ⓑ angry   Ⓒ sad   Ⓓ shocked

9. soothe : calm :: deprive : _____

   Ⓐ swig   Ⓑ distinguish   Ⓒ leave without   Ⓓ bribe

10. puzzled : confused :: astonished : _____

    Ⓐ amazed   Ⓑ surprised   Ⓒ relieved   Ⓓ saddened

11. to sparkle : glisten :: to hold steady : _____

    Ⓐ initiate   Ⓑ generate   Ⓒ focus   Ⓓ stabilize

12. winding : meandering :: something that stands out : _____

    Ⓐ lurking   Ⓑ prominent   Ⓒ bizarre   Ⓓ demented

Study the relationship between the first set of words. Pick the word that completes the second pair with this same relationship.

1. tribulations : hardships :: ramifications : _____

   Ⓐ accidents   Ⓑ agreements   Ⓒ consequences   Ⓓ reviews

2. illustrious : distinguished :: avid : _____

   Ⓐ boring   Ⓑ intentional   Ⓒ angry   Ⓓ enthusiastic

3. cheat : deceit :: rebuke : _____

   Ⓐ apart   Ⓑ mediate   Ⓒ reprimand   Ⓓ criminal

4. disapproval : rebuke :: approval : _____

   Ⓐ empathy   Ⓑ affirmation   Ⓒ insult   Ⓓ consolation

5. shame : embarrassment :: confusion : _____

   Ⓐ rebuke   Ⓑ perplexity   Ⓒ discord   Ⓓ veracity

6. sad : melancholy :: happy : _____

   Ⓐ coy   Ⓑ aghast   Ⓒ sullen   Ⓓ jovial

7. cheat : _____ :: rebuke : reprimand

   Ⓐ character   Ⓑ deceit   Ⓒ vengeance   Ⓓ wrath

8. topple : fall :: cease : _____

   Ⓐ sprint   Ⓑ stop   Ⓒ gnaw   Ⓓ escape

9. melancholy : sad :: boisterous : _____

   Ⓐ silent   Ⓑ dreamlike   Ⓒ loud   Ⓓ happy

10. rile : _____ :: abhor : despise

   Ⓐ anger   Ⓑ irritate   Ⓒ make messy   Ⓓ teach

11. tribute : honor :: memorial : _____

   Ⓐ rebuke   Ⓑ remember   Ⓒ control   Ⓓ summarize

12. a loud noise : clamor :: cold and damp : _____

   Ⓐ clambering   Ⓑ candor   Ⓒ calamity   Ⓓ clammy

Name _____   **LESSON 29**   Date _____

Study the relationship between the first set of words. Pick the word that completes the second pair with this same relationship.

1. awareness : knowledge :: responsibility : _____

    Ⓐ altruism   Ⓑ diffidence   Ⓒ duty   Ⓓ consequence

2. awareness : knowledge :: responsibility : _____

    Ⓐ duty   Ⓑ consequence   Ⓒ honor   Ⓓ generosity

3. vanish : disappear :: deteriorate : _____

    Ⓐ worsen   Ⓑ improve   Ⓒ save   Ⓓ explode

4. despised : hated :: flummoxed : _____

    Ⓐ retired   Ⓑ protected   Ⓒ distracted   Ⓓ confused

5. melancholy : _____ :: earnest : serious

    Ⓐ sad   Ⓑ fast   Ⓒ short   Ⓓ courteous

6. melancholy : sad :: boisterous : _____

    Ⓐ dreamlike   Ⓑ loud   Ⓒ silent   Ⓓ happy

7. cheat : deceit :: rebuke : _____

    Ⓐ mediate   Ⓑ reprimand   Ⓒ apart   Ⓓ criminal

8. illustrious : distinguished :: avid : _____

    Ⓐ angry   Ⓑ enthusiastic   Ⓒ intentional   Ⓓ boring

9. to take a person against their will : abduct :: to take control of a vehicle without permission : _____

    Ⓐ kidnap   Ⓑ steal   Ⓒ murder   Ⓓ hijack

10. a loud noise : clamor :: cold and damp : _____

    Ⓐ calamity   Ⓑ clammy   Ⓒ candor   Ⓓ clambering

11. rile : _____ :: abhor : despise

    Ⓐ anger   Ⓑ teach   Ⓒ make messy   Ⓓ irritate

12. shame : embarrassment :: confusion : _____

    Ⓐ veracity   Ⓑ perplexity   Ⓒ rebuke   Ⓓ discord

Name _____ **LESSON 30** Date _____

Study the relationship between the first set of words. Pick the word that completes the second pair with this same relationship.

1. illustrious : distinguished :: avid : _____

   (A) angry   (B) intentional   (C) boring   (D) enthusiastic

2. boisterous : noisy :: melancholy : _____

   (A) sad   (B) dreamlike   (C) silent   (D) happy

3. disapproval : rebuke :: approval : _____

   (A) empathy   (B) consolation   (C) insult   (D) affirmation

4. tribute : honor :: memorial : _____

   (A) rebuke   (B) remember   (C) summarize   (D) control

5. sad : melancholy :: happy : _____

   (A) coy   (B) sullen   (C) jovial   (D) aghast

6. despised : hated :: flummoxed : _____

   (A) distracted   (B) retired   (C) confused   (D) protected

7. cheat : _____ :: rebuke : reprimand

   (A) wrath   (B) vengeance   (C) character   (D) deceit

8. to take a person against their will : abduct :: to take control of a vehicle without permission : _____

   (A) hijack   (B) steal   (C) murder   (D) kidnap

9. topple : fall :: cease : _____

   (A) escape   (B) sprint   (C) stop   (D) gnaw

10. jostle : shake :: gnaw : _____

    (A) pop   (B) view   (C) chew   (D) carry

11. unnoticeable : inconspicuous :: joyful : _____

    (A) righteous   (B) blissful   (C) melancholy   (D) corrigible

12. shame : embarrassment :: confusion : _____

    (A) perplexity   (B) rebuke   (C) discord   (D) veracity

Study the relationship between the first set of words. Pick the word that completes the second pair with this same relationship.

1. known : _____ :: unknown : mystery

    (A) speech   (B) lie   (C) fact   (D) book

2. romance : love story :: _____ : "who-dun-it"

    (A) discovery   (B) mystery   (C) false   (D) solution

3. resolve : determine :: embed : _____

    (A) guess   (B) incorporate   (C) sleep   (D) slide

4. _____ : unexplained :: secret : unknown

    (A) clue   (B) mystery   (C) suspicion   (D) false

5. meant to be : fate :: good fortune : _____

    (A) serendipity   (B) doom   (C) happenchance   (D) destiny

6. known : familiar :: unknown : _____

    (A) recognizable   (B) foreign   (C) ship   (D) definite

7. _____ : plays :: Agatha Christie : mysteries

    (A) Rene Descartes   (B) William Shakespeare   (C) Francis Bacon   (D) Petrarch

8. emphasis : significance :: supervision : _____

    (A) ingenuity   (B) management   (C) disregard   (D) encouragement

9. estimation : guess :: significance : _____

    (A) dependability   (B) knowledge   (C) importance   (D) precision

10. necessity : poverty :: frivolity : _____

    (A) luxury   (B) charity   (C) disparity   (D) industry

11. torment : disturb :: replenish : _____

    (A) discuss   (B) lurk   (C) refill   (D) regret

12. divine : godly :: miraculous : _____

    (A) charitable   (B) eternal   (C) phenomenal   (D) ordinary

Study the relationship between the first set of words. Pick the word that completes the second pair with this same relationship.

1. glorious : wonderful :: weary : _____

   Ⓐ nightgown   Ⓑ tired   Ⓒ lonely   Ⓓ terrible

2. problem : conundrum :: mystery : _____

   Ⓐ certain   Ⓑ meticulous   Ⓒ dogmatic   Ⓓ enigma

3. _____ : unexplained :: secret : unknown

   Ⓐ mystery   Ⓑ clue   Ⓒ suspicion   Ⓓ false

4. meant to be : fate :: good fortune : _____

   Ⓐ serendipity   Ⓑ happenchance   Ⓒ destiny   Ⓓ doom

5. aware : conscious :: unintended : _____

   Ⓐ inadvertent   Ⓑ uninhabited   Ⓒ unrestrained   Ⓓ ineffective

6. known : _____ :: unknown : mystery

   Ⓐ lie   Ⓑ fact   Ⓒ book   Ⓓ speech

7. discern : recognize :: relish : _____

   Ⓐ enjoy   Ⓑ review   Ⓒ hide   Ⓓ command

8. elusive : evasive :: terse : _____

   Ⓐ polite   Ⓑ tormented   Ⓒ diligent   Ⓓ brief

9. instantaneous : only a second :: eternal : _____

   Ⓐ days   Ⓑ forever   Ⓒ until the end of the day   Ⓓ years

10. recognize : identify :: subside : _____

    Ⓐ mark   Ⓑ hide   Ⓒ uncover   Ⓓ diminish

11. estimation : guess :: significance : _____

    Ⓐ knowledge   Ⓑ precision   Ⓒ importance   Ⓓ dependability

12. momentary : eternal :: distracted : _____

    Ⓐ disarming   Ⓑ aghast   Ⓒ engrossed   Ⓓ petrified

Study the relationship between the first set of words. Pick the word that completes the second pair with this same relationship.

1. blunder : mistake :: peril : _____

   Ⓐ destiny   Ⓑ storage   Ⓒ danger   Ⓓ announcement

2. glorious : wonderful :: weary : _____

   Ⓐ tired   Ⓑ terrible   Ⓒ nightgown   Ⓓ lonely

3. elusive : evasive :: terse : _____

   Ⓐ brief   Ⓑ tormented   Ⓒ diligent   Ⓓ polite

4. arbitrate : judge :: deduce : _____

   Ⓐ argue   Ⓑ determine   Ⓒ waste   Ⓓ create

5. problem : conundrum :: mystery : _____

   Ⓐ meticulous   Ⓑ enigma   Ⓒ dogmatic   Ⓓ certain

6. occur : occurrence :: develop : _____

   Ⓐ developing   Ⓑ developed   Ⓒ development   Ⓓ developence

7. discern : recognize :: relish : _____

   Ⓐ command   Ⓑ hide   Ⓒ review   Ⓓ enjoy

8. known : familiar :: unknown : _____

   Ⓐ ship   Ⓑ recognizable   Ⓒ definite   Ⓓ foreign

9. aware : conscious :: unintended : _____

   Ⓐ inadvertent   Ⓑ ineffective   Ⓒ uninhabited   Ⓓ unrestrained

10. resolve : determine :: embed : _____

    Ⓐ slide   Ⓑ incorporate   Ⓒ sleep   Ⓓ guess

11. instantaneous : only a second :: eternal : _____

    Ⓐ forever   Ⓑ years   Ⓒ days   Ⓓ until the end of the day

12. torment : disturb :: replenish : _____

    Ⓐ regret   Ⓑ discuss   Ⓒ lurk   Ⓓ refill

Study the relationship between the first set of words. Pick the word that completes the second pair with this same relationship.

1. unable to read : illiterate :: out of work : _____

   (A) uninsured   (B) illegal   (C) unemployed   (D) inept

2. to deal with something : cope :: to shame : _____

   . adjoin   (B) commend   (C) lurch   (D) disgrace

3. list of players participating in a game : lineup :: plan of action : _____

   (A) strategy   (B) manager   (C) sponsor   (D) roster

4. sensible : practical :: suitable : _____

   (A) moderate   (B) appropriate   (C) rubbish   (D) restored

5. hallucinate : imagine :: incinerate : _____

   (A) burn   (B) accuse   (C) reject   (D) touch

6. fake : phony :: authentic : _____

   (A) artificial   (B) processed   (C) bona fide   (D) imaginary

7. commend : _____ :: humiliate : embarrass

   (A) meditation   (B) praise   (C) faith   (D) belief

8. enlisted : signed up :: killed or wounded : _____

   (A) discharged   (B) strategy   (C) promoted   (D) casualty

9. imbecilically : foolishly :: furtively : _____

   . remotely   (B) thoughtfully   . stealthily   (D) elaborately

10. caring : compassionate :: honest : _____

    (A) character   (B) empathetic   (C) trustworthy   (D) stubborn

11. enclosed : enveloped :: run down : _____

    (A) impulsive   (B) circulated   (C) cornucopia   (D) dilapidated

12. bountiful : sparse :: elaborate : _____

    (A) dignified   (B) simple   (C) composed   (D) dirty

Study the relationship between the first set of words. Pick the word that completes the second pair with this same relationship.

1. a right : privilege :: a condition : _____

    Ⓐ writ   Ⓑ provision   Ⓒ sovereign   Ⓓ debt

2. an agreement to stop fighting : truce :: to win out over other options : _____

    Ⓐ surrender   Ⓑ commend   Ⓒ implore   Ⓓ prevail

3. surrender : give up :: vanquish : _____

    Ⓐ commend   Ⓑ honor   Ⓒ defeat   Ⓓ chase

4. slug : hit :: grumble : _____

    Ⓐ help   Ⓑ wag   Ⓒ complain   Ⓓ yell

5. derisive : insulting :: furtive : _____

    Ⓐ paranoid   Ⓑ sentimental   Ⓒ sneaky   Ⓓ brave

6. sensible : practical :: suitable : _____

    Ⓐ rubbish   Ⓑ moderate   Ⓒ restored   Ⓓ appropriate

7. open : closed :: real : _____

    ⸱ expected   Ⓑ shut   Ⓒ authentic   Ⓓ imaginary

8. _____ : optimistic :: sentimental : nostalgic

    Ⓐ kind   Ⓑ nervous   Ⓒ hopeful   Ⓓ negative

9. impeach : accuse :: adjourn : _____

    Ⓐ punish   Ⓑ judge   Ⓒ suspend   Ⓓ free

10. fake : phony :: authentic : _____

    Ⓐ bona fide   Ⓑ artificial   Ⓒ imaginary   Ⓓ processed

11. to look forward to : _____ :: to fear greatly : dread

    Ⓐ amend   Ⓑ anticipate   Ⓒ apprehend   Ⓓ generate

12. sentimental : emotional :: optimistic : _____

    Ⓐ affectionate Ⓑ hopeful   Ⓒ negative   Ⓓ ridiculous

Name _____   **LESSON 36**   Date _____

Study the relationship between the first set of words. Pick the word that completes the second pair with this same relationship.

1. flexible : rigid :: obedient : _____

    Ⓐ reproachful   Ⓑ defiant   Ⓒ shrewd   Ⓓ stern

2. sentimental : emotional :: confidential : _____

    Ⓐ special   Ⓑ private   Ⓒ shameful   Ⓓ discreet

3. sensible : practical :: suitable : _____

    Ⓐ restored   Ⓑ appropriate   Ⓒ moderate   Ⓓ rubbish

4. to hit repeatedly : pelt :: to say something clever : _____

    Ⓐ paddock   Ⓑ dreg   Ⓒ quip   Ⓓ elaborate

5. caring : compassionate :: honest : _____

    Ⓐ character   Ⓑ empathetic   Ⓒ trustworthy   Ⓓ stubborn

6. derision : ridicule :: chagrin : _____

    Ⓐ embarrassment   Ⓑ surprise   Ⓒ disappointment   Ⓓ enjoyment

7. loyal : _____ :: persistent : relentless

    Ⓐ stubborn   Ⓑ trustworthy   Ⓒ empathetic   Ⓓ character

8. practical : useful :: suitable : _____

    Ⓐ final   Ⓑ expected   Ⓒ helpful   Ⓓ appropriate

9. inheritance : _____ :: dowry : marriage

    Ⓐ petrification   Ⓑ death   Ⓒ clean   Ⓓ buzzard

10. impeach : accuse :: adjourn : _____

    Ⓐ suspend   Ⓑ free   Ⓒ punish   Ⓓ judge

11. illegal : against the law :: illiterate : _____

    Ⓐ unkind   Ⓑ cannot vote   Ⓒ cannot read   Ⓓ underground

12. plan : strategy :: suggestion : _____

    Ⓐ execution   . corroboration   Ⓒ proposal   . rationalization

Name _____   **LESSON 37**   Date _____

Study the relationship between the first set of words. Pick the word that completes the second pair with this same relationship.

1. faith : belief :: honesty : _____

   Ⓐ virtue   Ⓑ attitude   Ⓒ optimism   Ⓓ aptitude

2. partner : _____ :: heir : inherit

   Ⓐ help   Ⓑ run   Ⓒ talk   Ⓓ train

3. assist : help :: motivate : _____

   Ⓐ inspire   Ⓑ enforce   Ⓒ punish   Ⓓ discipline

4. bad behavior : discipline :: good behavior : _____

   Ⓐ teacher   Ⓑ tantrum   Ⓒ test   Ⓓ reward

5. study : prepare :: lesson : _____

   Ⓐ debate   Ⓑ lecture   Ⓒ conduct   Ⓓ discipline

6. conquer : defeat :: rebellion : _____

   Ⓐ defend   Ⓑ triumph   Ⓒ revolt   Ⓓ treaty

7. the essential nature of the universe : dharma :: the belief that a person's actions, good or bad, determine their destiny : _____

   Ⓐ tao   Ⓑ dogma   Ⓒ karma   Ⓓ faith

8. _____ : shake :: divulge : reveal

   Ⓐ turret   Ⓑ tithe   Ⓒ quiver   Ⓓ lance

9. principles and beliefs : philosophy :: opinion of character : _____

   Ⓐ modesty   Ⓑ faith   Ⓒ reputation   Ⓓ synergy

10. accomplice : helper :: obligation : _____

    Ⓐ duty   Ⓑ reward   Ⓒ oddity   Ⓓ defense

11. reveal : expose :: begin : _____

    Ⓐ originate   Ⓑ conserve   Ⓒ conclude   Ⓓ exclude

12. insolent : rude :: haughty : _____

    Ⓐ arrogant   Ⓑ generous   Ⓒ reclusive   Ⓓ charming

Study the relationship between the first set of words. Pick the word that completes the second pair with this same relationship.

1. irreverent : disrespectful :: penitent : _____

   (A) jealous   (B) sorrowful   (C) honorable   (D) generous

2. emphasis : significance :: supervision : _____

   (A) management   (B) encouragement   (C) disregard   (D) ingenuity

3. to look up to : admire :: to imitate : _____

   (A) immerse   (B) justify   (C) condescend   (D) impersonate

4. reveal : expose :: begin : _____

   (A) exclude   (B) conserve   (C) conclude   (D) originate

5. accomplice : helper :: obligation : _____

   (A) oddity   (B) reward   (C) duty   (D) defense

6. _____ : discipline :: cheer : encourage

   (A) allow   (B) encourage   (C) punish   (D) dream

7. _____ : call :: admonish : scold

   (A) process   (B) summon   (C) understand   (D) communicate

8. principles and beliefs : philosophy :: opinion of character : _____

   (A) faith   (B) modesty   (C) synergy   (D) reputation

9. wealthy : nobles :: poor : _____

   (A) peasants   (B) damsels   (C) knights   (D) princes

10. disturb : bother :: befuddle : _____

    (A) justify   (B) anger   (C) confuse   (D) tease

11. study : prepare :: lesson : _____

    (A) conduct   (B) debate   . discipline   (D) lecture

12. good : excellent :: funny : _____

    (A) hilarious   (B) ridiculous   (C) suspicious   (D) generous

Study the relationship between the first set of words. Pick the word that completes the second pair with this same relationship.

1. obedient : defiant :: effortless : _____

   . conscious   B. justified   C. transparent   D. strenuous

2. faith : belief :: honesty : _____

   A. aptitude   B. optimism   C. attitude   D. virtue

3. the essential nature of the universe : dharma :: the belief that a person's actions, good or bad, determine their destiny : _____

   A. faith   B. karma   C. tao   D. dogma

4. art : creativity :: _____ : faith

   . war   B. clothing   C. history   D. religion

5. joined as one : united :: restricted : _____

   A. confined   B. opposed   C. relayed   D. justified

6. punish : discipline :: cheer : _____

   A. stalk   B. encourage   C. enlarge   D. hurt

7. greed : selfish :: _____ : generous

   A. commiseration   B. camaraderie   C. charity   D. sympathy

8. encouraging : intimidating :: _____ : stingy

   A. thick   B. honesty   C. fortunate   D. generous

9. _____ : shake :: divulge : reveal

   A. tithe   B. lance   C. quiver   D. turret

10. conquer : defeat :: rebellion : _____

    A. revolt   . treaty   C. triumph   D. defend

11. sorcerer : magician :: damsel : _____

    A. maiden   B. dragon   C. knight   D. peasant

12. summon : call :: toil : _____

    A. cover   B. anger   C. work   D. tie

Study the relationship between the first set of words. Pick the word that completes the second pair with this same relationship.

1. lair : dragon :: castle : _____

   Ⓐ king   Ⓑ peasant   Ⓒ magician   Ⓓ peasant

2. faith : belief :: unity : _____

   Ⓐ separation   Ⓑ togetherness   Ⓒ joy   Ⓓ culture

3. to look up to : admire :: to imitate : _____

   Ⓐ impersonate   Ⓑ justify   Ⓒ immerse   Ⓓ condescend

4. teach : educate :: beckon : _____

   Ⓐ summon   Ⓑ understand   Ⓒ communicate   Ⓓ process

5. conquer : defeat :: rebellion : _____

   Ⓐ revolt   Ⓑ defend   Ⓒ triumph   Ⓓ treaty

6. partner : help :: _____ : inherit

   Ⓐ atmosphere   Ⓑ hair   Ⓒ heir   Ⓓ pair

7. inspire : motivate :: discipline : _____

   Ⓐ encourage   Ⓑ reward   Ⓒ punish   Ⓓ detain

8. to honor through memories : remembrance :: to give something up for the sake of something greater : _____

   Ⓐ valiance   Ⓑ faith   Ⓒ integrity   Ⓓ sacrifice

9. _____ : selfish :: charity : generous

   Ⓐ anger   Ⓑ shame   Ⓒ lust   Ⓓ greed

10. assist : help :: motivate : _____

    Ⓐ inspire   Ⓑ discipline   Ⓒ enforce   Ⓓ punish

11. good : excellent :: funny : _____

    Ⓐ hilarious   Ⓑ generous   Ⓒ suspicious   Ⓓ ridiculous

12. obligation : burden :: package : _____

    Ⓐ menagerie   Ⓑ tariff   Ⓒ parcel   Ⓓ scythe

Study the relationship between the first set of words. Pick the word that completes the second pair with this same relationship.

1. hidden : revealed :: bare : _____

    A covered   B lit   C cub   D empty

2. conquer : defeat :: rebellion : _____

    A triumph   B revolt   C defend   D treaty

3. allegiance : loyalty :: independence : _____

    A freedom   B faith   C compromise   D unity

4. obligation : burden :: package : _____

    A parcel   B tariff   C menagerie   D scythe

5. teach : educate :: beckon : _____

    A process   B summon   C communicate   D understand

6. wealthy : _____ :: poor : peasants

    A lawmakers   B priests   C nobles   D farmers

7. irreverent : disrespectful :: penitent : _____

    A honorable   B sorrowful   C generous   D jealous

8. mislead : deceive :: emancipate : _____

    A reveal   B forgive   C free   D enslave

9. bad behavior : discipline :: good behavior : _____

    A teacher   B reward   C tantrum   D test

10. to move in a circular pattern : circulate :: to work together : _____

    A collaborate   B enthrall   C justify   D bereave

11. summoned : called :: tapered : _____

    A gradually reduced   B measured   C quickly bound   D released

12. peasant : house :: king : _____

    A moat   B circus   C palace   D queen

Study the relationship between the first set of words. Pick the word that completes the second pair with this same relationship.

1. accomplice : helper :: obligation : _____

   (A) oddity   (B) duty   (C) reward   (D) defense

2. summoned : called :: tapered : _____

   (A) quickly bound   (B) released   (C) gradually reduced   (D) measured

3. inspire : motivate :: discipline : _____

   (A) encourage   (B) punish   (C) detain   (D) reward

4. supervise : oversee :: summon : _____

   (A) manage   . call   (C) assist   (D) consult

5. assist : help :: motivate : _____

   (A) inspire   (B) punish   (C) discipline   (D) enforce

6. mislead : deceive :: emancipate : _____

   (A) enslave   (B) reveal   (C) forgive   (D) free

7. disturb : bother :: befuddle : _____

   (A) justify   (B) anger   (C) confuse   (D) tease

8. reveal : expose :: begin : _____

   (A) conclude   (B) conserve   (C) originate   (D) exclude

9. _____ : belief :: honesty : virtue

   . love   (B) pray   (C) faith   (D) literature

10. to move in a circular pattern : circulate :: to work together : _____

    (A) enthrall   (B) collaborate   (C) justify   (D) bereave

11. hidden : revealed :: bare : _____

    (A) lit   (B) cub   (C) empty   (D) covered

12. sorcerer : magician :: damsel : _____

    (A) knight   (B) dragon   (C) peasant   . maiden

Study the relationship between the first set of words. Pick the word that completes the second pair with this same relationship.

1. _____ : number :: rectangle : shape

   A five   B fourteen   C fifteen   D twelve

2. rectangle : _____ :: triangle : three

   A four   B army   C corner   D seven

3. drink : ice cube :: ocean : _____

   A salt   B iceberg   C ice crystals   D sleet

4. ruler : inches :: _____ : pounds

   A scales   B fish   C big   D weight

5. nueve : nine :: cuatro : _____

   A one   B five   C six   D four

6. inches : length :: cubic inches : _____

   A perimeter   B area   C hypotenuse   D volume

7. English units : gallon :: metric units : _____

   A inch   B pint   C liter   D pound

8. inch : centimeter :: quart : _____

   A weight   B inch   C liter   D yard

9. allowed : aloud :: him : _____

   A gym   B limb   C hymn   D her

10. something large : massive :: a small amount : _____

    A bunch   B lots   C smidgeon   D abundance

11. square : box :: round : _____

    A rectangle   B ball   C golf   D triangle

12. three : _____ :: four : rectangle

    A rhombus   B triangle   C octagon   D circle

Name _____   **LESSON 44**   Date _____

Study the relationship between the first set of words. Pick the word that completes the second pair with this same relationship.

1. triangle : three :: square : _____

   Ⓐ round   Ⓑ corner   Ⓒ four   Ⓓ army

2. far : distant :: nearby : _____

   Ⓐ close   Ⓑ campsite   Ⓒ canoe   Ⓓ already

3. slice of pizza : triangle :: whole pizza : _____

   Ⓐ rectangle   Ⓑ circle   Ⓒ oval   Ⓓ square

4. cereal : breakfast :: sandwich : _____

   Ⓐ chips   Ⓑ ham   Ⓒ lunch   Ⓓ cheese

5. sip : drink :: munch : _____

   Ⓐ view   Ⓑ wash   Ⓒ snack   Ⓓ crush

6. square : box :: round : _____

   Ⓐ triangle   Ⓑ ball   Ⓒ golf   Ⓓ rectangle

7. morning : _____ :: breakfast : lunch

   Ⓐ sandwich   Ⓑ noon   Ⓒ evening   Ⓓ dinner

8. easy : _____ :: near : far

   Ⓐ rigid   Ⓑ powerful   Ⓒ difficult   Ⓓ lengthy

9. inch : centimeter :: quart : _____

   Ⓐ liter   Ⓑ yard   Ⓒ weight   Ⓓ inch

10. inch : distance :: pound : _____

    Ⓐ energy   Ⓑ time   Ⓒ volume   Ⓓ weight

11. colossal : large :: distant : _____

    Ⓐ irresistible   Ⓑ far   Ⓒ small   Ⓓ immediate

12. allowed : aloud :: him : _____

    Ⓐ her   Ⓑ gym   Ⓒ limb   Ⓓ hymn

Study the relationship between the first set of words. Pick the word that completes the second pair with this same relationship.

1. oval : _____ :: rectangle : square

    Ⓐ cube   Ⓑ line   Ⓒ triangle   Ⓓ circle

2. inches : length :: cubic inches : _____

    Ⓐ area   Ⓑ volume   Ⓒ perimeter   Ⓓ hypotenuse

3. inch : distance :: pound : _____

    Ⓐ volume   Ⓑ time   Ⓒ weight   Ⓓ energy

4. something large : massive :: a small amount : _____

    Ⓐ smidgeon   Ⓑ bunch   Ⓒ abundance   Ⓓ lots

5. appetite : _____ :: thirst : drink

    Ⓐ play   Ⓑ sugar   Ⓒ crumbs   Ⓓ eat

6. four : quartet :: eight : _____

    Ⓐ octet   Ⓑ trio   Ⓒ arrangement   Ⓓ sextet

7. two-dimensional : square :: three-dimensional : _____

    Ⓐ rectangle   Ⓑ triangle   Ⓒ star   Ⓓ cube

8. pyramid : square :: cone : _____

    Ⓐ rectangle   Ⓑ star   Ⓒ circle   Ⓓ cube

9. inch : centimeter :: quart : _____

    Ⓐ inch   Ⓑ liter   Ⓒ yard   Ⓓ weight

10. something large : massive :: a small amount : _____

    Ⓐ bunch   Ⓑ smidgeon   Ⓒ lots   Ⓓ abundance

11. 12 inches : foot :: 3 feet : _____

    Ⓐ hand   Ⓑ mile   Ⓒ yard   Ⓓ inch

12. drink : ice cube :: ocean : _____

    Ⓐ iceberg   Ⓑ sleet   Ⓒ ice crystals   Ⓓ salt

Study the relationship between the first set of words. Pick the word that completes the second pair with this same relationship.

1. _____ : head :: hoarse : throat

   Ⓐ content   Ⓑ furious   Ⓒ daring   Ⓓ dizzy

2. devotion : dedication :: compassion : _____

   Ⓐ attitude   Ⓑ hardworking   Ⓒ helpful   Ⓓ sympathy

3. attitude : outlook :: aptitude : _____

   Ⓐ ability   Ⓑ morals   Ⓒ compassion   Ⓓ intelligence

4. brilliant : splendid :: giddy : _____

   Ⓐ furious   Ⓑ dizzy   Ⓒ daring   content

5. dedicated : hard-working :: faithful : _____

   Ⓐ anxious   Ⓑ sober   Ⓒ keen   loyal

6. trivial : insignificant :: stellar : _____

   Ⓐ complicated   disastrous   Ⓒ determined   Ⓓ outstanding

7. impressive, based on appearance : imposing :: burdensome : _____

   Ⓐ drear   Ⓑ exclusive   Ⓒ oppressive   Ⓓ poignant

8. browse : _____ :: rehearse : practice

   dispose of   Ⓑ review   Ⓒ cover up   Ⓓ look through

9. romantic : platonic :: eager : _____

   Ⓐ keen   Ⓑ reluctant   Ⓒ fruitful   salient

10. common : well-known :: unique : _____

    Ⓐ hidden   Ⓑ old   Ⓒ secret   Ⓓ one of a kind

11. well-known : common :: one of a kind : _____

    Ⓐ hidden   Ⓑ secret   Ⓒ unique   Ⓓ antique

12. sarcasm : irony :: revulsion : _____

    Ⓐ dislike   Ⓑ insult   Ⓒ compassion   Ⓓ humor

Name _____   **LESSON 47**   Date _____

Study the relationship between the first set of words. Pick the word that completes the second pair with this same relationship.

1. sneaky : stealthy :: difficult to catch : _____

   Ⓐ elusive   Ⓑ servile   Ⓒ furtive   Ⓓ poignant

2. _____ : intelligent :: gracious : kind

   Ⓐ clever   Ⓑ admirable   Ⓒ childish   Ⓓ foolish

3. impressive, based on appearance : imposing :: burdensome : _____

   Ⓐ poignant   Ⓑ exclusive   Ⓒ drear   Ⓓ oppressive

4. attitude : outlook :: aptitude : _____

   Ⓐ compassion   Ⓑ intelligence   Ⓒ morals   Ⓓ ability

5. _____ : head :: hoarse : throat

   Ⓐ furious   Ⓑ dizzy   Ⓒ daring   Ⓓ content

6. rude : manners :: lonesome : _____

   Ⓐ compassion   Ⓑ sadness   Ⓒ entertainment   Ⓓ companions

7. well-known : common :: one of a kind : _____

   Ⓐ antique   Ⓑ secret   Ⓒ hidden   Ⓓ unique

8. humongous : enormous :: fierce : _____

   Ⓐ hostile   Ⓑ complicated   Ⓒ hot   Ⓓ tiny

9. sarcasm : irony :: revulsion : _____

   Ⓐ dislike   Ⓑ humor   Ⓒ compassion   Ⓓ insult

10. devotion : dedication :: compassion : _____

    Ⓐ sympathy   Ⓑ hardworking   Ⓒ helpful   Ⓓ attitude

11. dispose : get rid of :: peruse : _____

    Ⓐ fulfill   Ⓑ watch   Ⓒ release   Ⓓ browse

12. sorrowful : sad :: complicated : _____

    Ⓐ complex   Ⓑ slow   Ⓒ capable   Ⓓ delicate

Study the relationship between the first set of words. Pick the word that completes the second pair with this same relationship.

1. treason : loyalty :: divided : _____

    (A) united   (B) faithful   (C) apart   (D) promised

2. romantic : platonic :: eager : _____

    (A) reluctant   (B) salient   (C) fruitful   (D) keen

3. lithe : flexible :: myriad : _____

    (A) unique   (B) structured   (C) innumerable   (D) ordinary

4. trivial : insignificant :: stellar : _____

    (A) disastrous   (B) complicated   (C) determined   (D) outstanding

5. complicated : _____ :: jumbled : orderly

    (A) elegant   (B) complex   (C) composed   (D) simple

6. devotion : dedication :: compassion : _____

    (A) hardworking   (B) attitude   (C) sympathy   (D) helpful

7. browse : _____ :: rehearse : practice

    (A) look through   (B) dispose of   (C) cover up   (D) review

8. eccentric : odd :: fervent : _____

    (A) calm   (B) gracious   (C) average   (D) intense

9. treasonous : loyal :: divided : _____

    (A) separated   (B) united   (C) promised   (D) faithful

10. naive : trusting :: mundane : _____

    (A) gracious   (B) dark   (C) ordinary   (D) helpful

11. humongous : enormous :: fierce : _____

    (A) tiny   (B) hot   (C) hostile   (D) complicated

12. loyalty : allegiance :: treason : _____

    (A) liberty   (B) disloyalty   (C) faithfulness   (D) independence

Study the relationship between the first set of words. Pick the word that completes the second pair with this same relationship.

1. to set on fire : ignite :: to empty : _____

   A gorge   **B** invigorate   **C** conform   **D** vacate

2. forlorn : forsaken :: vain : _____

   A insulting   **B** without purpose   **C** serious   **D** rebellious

3. immature : green :: mature : _____

   A ripe   **B** red   **C** yellow   **D** old

4. comedy : funny :: tragedy : _____

   A angry   **B** fable   **C** moral   **D** sad

5. horrid : terrible :: prim : _____

   A crisp   **B** beautiful   **C** coarse   **D** proper

6. cantankerous : disagreeable :: headstrong : _____

   A stubborn   **B** brave   **C** focused   **D** intelligent

7. cheerful : grim :: polite : _____

   A gracious   **B** gruff   **C** immature   **D** kind

8. mandated : _____ :: traditional : customary

   A required   **B** objected   **C** composed   **D** honorable

9. outlaw : _____ :: showdown : confrontation

   A counsel   **B** criminal   **C** laws   **D** rules

10. faith : belief :: honesty : _____

    A virtue   **B** attitude   **C** aptitude   **D** optimism

11. a decoration : ornament :: something that is in the way : _____

    A plaque   **B** obstacle   **C** modem   **D** trinket

12. to follow the rules : comply :: to gain possession of something : _____

    A reprieve   **B** grant   **C** procure   **D** preside

Name _____ **LESSON 50** Date _____

Study the relationship between the first set of words. Pick the word that completes the second pair with this same relationship.

1. to pardon : condone :: to admit : _____

    Ⓐ concede   Ⓑ evade   Ⓒ procure   Ⓓ retort

2. mulish : _____ :: sheepish : bashful

    Ⓐ distressed   Ⓑ lame   Ⓒ haughty   Ⓓ stubborn

3. assimilated : conformed :: abridged : _____

    Ⓐ disclosed   Ⓑ lengthened   Ⓒ shortened   Ⓓ surrounded

4. _____ : victorious :: jubilant : joyous

    Ⓐ fluent   Ⓑ triumphant   Ⓒ relieved   Ⓓ grubby

5. prompt : quick :: _____ : angry

    Ⓐ rogue   Ⓑ idle   Ⓒ immaculate   Ⓓ indignant

6. superstition : _____ :: fortune : luck

    Ⓐ skeptical   Ⓑ doubt   Ⓒ belief   Ⓓ ghost

7. lustrous : shiny :: jubilant : _____

    Ⓐ brave   Ⓑ important   Ⓒ joyful   Ⓓ invincible

8. amended : changed :: mandated : _____

    Ⓐ professional   Ⓑ composed   Ⓒ allotted   Ⓓ required

9. faith : belief :: honesty : _____

    Ⓐ attitude   Ⓑ optimism   Ⓒ aptitude   Ⓓ virtue

10. appetite : eat :: thirst : _____

    Ⓐ drink   Ⓑ hunger   Ⓒ quench   Ⓓ parched

11. thirst : drink :: appetite : _____

    Ⓐ eat   Ⓑ hunger   Ⓒ parched   Ⓓ quench

12. regulations : rules :: restitution : _____

    Ⓐ restriction   Ⓑ expulsion   Ⓒ initiation   Ⓓ repayment

Study the relationship between the first set of words. Pick the word that completes the second pair with this same relationship.

1. branch : division :: remnant : _____

   Ⓐ foundation   Ⓑ scrap   Ⓒ assortment   Ⓓ hole

2. happens over and over again : repetitive :: not allowed : _____

   Ⓐ superstitious   Ⓑ immature   Ⓒ virtual   Ⓓ ineligible

3. hug : _____ :: kiss : smooch

   Ⓐ embrace   Ⓑ lips   Ⓒ shake   Ⓓ love

4. cultural : Renaissance :: religious : _____

   Ⓐ Reformation   Ⓑ Protestant   Ⓒ Restoration   Ⓓ Reclamation

5. appetite : eat :: thirst : _____

   Ⓐ drink   Ⓑ quench   Ⓒ parched   Ⓓ hunger

6. pelt : hit :: liberate : _____

   Ⓐ hide   Ⓑ swell   Ⓒ trespass   Ⓓ free

7. _____ : interested in how things work :: persevere : does not give up

   Ⓐ humble   Ⓑ generous   Ⓒ hostile   Ⓓ curious

8. forlorn : forsaken :: vain : _____

   Ⓐ rebellious   Ⓑ serious   Ⓒ insulting   Ⓓ without purpose

9. stumbling block : obstacle :: natural ability : _____

   Ⓐ dilemma   Ⓑ smirk   Ⓒ knack   Ⓓ troupe

10. lustrous : shiny :: jubilant : _____

    Ⓐ invincible   Ⓑ joyful   Ⓒ important   Ⓓ brave

11. hug : _____ :: kiss : smooch

    Ⓐ shake   Ⓑ embrace   Ⓒ love   Ⓓ lips

12. scheme : plot :: infraction : _____

    Ⓐ violation   Ⓑ suspension   Ⓒ confession   Ⓓ decision

Name _____   **LESSON 52**   Date _____

Study the relationship between the first set of words. Pick the word that completes the second pair with this same relationship.

1.	devotion : dedication :: compassion : _____
	(A) sympathy (B) helpful (C) hardworking (D) attitude
2.	achievement : accomplishment :: praise : _____
	(A) opponent (B) criticism (C) accolades (D) reverence
3.	a penalty given to someone for doing wrong : punishment :: getting back at someone who has done something to hurt you : _____
	(A) grievance (B) munitions (C) penance (D) revenge
4.	naive : trusting :: mundane : _____
	(A) helpful (B) ordinary (C) dark (D) gracious
5.	freight : cargo :: property : _____
	(A) premises (B) crew (C) doctrine (D) contraption
6.	charity : generosity :: cheer : _____
	(A) happiness (B) greed (C) curiosity (D) hunger
7.	reluctant : willing :: dismayed : _____
	(A) scorned (B) content (C) unprecedented (D) evident
8.	vengeance : revenge :: vigilance : _____
	(A) compassion (B) watchfulness (C) camaraderie (D) distress
9.	sympathy for the misfortunes of others : compassion :: giving to those in need : _____
	(A) camaraderie (B) commiseration (C) charity (D) sympathy
10.	enlist : enroll :: discharged : _____
	(A) injured (B) punished (C) captured (D) released
11.	haphazard : random :: fervent : _____
	(A) intentional (B) enthusiastic (C) condemned (D) puny
12.	values : ideals :: manners : _____
	(A) morals (B) etiquette (C) kindness (D) rudeness

57

Name _____   **LESSON 53**   Date _____

Study the relationship between the first set of words. Pick the word that completes the second pair with this same relationship.

1.	charity : generosity :: cheer : _____
	A hunger **B** happiness **C** greed **D** curiosity
2.	acrid : bitter :: brackish : _____
	A sweet **B** salty **C** crunchy **D** muddy
3.	weapon : revolver :: motive : _____
	A crime scene **B** trust **C** evidence **D** revenge
4.	extricated : released :: deluged : _____
	A captured **B** prodded **C** flooded **D** punished
5.	shout : yell :: clench : _____
	A hold tightly **B** release **C** whisper **D** take a risk
6.	vengeance : revenge :: vigilance : _____
	A compassion **B** distress **C** camaraderie **D** watchfulness
7.	soda : sweet :: coffee : _____
	A hot **B** brown **C** sugar **D** bitter
8.	revenge : vengeance :: partnership : _____
	A opposition **B** retort **C** alliance **D** tirade
9.	stymied : hindered :: marooned : _____
	A injured **B** trusting **C** abandoned **D** sweet
10.	cold : bitter :: heat : _____
	A sweet **B** sun **C** oppressive **D** warm
11.	plan : strategy :: suggestion : _____
	A corroboration **B** proposal **C** execution **D** rationalization
12.	thankfulness : gratefulness :: charity : _____
	A generosity **B** patience **C** poverty **D** praise

Name _____ **LESSON 54** Date _____

Study the relationship between the first set of words. Pick the word that completes the second pair with this same relationship.

1. charity : generosity :: cheer : _____

    (A) greed   (B) happiness   (C) curiosity   (D) hunger

2. stymied : hindered :: marooned : _____

    (A) sweet   (B) injured   (C) abandoned   (D) trusting

3. haphazard : random :: fervent : _____

    (A) puny   (B) intentional   (C) enthusiastic   (D) condemned

4. freight : cargo :: property : _____

    (A) premises   (B) contraption   (C) doctrine   (D) crew

5. cheerful : grim :: polite : _____

    (A) kind   (B) immature   (C) gracious   (D) gruff

6. values : ideals :: manners : _____

    (A) rudeness   (B) morals   (C) etiquette   (D) kindness

7. enlist : enroll :: discharged : _____

    (A) punished   (B) injured   (C) captured   (D) released

8. push : pull :: scatter : _____

    (A) huddle   (B) hinder   (C) open   (D) stretch

9. to tell someone that you are grateful their help : _____ :: to get back at someone : revenge

    (A) insult   (B) spoil   (C) thank   (D) forgive

10. protect : shield :: assist : _____

    (A) hinder   (B) community   (C) help   (D) review

11. shout : yell :: clench : _____

    (A) take a risk   (B) release   (C) hold tightly   (D) whisper

12. devotion : dedication :: compassion : _____

    (A) helpful   (B) attitude   (C) sympathy   (D) hardworking

Study the relationship between the first set of words. Pick the word that completes the second pair with this same relationship.

1. heart : blood :: lungs : _____

    Ⓐ water   Ⓑ air   Ⓒ chest   Ⓓ nose

2. Teacher : education :: Attorney : _____

    Ⓐ suing   Ⓑ medicine   Ⓒ law   Ⓓ instruction

3. policeman : law :: criminal : _____

    Ⓐ crime   Ⓑ arrest   Ⓒ patrol   Ⓓ blue

4. vacation : trip :: photographs : _____

    Ⓐ snapshots   Ⓑ copies   Ⓒ remember   Ⓓ camera

5. Livingston : Victoria Falls :: Balboa : _____

    Ⓐ Arctic Ocean   Ⓑ Panama   Ⓒ North Pole   Ⓓ Pacific Ocean

6. termite : wood :: mosquito : _____

    Ⓐ honey   Ⓑ water   Ⓒ aphids   Ⓓ blood

7. laws : rules :: right : _____

    Ⓐ freedom   Ⓑ anger   Ⓒ same   Ⓓ equal

8. think back : remember :: _____ : imagine

    Ⓐ equal   Ⓑ change   Ⓒ lead   Ⓓ dream

9. swallow : food :: pump : _____

    Ⓐ turtle   Ⓑ water   Ⓒ heart   Ⓓ blood

10. hoist : lift :: regale : _____

    Ⓐ whisper   Ⓑ persuade   Ⓒ entertain   Ⓓ forgive

11. _____ : persuade :: excuse : forgive

    Ⓐ increase   Ⓑ vacate   Ⓒ coax   Ⓓ invoke

12. pumpkin : _____ :: blood : red

    Ⓐ red   Ⓑ yellow   Ⓒ orange   Ⓓ white

Name _____   **LESSON 56**   Date _____

Study the relationship between the first set of words. Pick the word that completes the second pair with this same relationship.

1. disrespect : honor :: forget : _____

    (A) remember   (B) replenish   (C) doubt   (D) control

2. Plymouth : colony :: Mayflower Compact : _____

    (A) laws   (B) harvest feast   (C) William Bradford   (D) ship

3. laws : rules :: right : _____

    (A) same   (B) freedom   (C) equal   (D) anger

4. heart : blood :: lungs : _____

    (A) nose   (B) chest   (C) air   (D) water

5. grateful : thank :: sorry : _____

    (A) spoil   (B) insult   (C) forgive   (D) apologize

6. termite : wood :: mosquito : _____

    (A) aphids   (B) honey   (C) blood   (D) water

7. assist : help :: recycle : _____

    (A) reuse   (B) remember   (C) join   (D) aid

8. compose : write :: plead : _____

    (A) mock   (B) beg   (C) join   (D) forgive

9. tribute : _____ :: memorial : remember

    (A) admire   (B) contemplate   (C) religion   (D) honor

10. _____ : persuade :: excuse : forgive

    (A) coax   (B) invoke   (C) increase   (D) vacate

11. Teacher : education :: Attorney : _____

    (A) law   (B) suing   (C) medicine   (D) instruction

12. photographs : snapshots :: vacation : _____

    (A) copies   (B) camera   (C) trip   (D) remember

Name _____   **LESSON 57**   Date _____

Study the relationship between the first set of words. Pick the word that completes the second pair with this same relationship.

1. laws : rules :: right : _____

   Ⓐ anger   Ⓑ same   Ⓒ freedom   Ⓓ equal

2. tribute : honor :: memorial : _____

   Ⓐ control   Ⓑ remember   Ⓒ rebuke   Ⓓ summarize

3. trifle : small amount :: dandy : _____

   Ⓐ automatic   Ⓑ temporary   Ⓒ colorful   Ⓓ excellent

4. _____ : persuade :: excuse : forgive

   Ⓐ invoke   Ⓑ vacate   Ⓒ coax   Ⓓ increase

5. swallow : food :: pump : _____

   Ⓐ blood   Ⓑ water   Ⓒ turtle   Ⓓ heart

6. Livingston : Victoria Falls :: Balboa : _____

   Ⓐ North Pole   Ⓑ Pacific Ocean   Ⓒ Panama   Ⓓ Arctic Ocean

7. warn : alert :: persuade : _____

   Ⓐ convince   Ⓑ forgive   Ⓒ leave   Ⓓ hide

8. hoist : lift :: regale : _____

   Ⓐ whisper   Ⓑ forgive   Ⓒ entertain   Ⓓ persuade

9. think back : remember :: _____ : imagine

   Ⓐ lead   Ⓑ change   Ⓒ dream   Ⓓ equal

10. tribute : _____ :: memorial : remember

    Ⓐ contemplate   Ⓑ religion   Ⓒ admire   Ⓓ honor

11. Teacher : education :: Attorney : _____

    Ⓐ instruction   Ⓑ law   Ⓒ medicine   Ⓓ suing

12. peer : look :: recollect : _____

    Ⓐ give   Ⓑ remember   Ⓒ decide   Ⓓ replenish

Study the relationship between the first set of words. Pick the word that completes the second pair with this same relationship.

1. search : look for :: interrogate : _____

   Ⓐ witness   Ⓑ protect   Ⓒ imprison   Ⓓ question

2. facile : simple :: futile : _____

   Ⓐ thorough   Ⓑ ineffective   Ⓒ difficult   Ⓓ profane

3. wrong : right :: _____ : innocent

   Ⓐ guilty   Ⓑ judgmental   Ⓒ forgiving   Ⓓ guiltless

4. honest : deceptive :: innocent : _____

   Ⓐ guilty   Ⓑ forgiving   Ⓒ judgmental   Ⓓ guiltless

5. peddle : sell :: proclaim : _____

   Ⓐ announce   Ⓑ witness   Ⓒ own   Ⓓ hide

6. redemption : salvation :: rebirth of a soul into a new body : _____

   Ⓐ karma   Ⓑ shrine   Ⓒ inspiration   Ⓓ reincarnation

7. detective : sleuth :: criminal : _____

   Ⓐ counsel   Ⓑ juror   Ⓒ felon   Ⓓ witness

8. culprit : guilty :: maniac : _____

   Ⓐ crazy   Ⓑ sacrilegious   Ⓒ sad   Ⓓ sympathetic

9. jury : judgment :: witness : _____

   Ⓐ counsel   Ⓑ testimony   Ⓒ objections   Ⓓ asks questions

10. sport : spectator :: crime : _____

    Ⓐ witness   Ⓑ detective   Ⓒ interrogator   Ⓓ informant

11. envious : content :: guilty : _____

    Ⓐ practical   Ⓑ innocent   Ⓒ patient   Ⓓ crook

12. criminal : felon :: detective : _____

    Ⓐ negotiator   Ⓑ sleuth   Ⓒ witness   Ⓓ outlaw

Study the relationship between the first set of words. Pick the word that completes the second pair with this same relationship.

1. envious : content :: guilty : _____

   Ⓐ practical   Ⓑ patient   Ⓒ crook   Ⓓ innocent

2. redemption : salvation :: rebirth of a soul into a new body : _____

   Ⓐ shrine   Ⓑ inspiration   Ⓒ reincarnation   Ⓓ karma

3. search : look for :: interrogate : _____

   Ⓐ imprison   Ⓑ protect   Ⓒ question   Ⓓ witness

4. criminal : felon :: detective : _____

   Ⓐ outlaw   Ⓑ sleuth   Ⓒ negotiator   Ⓓ witness

5. jury : judgment :: witness : _____

   Ⓐ asks questions   Ⓑ counsel   Ⓒ objections   Ⓓ testimony

6. peddle : sell :: proclaim : _____

   Ⓐ announce   Ⓑ hide   Ⓒ witness   Ⓓ own

7. wrong : right :: _____ : innocent

   Ⓐ forgiving   Ⓑ guilty   Ⓒ judgmental   Ⓓ guiltless

8. honest : deceptive :: innocent : _____

   Ⓐ guiltless   Ⓑ judgmental   Ⓒ guilty   Ⓓ forgiving

9. facile : simple :: futile : _____

   Ⓐ thorough   Ⓑ difficult   Ⓒ profane   Ⓓ ineffective

10. gun : weapon :: fingerprints : _____

   Ⓐ detective   Ⓑ suspect   Ⓒ evidence   Ⓓ witness

11. detective : sleuth :: criminal : _____

   Ⓐ juror   Ⓑ witness   Ⓒ felon   Ⓓ counsel

12. culprit : guilty :: maniac : _____

   Ⓐ sympathetic   Ⓑ crazy   Ⓒ sacrilegious   Ⓓ sad

Name _____   **LESSON 60**   Date _____

Study the relationship between the first set of words. Pick the word that completes the second pair with this same relationship.

1. redemption : salvation :: rebirth of a soul into a new body : _____

   Ⓐ karma   Ⓑ inspiration   Ⓒ reincarnation   Ⓓ shrine

2. jury : judgment :: witness : _____

   Ⓐ asks questions Ⓑ testimony   Ⓒ objections   Ⓓ counsel

3. wrong : right :: _____ : innocent

   Ⓐ forgiving   Ⓑ judgmental   Ⓒ guiltless   Ⓓ guilty

4. sport : spectator :: crime : _____

   Ⓐ witness   Ⓑ detective   Ⓒ interrogator   Ⓓ informant

5. facile : simple :: futile : _____

   Ⓐ ineffective   Ⓑ difficult   Ⓒ thorough   Ⓓ profane

6. detective : sleuth :: criminal : _____

   Ⓐ juror   Ⓑ counsel   Ⓒ felon   Ⓓ witness

7. envious : content :: guilty : _____

   Ⓐ innocent   Ⓑ practical   Ⓒ crook   Ⓓ patient

8. honest : deceptive :: innocent : _____

   Ⓐ forgiving   Ⓑ guilty   Ⓒ judgmental   Ⓓ guiltless

9. search : look for :: interrogate : _____

   Ⓐ protect   Ⓑ question   Ⓒ witness   Ⓓ imprison

10. peddle : sell :: proclaim : _____

    Ⓐ witness   Ⓑ announce   Ⓒ hide   Ⓓ own

11. criminal : felon :: detective : _____

    Ⓐ negotiator   Ⓑ sleuth   Ⓒ witness   Ⓓ outlaw

12. gun : weapon :: fingerprints : _____

    Ⓐ detective   Ⓑ suspect   Ⓒ evidence   Ⓓ witness

Study the relationship between the first set of words. Pick the word that completes the second pair with this same relationship.

1. Labor : relax :: _____ : unwind

   Ⓐ tie   Ⓑ Work   Ⓒ retire   Ⓓ trade

2. lord : lady :: monk : _____

   Ⓐ physician   Ⓑ monastery   Ⓒ damsel   Ⓓ nun

3. explore : look for :: discover : _____

   Ⓐ hide   Ⓑ cover   Ⓒ find   Ⓓ seek

4. explore : look for :: discover : _____

   Ⓐ hide   Ⓑ seek   Ⓒ find   Ⓓ cover

5. missing : lost :: seek : _____

   Ⓐ clue   Ⓑ trail   Ⓒ search   Ⓓ found

6. wishes for the future : hope :: a group with a single goal : _____

   Ⓐ unity   Ⓑ trust   Ⓒ remorse   Ⓓ empathy

7. hope : wish :: vision : _____

   Ⓐ lead   Ⓑ dream   Ⓒ change   Ⓓ equal

8. quaffle : beater :: _____ : seeker

   Ⓐ nosey   Ⓑ snitch   Ⓒ jerk   Ⓓ snoop

9. believe : know :: wish : _____

   Ⓐ help   Ⓑ hope   Ⓒ respect   Ⓓ change

10. romance : love :: camaraderie : _____

    Ⓐ jealousy   Ⓑ friendship   Ⓒ emotion   Ⓓ infatuation

11. teach : learn :: lead : _____

    Ⓐ free   Ⓑ follow   Ⓒ hope   Ⓓ change

12. school : _____ :: vacation : play

    Ⓐ consumer   Ⓑ anger   Ⓒ work   Ⓓ cover

Name _____ **LESSON 62** Date _____

Study the relationship between the first set of words. Pick the word that completes the second pair with this same relationship.

1. factory : _____ :: tenement house : live

    Ⓐ employ   Ⓑ work   Ⓒ retire   Ⓓ tie

2. god : deity :: follower : _____

    Ⓐ martyr   Ⓑ disciple   Ⓒ prophet   Ⓓ leader

3. desk : work :: bed : _____

    Ⓐ sleep   Ⓑ stand   Ⓒ travel   Ⓓ night

4. detest : hate :: adore : _____

    Ⓐ cactus   Ⓑ love   Ⓒ anger   Ⓓ dislike

5. explore : look for :: discover : _____

    Ⓐ hide   Ⓑ find   Ⓒ seek   Ⓓ cover

6. Labor : relax :: _____ : unwind

    Ⓐ tie   Ⓑ Work   Ⓒ trade   Ⓓ retire

7. mythology : gods :: fables : _____

    ₌ stars   Ⓑ animals   Ⓒ heroes   Ⓓ fish

8. God : Christianity :: Allah : _____

    Ⓐ Judaism   Ⓑ Buddhism   Ⓒ Mormonism   Ⓓ Islam

9. _____ : Hades :: goddess : Athena

    Ⓐ Jesus Christ   Ⓑ Mohammed   Ⓒ god   Ⓓ Buddha

10. hope : wish :: vision : _____

    Ⓐ lead   Ⓑ equal   Ⓒ dream   Ⓓ change

11. capital : asset :: labor : _____

    Ⓐ consumer   Ⓑ demand   Ⓒ anger   Ⓓ work

12. believe : know :: wish : _____

    Ⓐ help   Ⓑ change   Ⓒ respect   Ⓓ hope

Study the relationship between the first set of words. Pick the word that completes the second pair with this same relationship.

1. romance : love :: camaraderie : _____

   (A) jealousy   (B) friendship   (C) emotion   (D) infatuation

2. _____ : Allah :: Judaism : God

   (A) Islam   (B) Mormonism   (C) Buddhism   (D) Judaism

3. desk : work :: bed : _____

   (A) sleep   (B) stand   (C) night   (D) travel

4. portrait : realistic :: caricature : _____

   (A) personal   (B) art   (C) cartoon   (D) drawing

5. love : feeling :: _____ : card

   (A) gift   (B) card   (C) valentine   (D) cupid

6. hope : hoping :: vote : _____

   (A) ballot   (B) voting   (C) party   (D) voted

7. admiration : respect :: amazement : _____

   (A) hope   (B) admiration   (C) awe   (D) understanding

8. factory : _____ :: tenement house : live

   (A) employ   (B) work   (C) tie   (D) retire

9. explore : look for :: discover : _____

   (A) hide   (B) cover   (C) seek   (D) find

10. hope : wish :: vision : _____

    (A) dream   (B) equal   (C) change   (D) lead

11. comprehend : understand :: contribute : _____

    (A) prove   (B) give   (C) seek   (D) learn

12. falter : advance :: abandon : _____

    (A) lose   (B) forward   (C) hope   (D) rescue

Name _____   **LESSON 64**   Date _____

Study the relationship between the first set of words. Pick the word that completes the second pair with this same relationship.

1. mountain : valley :: rainforest : _____

    Ⓐ jungle   Ⓑ desert   Ⓒ wet   Ⓓ Amazon

2. life : lives :: peach : _____

    Ⓐ peachy   Ⓑ peaches   Ⓒ peachs   Ⓓ peachves

3. Mkeka : mat :: kinara : _____

    Ⓐ pan   Ⓑ toy   Ⓒ candleholder   Ⓓ cup

4. and : conjunction :: _____ : noun

    Ⓐ oven   Ⓑ bed   Ⓒ television   Ⓓ table

5. fighting : knights :: farming : _____

    Ⓐ pages   Ⓑ lords   Ⓒ kings   Ⓓ serfs

6. water : fire :: disinfectant : _____

    Ⓐ germs   Ⓑ coal   Ⓒ dirt   Ⓓ oil

7. knight : page :: _____ : serf

    Ⓐ knight   Ⓑ lord   Ⓒ squire   ⊕ monk

8. woods : forest :: grassland : _____

    Ⓐ prairie   Ⓑ corn   Ⓒ plateau   Ⓓ valley

9. resourceful : creativity :: virtue : _____

    Ⓐ goodness   Ⓑ curiosity   Ⓒ justice   Ⓓ control

10. milk : gallon :: eggs : _____

    Ⓐ dozen   Ⓑ pound   Ⓒ can   Ⓓ cup

11. absurdity : disbelief :: revulsion : _____

    Ⓐ comfort   Ⓑ regret   Ⓒ fear   Ⓓ disgust

12. heinous : evil :: cunning : _____

    Ⓐ kind   Ⓑ foolish   Ⓒ rude   Ⓓ clever

69

Name _____ **LESSON 65** Date _____

Study the relationship between the first set of words. Pick the word that completes the second pair with this same relationship.

1. _____ : gallons :: land : acres

   A road   **B** water   **C** oven   **D** vitamins

2. lesson : lecture :: study : _____

   A teach   **B** observe   **C** learn   **D** prepare

3. bed : sleep :: table : _____

   A eat   sing   **C** read   **D** watch football

4. police officer : friend :: terrorist : _____

   A home   **B** angry   **C** enemy   **D** family

5. need : shelter :: want : _____

   A clothing   **B** food   **C** water   **D** toys

6. white + red : _____ :: yellow + blue : green

   A blue   **B** purple   **C** pink   **D** brown

7. truth : confession :: lie : _____

   A perjury   **B** innocence   **C** interrogation   **D** obstruction

8. spoons : drawer :: plates : _____

   A chair   **B** cupboard   **C** cup   **D** pan

9. cup : _____ :: bed : bassinet

   A spoon   **B** lid   **C** bottle   **D** fire

10. wants : wishes :: needs : _____

    A capital   **B** earnings   **C** necessities   **D** surplus

11. culprit : guilty :: maniac : _____

    A evil   **B** friendly   **C** innocent   **D** crazy

12. stifled : quieted :: tethered : _____

    A woven   **B** opened   **C** covered   **D** tied

70

Name _____   **LESSON 66**   Date _____

Study the relationship between the first set of words. Pick the word that completes the second pair with this same relationship.

1. dove : peace :: bald eagle : _____

    Ⓐ life   Ⓑ intelligence   Ⓒ freedom   Ⓓ speed

2. _____ : loud :: worthless : valuable

    Ⓐ play   Ⓑ open   Ⓒ careful   Ⓓ quiet

3. bury : soil :: submerge : _____

    Ⓐ air   Ⓑ blankets   Ⓒ water   Ⓓ stones

4. menorah : candleholder :: dreidel : _____

    Ⓐ toy   Ⓑ oil   Ⓒ story   Ⓓ book

5. rocks : stones :: valleys : _____

    Ⓐ peaks   Ⓑ streams   Ⓒ boulders   Ⓓ hollows

6. culprit : guilty :: maniac : _____

    Ⓐ friendly   Ⓑ evil   Ⓒ innocent   Ⓓ crazy

7. lesson : lecture :: study : _____

    Ⓐ observe   Ⓑ teach   Ⓒ prepare   Ⓓ learn

8. theatrical play : script :: orchestra : _____

    Ⓐ pitch   Ⓑ staff   Ⓒ tone   Ⓓ score

9. to dog : follow :: to hawk : _____

    Ⓐ peddle   Ⓑ steal   Ⓒ find   Ⓓ meddle

10. optimism : hope :: _____ : fear

    Ⓐ persistence   Ⓑ prejudice   Ⓒ civility   Ⓓ equality

11. bed : _____ :: table : eat

    Ⓐ night   Ⓑ play   Ⓒ travel   Ⓓ sleep

12. enemy : ally :: stranger : _____

    Ⓐ alcove   Ⓑ acquaintance   Ⓒ marksman   Ⓓ survivor

Study the relationship between the first set of words. Pick the word that completes the second pair with this same relationship.

1.   digit : number :: letter : _____

   A manuscript   **B** cursive   **C** word   **D** write

2.   signals a business is not open : closed sign :: signals there is mail for the postal worker to pick up in a mailbox : _____

   A stamps   **B** balloons   **C** flag   **D** rain

3.   quake : shake :: hunker : _____

   A retreat   **B** carry   **C** swim   **D** squat

4.   center : mailing address :: top-left corner : _____

   A stamp   **B** envelope   **C** return address   **D** change of address

5.   legible : read :: _____ : eat

   A clean   **B** edible   **C** light   **D** nourishing

6.   Mother's Day : Sunday :: Memorial Day : _____

   A Monday   **B** Sunday   **C** Saturday   **D** Friday

7.   cookbook : recipes :: sketchbook : _____

   A instructions   **B** drawings   **C** photographs   **D** addresses

8.   April Fool's Day : humor :: Valentine's Day : _____

   A cards   **B** red   **C** love   **D** candy

9.   city : _____ :: house : neighborhood

   A state   **B** government   **C** country   **D** zip code

10.   add : numbers :: spell : _____

   A paper   **B** English   **C** test   **D** letters

11.   Mother's Day : Sunday :: Memorial Day : _____

   A Friday   **B** Saturday   **C** Tuesday   **D** Monday

12.   not closed : open :: not new : _____

   A learn   **B** dirty   **C** today   **D** old

72

Study the relationship between the first set of words. Pick the word that completes the second pair with this same relationship.

1. closed : open :: broken : _____

   Ⓐ resignation   Ⓑ functional   Ⓒ installation   Ⓓ pulverized

2. English writing : letters :: Chinese writing : _____

   Ⓐ dots   Ⓑ French   Ⓒ cartoons   Ⓓ characters

3. oath : _____ :: address : speech

   Ⓐ promise   Ⓑ suppose   Ⓒ plan   Ⓓ law

4. baffling : confusing :: tedious : _____

   Ⓐ special   Ⓑ cozy   Ⓒ tiring   Ⓓ honorable

5. note asking you to come to a party : invitation :: note sent while you are on vacation :

   _____

   Ⓐ post card   Ⓑ roll   Ⓒ package   Ⓓ envelope

6. Mother's Day : Sunday :: Memorial Day : _____

   Ⓐ Sunday   Ⓑ Friday   Ⓒ Monday   Ⓓ Saturday

7. day : noon :: night : _____

   Ⓐ fall   Ⓑ midnight   Ⓒ afternoon   Ⓓ month

8. gift : box :: card : _____

   Ⓐ Valentine   Ⓑ present   Ⓒ mail   Ⓓ envelope

9. always : never :: up : _____

   Ⓐ jump   Ⓑ sky   Ⓒ down   Ⓓ above

10. sender : return address :: recipient : _____

    Ⓐ zip code   Ⓑ stamp   Ⓒ mailing address   Ⓓ post card

11. withdraw : secede :: control : _____

    Ⓐ dominate   Ⓑ unite   Ⓒ indenture   Ⓓ address

12. _____ : mailman :: postage : stamp

    Ⓐ stamp collector   Ⓑ firefighter   Ⓒ postal worker   Ⓓ nurse

Name _____   **LESSON 69**   Date _____

Study the relationship between the first set of words. Pick the word that completes the second pair with this same relationship.

1. yellow rose : _____ :: red rose : love

   Ⓐ jealousy   Ⓑ emotion   Ⓒ friendship   Ⓓ infatuation

2. _____ : mailman :: postage : stamp

   Ⓐ firefighter   Ⓑ stamp collector   Ⓒ nurse   Ⓓ postal worker

3. candid : open :: treacherous : _____

   Ⓐ dangerous   Ⓑ healthy   Ⓒ hidden   Ⓓ educational

4. Mother's Day : Sunday :: Memorial Day : _____

   Ⓐ Saturday   Ⓑ Friday   Ⓒ Monday   Ⓓ Sunday

5. breakfast : _____ :: lunch : afternoon

   Ⓐ alarm clock   Ⓑ morning   Ⓒ afternoon   Ⓓ egg

6. kind : angry :: gentle : _____

   Ⓐ old-fashioned   Ⓑ weak   Ⓒ special   Ⓓ vicious

7. title of a noble woman : _____ :: title of a noble man : lord

   Ⓐ boy   Ⓑ guy   Ⓒ lady   Ⓓ mister

8. grocery store : food :: post office : _____

   Ⓐ medicine   Ⓑ plants   Ⓒ fabric   Ⓓ stamps

9. birth date : age :: address : _____

   Ⓐ house   Ⓑ post office   Ⓒ direction   Ⓓ location

10. April Fool's Day : humor :: Valentine's Day : _____

    Ⓐ red   Ⓑ cards   Ⓒ candy   Ⓓ love

11. dribble : spill :: quiver : _____

    Ⓐ mop   Ⓑ cold   Ⓒ shake   Ⓓ flip

12. weekday : Tuesday :: weekend : _____

    Ⓐ Friday   Ⓑ Wednesday   Ⓒ Saturday   Ⓓ Monday

Name _____   LESSON 70   Date _____

Study the relationship between the first set of words. Pick the word that completes the second pair with this same relationship.

1. rotate : spin :: orbit : _____

   Ⓐ tilt   Ⓑ revolve around   Ⓒ expand   Ⓓ absorb

2. alarm clock : _____ :: microwave oven : kitchen

   Ⓐ porch   Ⓑ bedroom   Ⓒ family room   Ⓓ garage

3. girl : _____ :: woman : man

   Ⓐ male   Ⓑ lady   Ⓒ woman   Ⓓ boy

4. small : tiny :: large : _____

   Ⓐ miniature   Ⓑ average   Ⓒ enormous   Ⓓ little

5. deer : fur :: turkey : _____

   Ⓐ feathers   Ⓑ gobble   Ⓒ bird   Ⓓ beak

6. sandwich : bread :: _____ : lettuce

   Ⓐ round   Ⓑ rabbits   Ⓒ garden   Ⓓ salad

7. assist : help :: recycle : _____

   Ⓐ remember   Ⓑ reuse   Ⓒ aid   Ⓓ join

8. title of a noble woman : _____ :: title of a noble man : lord

   Ⓐ mister   Ⓑ guy   Ⓒ boy   Ⓓ lady

9. cupboard : _____ :: barricade : barrier

   Ⓐ Vice-President Ⓑ cabinet   Ⓒ Oval Office   Ⓓ Secretary of State

10. pagoda : building :: wok : _____

    Ⓐ dress   Ⓑ a farming tool   Ⓒ cooking pot   Ⓓ candle

11. closet : bedroom :: pantry : _____

    Ⓐ garage   Ⓑ family room   Ⓒ kitchen   Ⓓ living room

12. carrots : vitamin A :: milk : _____

    Ⓐ iron   Ⓑ vitamin K   Ⓒ vitamin C   Ⓓ calcium

Name _____   **LESSON 71**   Date _____

Study the relationship between the first set of words. Pick the word that completes the second pair with this same relationship.

1. tug : pull :: huddle : _____

    (A) push   (B) gather around   (C) strut   (D) spread out

2. _____ : quack :: turkey : gobble

    (A) frog   (B) duck   (C) cow   (D) walrus

3. alarm clock : _____ :: microwave oven : kitchen

    (A) porch   (B) bedroom   (C) garage   (D) family room

4. lord : lady :: monk : _____

    (A) bishop   (B) monastery   (C) cathedral   (D) nun

5. male : man :: female : _____

    (A) woman   (B) feline   (C) boy   (D) gentleman

6. male : _____ :: female : lady

    (A) kid   (B) madam   (C) officer   (D) gentleman

7. rain : _____ :: snow : cold

    (A) warm   (B) middle   (C) temperature (D) dry

8. hustle : hurry :: confer : _____

    (A) swoop   (B) scrunch   (C) discuss   (D) sleep

9. turkey : cranberry sauce :: mashed potatoes : _____

    (A) dressing   (B) corn   (C) gravy   (D) pie

10. breakfast : morning :: _____ : noon

    (A) snack   (B) lunch   (C) dinner   (D) sandwich

11. winter : cold :: summer : _____

    (A) hot   (B) good   (C) sunny   (D) June

12. quiet : loud :: empty : _____

    (A) dark   (B) crowded   (C) clean   (D) closed

Study the relationship between the first set of words. Pick the word that completes the second pair with this same relationship.

1.   man : _____ :: woman : purse

    Ⓐ check   Ⓑ deposit   Ⓒ credit   Ⓓ wallet

2.   peer : _____ :: recollect : remember

    Ⓐ cut   Ⓑ look   Ⓒ near   Ⓓ cover

3.   flourish : wave :: perspire : _____

    Ⓐ reach   Ⓑ cut   Ⓒ sweat   Ⓓ speak

4.   push : pull :: scatter : _____

    Ⓐ hinder   Ⓑ open   Ⓒ stretch   Ⓓ huddle

5.   milk : _____ :: hot chocolate : hot

    Ⓐ cloudy   Ⓑ cold   Ⓒ precipitation   Ⓓ ice

6.   shop : store :: barrel : _____

    Ⓐ mixture   Ⓑ stranger   Ⓒ light   Ⓓ container

7.   photographs : snapshots :: vacation : _____

    Ⓐ remember   Ⓑ trip   Ⓒ camera   Ⓓ copies

8.   female : lady :: male : _____

    Ⓐ madam   Ⓑ kid   Ⓒ officer   Ⓓ gentleman

9.   lord : lady :: monk : _____

    Ⓐ bishop   Ⓑ nun   Ⓒ damsel   Ⓓ cathedral

10.   _____ : soup :: breakfast : porridge

    Ⓐ kitchen   Ⓑ snack   Ⓒ dinner   Ⓓ eat

11.   to gather together : cluster :: to clap : _____

    Ⓐ huddle   Ⓑ applaud   Ⓒ strike   Ⓓ jeer

12.   Dr. : Doctor :: Mr. : _____

    Ⓐ Sir   Ⓑ Ma'am   Ⓒ Mister   Ⓓ Lady

Study the relationship between the first set of words. Pick the word that completes the second pair with this same relationship.

1. Athens : Greece :: Rome : _____

   A China   **B** Egypt   **C** Spain   **D** Italy

2. France : Europe :: Ghana : _____

   A Australia   **B** South America   **C** Asia   **D** Africa

3. London : England :: Paris : _____

   A Germany   **B** France   **C** Europe   **D** Italy

4. Normans : France :: Vikings : _____

   A Germany   **B** Spain   **C** China   **D** Scandinavia

5. _____ : North America :: Spain : Europe

   A Japan   **B** Mexico   **C** United States   **D** Canada

6. India : Indian Ocean :: Italy : _____

   A Mediterranean Sea   **B** Atlantic Ocean   **C** Red Sea   **D** Black Sea

7. American Colonies : England :: Mexico : _____

   A America   **B** France   **C** California   **D** England

8. Francois I : France :: Henry VIII : _____

   A Italy   **B** Germany   **C** Spain   **D** England

9. WW I : Austria, Hungary, and Germany :: WWII : _____

   A Germany, Japan, and Italy   **B** Germany   **C** Germany, Japan, Italy, and ChinaJapan   **D** Germany and

10. ancient Rome : Italy :: ancient Mesopotamia : _____

    A Egypt   **B** India   **C** Spain   **D** Iraq

11. _____ : Norway :: Conquistador : Spain

    A Oslo   **B** Odin   **C** Leif Eriksson   **D** Viking

12. Hernando Cortes : _____ :: Giovanni da Verrazano : Italy

    A Mexico   **B** Aztecs   **C** England   **D** Spain

Name _____   **LESSON 74**   Date _____

Study the relationship between the first set of words. Pick the word that completes the
second pair with this same relationship.

1. _____ : Adriatic Sea :: Greece : Aegean Sea

    Ⓐ Spain   Ⓑ Egypt   Ⓒ Turkey   Ⓓ Italy

2. Shakespeare : England :: Faulkner : _____

    Ⓐ Germany   Ⓑ Soviet Union   Ⓒ Sweden   Ⓓ United States

3. Ecuador : bananas :: _____ : corn

    Ⓐ China   Ⓑ India   Ⓒ Argentina   Ⓓ Mexico

4. France : Europe :: Ghana : _____

    Ⓐ Australia   Ⓑ Asia   Ⓒ South America   Ⓓ Africa

5. WW I : Austria, Hungary, and Germany :: WWII : _____

    Ⓐ Germany,   Ⓑ Germany,   Ⓒ Germany and   Ⓓ Germany
    Japan, and Italy   Japan, Italy, and ChinaJapan

6. Adolf Hitler : Germany :: Saddam Hussein : _____

    Ⓐ Iraq   Ⓑ Iran   Ⓒ Spain   Ⓓ India

7. Machu Picchu : Peru :: Chichen Itza : _____

    Ⓐ Argentina   Ⓑ Columbia   Ⓒ Nicaragua   Ⓓ Mexico

8. Francois I : France :: Henry VIII : _____

    Ⓐ England   Ⓑ Italy   Ⓒ Spain   Ⓓ Germany

9. Christopher Columbus : Spain :: Leif Eriksson : _____

    Ⓐ Norway   Ⓑ Italy   Ⓒ France   Ⓓ England

10. Kenya : Africa :: Germany : _____

    Ⓐ Russia   Ⓑ Europe   Ⓒ France   Ⓓ Asia

11. Normans : France :: Vikings : _____

    Ⓐ Scandinavia   Ⓑ Spain   ⎯ Germany   Ⓓ China

12. ancient Rome : Italy :: ancient Mesopotamia : _____

    Ⓐ India   Ⓑ Spain   Ⓒ Iraq   Ⓓ Egypt

Name _____   **LESSON 75**   Date _____

Study the relationship between the first set of words. Pick the word that completes the second pair with this same relationship.

1. ancient Rome : Italy :: ancient Mesopotamia : _____

    Ⓐ Spain   Ⓑ Egypt   Ⓒ India   Ⓓ Iraq

2. United States : _____ :: Mexico : France

    Ⓐ Spain   Ⓑ England   Ⓒ Europe   Ⓓ Italy

3. Hernando Cortes : _____ :: Giovanni da Verrazano : Italy

    Ⓐ Aztecs   Ⓑ Mexico   Ⓒ England   Ⓓ Spain

4. _____ : Adriatic Sea :: Greece : Aegean Sea

    Ⓐ Egypt   Ⓑ Spain   Ⓒ Italy   Ⓓ Turkey

5. London : England :: Paris : _____

    Ⓐ Europe   Ⓑ France   Ⓒ Germany   Ⓓ Italy

6. España : Spain :: Los Estados Unidos : _____

    Ⓐ Mexico   Ⓑ United States   Ⓒ France   Ⓓ Australia

7. Adolf Hitler : Germany :: Saddam Hussein : _____

    Ⓐ Spain   Ⓑ India   Ⓒ Iran   Ⓓ Iraq

8. _____ : North America :: Spain : Europe

    Ⓐ United States   Ⓑ Mexico   Ⓒ Canada   Ⓓ Japan

9. Machu Picchu : Peru :: Chichen Itza : _____

    Ⓐ Nicaragua   Ⓑ Argentina   Ⓒ Columbia   Ⓓ Mexico

10. Germany : German shepherd :: _____ : Chihuahua

    Ⓐ England   Ⓑ Argentina   Ⓒ India   Ⓓ Mexico

11. ancient Rome : Italy :: ancient Mesopotamia : _____

    Ⓐ Italy   Ⓑ Iraq   Ⓒ Indonesia   Ⓓ Iran

12. Normans : France :: Vikings : _____

    Ⓐ Germany   Ⓑ Scandinavia   Ⓒ Spain   Ⓓ China

Study the relationship between the first set of words. Pick the word that completes the second pair with this same relationship.

1. charming : delightful :: sinister : _____

   Ⓐ kind   Ⓑ evil   Ⓒ shy   Ⓓ generous

2. slave : servant :: ruler : _____

   Ⓐ friend   Ⓑ enemy   Ⓒ teacher   Ⓓ leader

3. _____ : fright :: row : tow

   Ⓐ grass   Ⓑ weekend   Ⓒ July   Ⓓ light

4. criminal : felon :: detective : _____

   Ⓐ witness   Ⓑ negotiator   Ⓒ outlaw   Ⓓ sleuth

5. heinous : evil :: cunning : _____

   Ⓐ annoying   Ⓑ kind   Ⓒ clever   Ⓓ foolish

6. multiply : increase in number :: stretch : _____

   Ⓐ fade   Ⓑ gaze   Ⓒ gopher   Ⓓ expand

7. stumble : fall :: twitter : _____

   Ⓐ heat   Ⓑ tremble   Ⓒ cry   Ⓓ talk

8. fortune : good luck :: grudge : _____

   Ⓐ evil   Ⓑ fright   Ⓒ fairness   Ⓓ resentment

9. flea : bite :: bee : _____

   Ⓐ queen   Ⓑ honey   Ⓒ ant   Ⓓ sting

10. book : chapters :: war : _____

    Ⓐ battles   Ⓑ speeches   Ⓒ enemies   Ⓓ generals

11. devour : _____ :: extend : lengthen

    Ⓐ sleep   Ⓑ wear   Ⓒ eat   Ⓓ read

12. comprehend : understand :: contribute : _____

    Ⓐ give   Ⓑ seek   Ⓒ learn   Ⓓ prove

Name _____ **LESSON 77** Date _____

Study the relationship between the first set of words. Pick the word that completes the second pair with this same relationship.

1. invade : attack :: protect : _____

   (A) battle   (B) defeat   (C) defend   (D) soldiers

2. _____ : breathe in :: devour : eat

   (A) filter   (B) inhale   (C) cigarette   (D) smoke

3. need : shelter :: want : _____

   (A) clothing   (B) toys   (C) water   (D) food

4. song : carol :: folklore : _____

   (A) trouble   (B) artisan   (C) legend   (D) tradition

5. morning : light :: evening : _____

   (A) sun   (B) dark   (C) noon   (D) spark

6. ratify : _____ :: veto : reject

   (A) judge   (B) accept   (C) return   (D) refuse

7. _____ : move forward :: protrude : stick out

   (A) fight   (B) discharge   (C) casualty   (D) advance

8. school : teachers :: army : _____

   (A) students   (B) military   (C) generals   (D) war

9. defeat : _____ :: retreat : advance

   (A) victory   (B) tie   (C) surrender   (D) time out

10. cowardice : courage :: shame : _____

    (A) kindness   (B) glory   (C) pride   (D) fear

11. police officer : _____ :: terrorist : enemy

    (A) friend   (B) teacher   (C) gun   (D) pet

12. slave : servant :: ruler : _____

    (A) leader   (B) teacher   (C) enemy   (D) friend

Name _____   **LESSON 78**   Date _____

**Study the relationship between the first set of words. Pick the word that completes the
second pair with this same relationship.**

1. multiply : increase in number :: stretch : _____

    Ⓐ expand   Ⓑ fade   Ⓒ gopher   Ⓓ gaze

2. evil : kind :: afraid : _____

    Ⓐ hopeful   Ⓑ hidden   Ⓒ angry   Ⓓ fearless

3. heave : lift :: falter : _____

    Ⓐ cover   Ⓑ imagine   Ⓒ stumble   Ⓓ climb

4. cheerful : happy :: spooky : _____

    Ⓐ laughter   Ⓑ evil   Ⓒ eerie   Ⓓ nervous

5. trail : path :: bluff : _____

    Ⓐ mountain   Ⓑ rock   Ⓒ cliff   Ⓓ river

6. fortune : good luck :: grudge : _____

    Ⓐ resentment   Ⓑ fairness   Ⓒ fright   Ⓓ evil

7. bluff : cliff :: trail : _____

    Ⓐ mountain   Ⓑ path   Ⓒ entry   Ⓓ river

8. _____ : defeat :: allies : enemies

    Ⓐ surrender   Ⓑ general   Ⓒ battle   Ⓓ victory

9. barn : building :: fence : _____

    Ⓐ gate   Ⓑ shelter   Ⓒ border   Ⓓ post

10. mooring : securing :: meddling : _____

    Ⓐ sheltering   Ⓑ dividing   Ⓒ interfering   Ⓓ endangering

11. sleek : smooth :: withered : _____

    Ⓐ dried up   Ⓑ surrounded   Ⓒ round   Ⓓ bare

12. obstinacy : stubbornness :: trepidation : _____

    Ⓐ bravery   Ⓑ fear   Ⓒ emerge   Ⓓ humor

83

Study the relationship between the first set of words. Pick the word that completes the second pair with this same relationship.

1. football : _____ :: basketball : court

   A Ferris wheel   **B** farming   **C** field   **D** crops

2. lament : mourn :: cajole : _____

   A persuade   **B** count   **C** understand   **D** celebrate

3. present : gift :: prank : _____

   A cake   **B** trick   **C** book   **D** bow

4. lamp : light bulb :: jack-o-lantern : _____

   A orange   **B** pumpkin   **C** candle   **D** fire

5. excel : surpass :: flaunt : _____

   A perceive   **B** show off   **C** glide   **D** distract

6. small : tiny :: large : _____

   A spider   **B** little   **C** huge   **D** medium

7. asleep : awake :: little : _____

   A night   **B** big   **C** pillow   **D** small

8. dark : _____ :: laugh : cry

   A darkness   **B** table   **C** light   **D** marshmallows

9. canteen : water :: lantern : _____

   A soup   **B** matches   **C** marshmallows   **D** light

10. _____ : conceal :: disappear : vanish

   A carry   **B** clean   **C** hide   **D** fire

11. peer : look :: recollect : _____

   A replenish   **B** give   **C** decide   **D** remember

12. encounter : meet :: accomplish : _____

   A help   **B** scare   **C** decide   **D** achieve

Name _____   **LESSON 80**   Date _____

Study the relationship between the first set of words. Pick the word that completes the second pair with this same relationship.

1. vibration : feel :: click : _____

   Ⓐ remember   Ⓑ taste   Ⓒ see   Ⓓ hear

2. lament : mourn :: cajole : _____

   Ⓐ celebrate   Ⓑ persuade   Ⓒ count   Ⓓ understand

3. to bring into agreement : reconcile :: to comfort : _____

   Ⓐ console   Ⓑ tarry   Ⓒ poise   Ⓓ sneer

4. partner : help :: heir : _____

   Ⓐ serve   Ⓑ solve   Ⓒ buy   Ⓓ inherit

5. Zoroastrianism : religion :: Avesta : _____

   Ⓐ prophet   Ⓑ scripture   Ⓒ founder   Ⓓ god

6. disappear : vanish :: _____ : dread

   Ⓐ hope   Ⓑ shyness   Ⓒ love   Ⓓ fear

7. person who died for a religious cause : martyr :: person who betrayed another : _____

   Ⓐ traitor   Ⓑ prophet   Ⓒ apostle   Ⓓ pilgrim

8. peer : look :: recollect : _____

   Ⓐ decide   Ⓑ replenish   Ⓒ remember   Ⓓ give

9. _____ : light bulb :: candle : jack-o-lantern

   Ⓐ lamp   Ⓑ fireworks   Ⓒ fish   Ⓓ monster

10. small : tiny :: large : _____

   Ⓐ little   Ⓑ huge   Ⓒ medium   Ⓓ spider

11. lecture : speech :: conference : _____

   Ⓐ judgment   Ⓑ meeting   Ⓒ job   Ⓓ award

12. hide : conceal :: disappear : _____

   Ⓐ vanish   Ⓑ hide   Ⓒ bandit   Ⓓ suspect

Study the relationship between the first set of words. Pick the word that completes the second pair with this same relationship.

1. cattle : herd :: quail : _____

   Ⓐ murder   Ⓑ covey   Ⓒ snag   Ⓓ school

2. leader : king :: _____ : kingdom

   Ⓐ instrument   Ⓑ weapon   Ⓒ land   Ⓓ dungeon

3. small : tiny :: large : _____

   Ⓐ little   Ⓑ average   Ⓒ miniature   Ⓓ enormous

4. iodine : _____ :: vitamin D : milk

   Ⓐ cholesterol   Ⓑ sulfur   Ⓒ sugar   Ⓓ salt

5. excel : surpass :: flaunt : _____

   Ⓐ glide   Ⓑ perceive   Ⓒ show off   Ⓓ distract

6. appetite : eat :: thirst : _____

   Ⓐ quench   Ⓑ hunger   Ⓒ drink   Ⓓ table

7. hide : conceal :: disappear : _____

   Ⓐ bandit   Ⓑ vanish   Ⓒ hide   Ⓓ suspect

8. surly : grumpy :: meek : _____

   Ⓐ savage   Ⓑ gentle   Ⓒ active   Ⓓ scratchy

9. charity : generosity :: cheer : _____

   Ⓐ hunger   Ⓑ greed   Ⓒ curiosity   Ⓓ happiness

10. thirst : drink :: appetite : _____

    Ⓐ wash   Ⓑ rest   Ⓒ swim   Ⓓ eat

11. football : _____ :: basketball : court

    Ⓐ farming   Ⓑ Ferris wheel Ⓒ crops   Ⓓ field

12. jury : judgment :: witness : _____

    Ⓐ testimony   Ⓑ asks questions Ⓒ counsel Ⓓ objections

Study the relationship between the first set of words. Pick the word that completes the second pair with this same relationship.

1. spirited : enthusiastic :: easily seen : _____

    Ⓐ confident   Ⓑ emphatic   Ⓒ gregarious   Ⓓ obvious

2. democracy : _____ :: monarchy : inherit

    Ⓐ elect   Ⓑ empire   Ⓒ dictator   Ⓓ veto

3. resent someone for the things or status they have : _____ :: desire to have more of something than you need : greed

    Ⓐ anxiety   Ⓑ objectivity   Ⓒ gloves   Ⓓ jealousy

4. _____ : sad :: love : hate

    Ⓐ happy   Ⓑ scared   Ⓒ confused   Ⓓ frightful

5. chagrin : disappointment :: wrath : _____

    Ⓐ humiliation   Ⓑ anger   Ⓒ fright   Ⓓ joy

6. faith : belief :: unity : _____

    Ⓐ togetherness   Ⓑ culture   Ⓒ separation   Ⓓ joy

7. faithful : _____ :: dedicated : hard-working

    Ⓐ anxious   Ⓑ keen   Ⓒ sober   Ⓓ loyal

8. tolerance : acceptance :: charity : _____

    Ⓐ patience   Ⓑ generosity   Ⓒ inspiration   Ⓓ praise

9. resourceful : creativity :: _____ : goodness

    Ⓐ attitude   Ⓑ virtue   Ⓒ optimism   Ⓓ aptitude

10. fortification : reinforcement :: benevolence : _____

    Ⓐ donation   Ⓑ sympathy   Ⓒ gratitude   Ⓓ kindness

11. concealed : hidden :: obvious : _____

    Ⓐ easy to see   Ⓑ small   Ⓒ hard to remember   Ⓓ dark

12. _____ : excitement :: envy : jealousy

    Ⓐ enthusiasm   Ⓑ anticipation   Ⓒ repentance   Ⓓ frustration

Study the relationship between the first set of words. Pick the word that completes the second pair with this same relationship.

1. dove : peace :: vulture : _____

   (A) buzzard   (B) ugly   (C) scavenger   (D) death

2. infatuation : fleeting :: love : _____

   (A) affectionate   (B) beautiful   (C) enduring   (D) discerning

3. . war : _____ :: soldier : conscientious objector

   (A) trust   (B) freedom   (C) peace   (D) honesty

4. apprehension : fear :: wrath : _____

   (A) deceit   (B) anger   (C) joy   (D) humor

5. jealousy : envy :: trust : _____

   (A) skeptical   (B) doubt   (C) belief   (D) chance

6. common : rare :: ordinary : _____

   (A) obvious   (B) legendary   (C) exemplary   (D) singular

7. _____ : smiley face :: love : heart

   (A) angry   (B) furious   (C) happy   (D) frightful

8. fortification : reinforcement :: benevolence : _____

   (A) reproach   (B) kindness   (C) sympathy   (D) gratitude

9. conspicuous : obvious :: atrocious : _____

   (A) terrible   (B) calm   (C) anxious   (D) normal

10. romance : love :: camaraderie : _____

    (A) jealousy   (B) infatuation   (C) friendship   (D) emotion

11. cheating : plagiarism :: lying : _____

    (A) fraud   (B) morality   (C) shoplifting   (D) jealousy

12. shame : embarrassment :: confusion : _____

    (A) veracity   (B) discord   (C) perplexity   (D) rebuke

Name _____ LESSON 84 Date _____

Study the relationship between the first set of words. Pick the word that completes the second pair with this same relationship.

1. concealed : hidden :: obvious : _____

   Ⓐ easy to see   Ⓑ hard to remember   Ⓒ dark   Ⓓ small

2. love : feeling :: valentine : _____

   Ⓐ envelope   Ⓑ hug   Ⓒ February   Ⓓ card

3. peace : harmony :: war : _____

   Ⓐ army   Ⓑ happiness   Ⓒ conflict   Ⓓ soldier

4. adoration : love :: gratitude : _____

   Ⓐ hatred   Ⓑ thankfulness   Ⓒ kindness   Ⓓ sympathy

5. futile : ineffective :: frugal : _____

   Ⓐ isolated   Ⓑ efficient   Ⓒ obvious   Ⓓ thrifty

6. kindness : _____ :: sorrow : sadness

   Ⓐ mercy   Ⓑ stun   Ⓒ bitter   Ⓓ ridicule

7. apprehension : fear :: wrath : _____

   Ⓐ anger   Ⓑ joy   Ⓒ deceit   Ⓓ humor

8. _____ : excitement :: envy : jealousy

   Ⓐ anticipation   Ⓑ frustration   Ⓒ enthusiasm   Ⓓ repentance

9. romance : love :: camaraderie : _____

   Ⓐ emotion   Ⓑ friendship   Ⓒ jealousy   Ⓓ infatuation

10. despair : sadness :: envy : _____

    Ⓐ admiration   Ⓑ joyousness   Ⓒ jealousy   Ⓓ clumsy

11. chagrin : disappointment :: wrath : _____

    Ⓐ anger   Ⓑ joy   Ⓒ humiliation   Ⓓ fright

12. generosity : charity :: selfishness : _____

    Ⓐ jealousy   Ⓑ anger   Ⓒ greed   Ⓓ thoughtfulness

Study the relationship between the first set of words. Pick the word that completes the second pair with this same relationship.

1. gift : _____ :: gaze : stare

   (A) ancient   (B) prehistoric   (C) future   (D) present

2. sleek : smooth :: withered : _____

   (A) round   (B) dried up   (C) surrounded   (D) bare

3. afraid : brave :: _____ : wise

   (A) angry   (B) foolish   (C) lonely   (D) sad

4. _____ : sharp claws :: defense : protective plates

   (A) retreat   (B) attack   (C) hide   (D) generals

5. savage : wild :: accurate : _____

   (A) capable   (B) correct   (C) safe   (D) tame

6. agora : marketplace :: polis : _____

   (A) assembly   (B) school   (C) city-state   (D) temple

7. army : soldiers :: village : _____

   (A) farms   (B) houses   (C) weapons   (D) town

8. inhale : breathe in :: devour : _____

   (A) fall   (B) eat   (C) drink   (D) read

9. multiply : increase in number :: stretch : _____

   (A) gopher   (B) gaze   (C) expand   (D) fade

10. begrudge : envy :: inform : _____

    (A) admire   (B) tell   (C) trouble   (D) reward

11. scared : afraid :: angry : _____

    (A) free   (B) happy   (C) mad   (D) leader

12. groan : moan :: gaze : _____

    (A) stare   (B) examine   (C) crest   (D) waddle

Name _____ **LESSON 86** Date _____

Study the relationship between the first set of words. Pick the word that completes the second pair with this same relationship.

1. pursuit of wisdom : philosophy :: collection of stories about a group of people, their history, and origin : _____

    (A) mythology   (B) temple   (C) library   (D) astronomy

2. Army : defenders :: Congress : _____

    (A) lawmakers   (B) colonists   (C) protectors   (D) enforcers

3. peer : look :: spurn : _____

    (A) warn   (B) reject   (C) purchase   (D) hide

4. war : peace :: enemy : _____

    (A) pet   (B) ruler   (C) friend   (D) teacher

5. _____ : shelter :: money : currency

    (A) chief   (B) home   (C) calm   (D) clothing

6. begrudge : envy :: inform : _____

    (A) trouble   (B) reward   (C) admire   (D) tell

7. quaffle : beater :: snitch : _____

    (A) seeker   (B) tattler   (C) beater   (D) chaser

8. stumble : fall :: shake : _____

    (A) cry   (B) talk   (C) tremble   (D) heat

9. barn : building :: fence : _____

    (A) gate   (B) border   (C) post   (D) shelter

10. lantern : light :: _____ : noise

    (A) silence   (B) violence   (C) horn   (D) lightbulb

11. marquee : sign :: vow : _____

    (A) sacrifice   (B) promise   (C) clue   (D) gift

12. sleeping : bed :: sacrifices : _____

    (A) terrace   (B) altar   (C) lookout tower   (D) empire

Name _____   **LESSON 87**   Date _____

Study the relationship between the first set of words. Pick the word that completes the second pair with this same relationship.

1. devour : consume :: amble : _____

   Ⓐ jump   Ⓑ anger   Ⓒ read   Ⓓ stroll

2. sponge : heart :: absorb : _____

   Ⓐ beat   Ⓑ Spongebob   Ⓒ attack   Ⓓ blot

3. invade : attack :: _____ : defend

   Ⓐ lose   Ⓑ capture   Ⓒ protect   Ⓓ teach

4. agora : marketplace :: polis : _____

   Ⓐ city-state   Ⓑ school   Ⓒ temple   Ⓓ assembly

5. record of one person's money in a bank : account :: locked place where banks keep money :

   _____

   Ⓐ exchange   Ⓑ safe   Ⓒ credit   Ⓓ loan

6. stumble : fall :: twitter : _____

   Ⓐ heat   Ⓑ talk   Ⓒ cry   Ⓓ tremble

7. patriotism : _____ :: terrorism : fear

   Ⓐ flock   Ⓑ mane   Ⓒ herd   Ⓓ pride

8. surround : encircle :: accompany : _____

   Ⓐ make up   Ⓑ combine   Ⓒ clean up   Ⓓ go along with

9. fortune : luck :: misfortune : _____

   Ⓐ trouble   Ⓑ stability   Ⓒ chance   Ⓓ blessing

10. Admiral : _____ :: General : Army

    Ⓐ soldier   Ⓑ Navy   Ⓒ Air Force   Ⓓ boat

11. sleeping : bed :: sacrifices : _____

    Ⓐ terrace   Ⓑ empire   Ⓒ altar   Ⓓ lookout tower

12. Army : defenders :: Congress : _____

    Ⓐ lawmakers   Ⓑ protectors   Ⓒ enforcers   Ⓓ colonists

Study the relationship between the first set of words. Pick the word that completes the second pair with this same relationship.

1. apple : tree :: grape : _____

   (A) green   (B) red   (C) fruit   (D) vine

2. excusable : unforgivable :: _____ : despicable

   (A) difficult   (B) unbelievable   (C) honorable   (D) generous

3. wonderful : great :: peculiar : _____

   (A) fuss   (B) silly   (C) terrible   (D) odd

4. _____ : persuade :: excuse : forgive

   (A) relieve   (B) increase   (C) prattle   (D) coax

5. apple : fruit :: acorn : _____

   (A) squirrel   (B) tree   (C) nut   (D) autumn

6. vine : tomatoes :: stalk : _____

   (A) lettuce   (B) carrot   (C) onion   (D) corn

7. _____ : fruit :: peas : vegetable

   (A) report card   (B) squirrel   (C) apple   (D) sunflower

8. culprit : guilty :: maniac : _____

   (A) innocent   (B) friendly   (C) evil   (D) crazy

9. excusable : unforgivable :: despicable : _____

   (A) honorable   (B) unbelievable   (C) difficult   (D) generous

10. very good : wonderful :: very bad : _____

    (A) terrible   (B) normal   (C) magnificent   (D) great

11. clandestine : secret :: torrid : _____

    (A) great   (B) punishing   (C) hot   (D) deep

12. give orders : command :: follow orders : _____

    (A) obey   (B) lead   (C) rebel   (D) review

Study the relationship between the first set of words. Pick the word that completes the second pair with this same relationship.

1. wonderful : great :: _____ : odd

   Ⓐ astonishing   Ⓑ quaint   Ⓒ menacing   Ⓓ peculiar

2. excusable : unforgivable :: despicable : _____

   Ⓐ generous   Ⓑ honorable   Ⓒ difficult   Ⓓ unbelievable

3. enormous : colossal :: ravenous : _____

   Ⓐ miniscule   Ⓑ fulfilled   Ⓒ famished   Ⓓ ghastly

4. _____ : meat :: apple : fruit

   Ⓐ turkey   Ⓑ Christmas   Ⓒ hot dogs   Ⓓ cut

5. vine : tomatoes :: stalk : _____

   Ⓐ lettuce   Ⓑ corn   Ⓒ onion   Ⓓ carrot

6. vacation : trip :: photographs : _____

   Ⓐ snapshots   Ⓑ camera   Ⓒ copies   Ⓓ remember

7. culprit : guilty :: maniac : _____

   Ⓐ crazy   Ⓑ friendly   Ⓒ innocent   Ⓓ evil

8. tree : branch :: vine : _____

   Ⓐ cascade   Ⓑ tendril   Ⓒ pincer   Ⓓ canopy

9. corn : _____ :: pumpkin : vine

   Ⓐ stalk   Ⓑ fruit   Ⓒ vine   Ⓓ seed

10. shimmering : shining :: quavering : _____

    Ⓐ shaking   Ⓑ obeying   Ⓒ falling   Ⓓ darkening

11. vacation : trip :: photographs : _____

    Ⓐ snapshots   Ⓑ copies   Ⓒ camera   Ⓓ remember

12. think back : _____ :: dream : imagine

    Ⓐ remember   Ⓑ hide   Ⓒ summarize   Ⓓ doubt

Name _____ LESSON 90 Date _____

Study the relationship between the first set of words. Pick the word that completes the second pair with this same relationship.

1. honest : deceptive :: innocent : _____

    Ⓐ forgiving   Ⓑ guiltless   Ⓒ judgmental   Ⓓ guilty

2. carrot : vegetable :: banana : _____

    Ⓐ dairy   Ⓑ bread   Ⓒ meat   Ⓓ fruit

3. enormous : colossal :: ravenous : _____

    Ⓐ miniscule   Ⓑ famished   Ⓒ ghastly   Ⓓ fulfilled

4. common : rare :: vague : _____

    Ⓐ true   Ⓑ important   Ⓒ distinct   Ⓓ phony

5. true : _____ :: unproven : theory

    Ⓐ fact   Ⓑ speech   Ⓒ lie   Ⓓ book

6. disrespect : honor :: forget : _____

    Ⓐ decide   Ⓑ hide   Ⓒ remember   Ⓓ doubt

7. tribute : honor :: memorial : _____

    Ⓐ remember   Ⓑ decide   Ⓒ ignore   Ⓓ doubt

8. vacation : trip :: photographs : _____

    Ⓐ snapshots   Ⓑ remember   Ⓒ copies   Ⓓ camera

9. complementary products : in addition :: substitutes : _____

    Ⓐ with interest   Ⓑ in excess   Ⓒ imported   Ⓓ instead

10. dispose : get rid of :: peruse : _____

    Ⓐ browse   Ⓑ release   Ⓒ fulfill   Ⓓ watch

11. _____ : fruit :: peas : vegetable

    Ⓐ sunflower   Ⓑ squirrel   Ⓒ apple   Ⓓ report card

12. shimmering : shining :: quavering : _____

    Ⓐ shaking   Ⓑ obeying   Ⓒ darkening   Ⓓ falling

Name _____ **LESSON 91** Date _____

Study the relationship between the first set of words. Pick the word that completes the second pair with this same relationship.

1. _____ : gratitude :: Memorial Day : honor

    (A) Martin Luther King, Jr. Day (B) Thanksgiving (C) Memorial Day (D) Veteran's Day

2. Egypt : Nile :: Brazil : _____

    (A) Amazon (B) Tiber (C) Mississippi (D) Yangtze

3. irreverent : disrespectful :: penitent : _____

    (A) sorrowful (B) jealous (C) honorable (D) generous

4. better than all others : superior :: holy : _____

    (A) elite (B) prosperous (C) old (D) sacred

5. freedom : independence :: _____ : bondage

    (A) pledge (B) irony (C) slavery (D) rights

6. Statue of Liberty : _____ :: Pyramids : Egypt

    (A) England (B) France (C) Ireland (D) United States

7. school : _____ :: church : worship

    (A) play (B) learn (C) run (D) cook

8. coveted : desired :: abated : _____

    (A) unwanted (B) diminished (C) borrowed (D) destroyed

9. freedom : slavery :: fairness : _____

    (A) equality (B) secrecy (C) injustice (D) philosophy

10. Nile River : Egypt :: Indus River : _____

    (A) Pakistan (B) Egypt (C) India (D) Spain

11. detest : hate :: adore : _____

    (A) cactus (B) love (C) door (D) cards

12. fair : equality :: unfair : _____

    (A) slavery (B) rights (C) trade (D) voting

96

Name _____ LESSON 92 Date _____

Study the relationship between the first set of words. Pick the word that completes the second pair with this same relationship.

1. freedom : independence :: slavery : _____

    (A) dependence (B) runaway (C) journey (D) bondage

2. random : unordered :: immaculate : _____

    (A) colorful (B) spotless (C) holy (D) quiet

3. mummy : _____ :: vampire : Transylvania

    (A) king (B) France (C) Europe (D) Egypt

4. celebrate : _____ :: worship : prayer

    (A) catastrophe (B) feast (C) prepare (D) forage

5. strange : peculiar :: testimony : _____

    (A) evidence (B) witness (C) suspect (D) conviction

6. customs : traditions :: _____ : holy

    . sacred (B) old (C) prosperous (D) elite

7. school : learn :: church : _____

    (A) worship (B) teach (C) heal (D) love

8. coveted : desired :: abated : _____

    (A) borrowed (B) diminished (C) destroyed (D) unwanted

9. adoration : love :: gratitude : _____

    (A) thankfulness (B) kindness (C) sympathy (D) hatred

10. religion : worship :: _____ : farming

    (A) forestry (B) agriculture (C) simple (D) astronomy

11. enjoyment : covet :: zest : _____

    (A) odor (B) dislike (C) habit (D) crave

12. shame : honor :: cowardice : _____

    (A) glory (B) fear (C) kindness (D) courage

Name _____ **LESSON 93** Date _____

Study the relationship between the first set of words. Pick the word that completes the second pair with this same relationship.

1. crucial : _____ :: honor : deception

   Ⓐ trivial   Ⓑ savage   Ⓒ ashamed   Ⓓ harsh

2. enjoyment : covet :: zest : _____

   Ⓐ odor   Ⓑ dislike   Ⓒ crave   Ⓓ habit

3. one hundred years : century :: one thousand years : _____

   Ⓐ generation   Ⓑ eon   Ⓒ decade   Ⓓ millennium

4. irreverent : disrespectful :: penitent : _____

   Ⓐ generous   Ⓑ jealous   Ⓒ sorrowful   Ⓓ honorable

5. Paris : Eiffel Tower :: Egypt : _____

   Ⓐ Big Ben   Ⓑ Statue of Liberty   Ⓒ The Sphinx   Ⓓ The Great Wall

6. freedom : slavery :: fairness : _____

   Ⓐ equality   Ⓑ philosophy   Ⓒ secrecy   Ⓓ injustice

7. yellow rose : friendship :: red rose : _____

   Ⓐ door   Ⓑ love   Ⓒ purity   Ⓓ cards

8. Statue of Liberty : _____ :: Pyramids : Egypt

   Ⓐ Ireland   Ⓑ France   Ⓒ United States   Ⓓ England

9. _____ : testimony :: jury : judgment

   Ⓐ informant   Ⓑ detective   Ⓒ interrogator   Ⓓ witness

10. adoration : love :: gratitude : _____

    Ⓐ kindness   Ⓑ sympathy   Ⓒ hatred   Ⓓ thankfulness

11. severe : trivial :: shame : _____

    Ⓐ discredit   Ⓑ mourn   Ⓒ honor   Ⓓ celebration

12. strange : peculiar :: testimony : _____

    Ⓐ witness   Ⓑ suspect   Ⓒ evidence   Ⓓ conviction

Study the relationship between the first set of words. Pick the word that completes the second pair with this same relationship.

1. problem : conundrum :: mystery : _____

   Ⓐ certain   Ⓑ meticulous   Ⓒ enigma   Ⓓ dogmatic

2. street : driver :: sidewalk : _____

   Ⓐ pedestrian   Ⓑ traffic   Ⓒ walking   Ⓓ concrete

3. putrid : rotten :: decrepit : _____

   Ⓐ feeble   Ⓑ dirty   Ⓒ boring   Ⓓ new

4. imperative : necessary :: distinctive : _____

   Ⓐ optional   Ⓑ notable   Ⓒ ordinary   Ⓓ suspicious

5. ancestors : forefathers :: heritage : _____

   Ⓐ ceremony   Ⓑ history   Ⓒ council   Ⓓ rituals

6. branch : division :: remnant : _____

   Ⓐ assortment   Ⓑ scrap   Ⓒ hole   Ⓓ foundation

7. harmony : peace :: adversity : _____

   Ⓐ prosperity   Ⓑ same   Ⓒ suffering   Ⓓ fortune

8. airplane : runway :: car : _____

   Ⓐ traffic   Ⓑ stop sign   Ⓒ driveway   Ⓓ turn lane

9. scribe : writer :: warrior : _____

   Ⓐ scientist   Ⓑ ruler   Ⓒ fighter   Ⓓ teacher

10. awareness : knowledge :: responsibility : _____

    Ⓐ story   Ⓑ oddity   Ⓒ common occurrence   Ⓓ duty

11. groggy : sleepy :: feeble : _____

    Ⓐ immature   Ⓑ weak   Ⓒ suspicious   Ⓓ worried

12. monotony : repetition :: pomp : _____

    Ⓐ splendor   Ⓑ beauty   Ⓒ destruction   Ⓓ surprise

Study the relationship between the first set of words. Pick the word that completes the second pair with this same relationship.

1. street : driver :: sidewalk : _____

   Ⓐ concrete   Ⓑ traffic   Ⓒ walking   Ⓓ pedestrian

2. heritage : _____ :: symbol : sign

   Ⓐ responsibility   Ⓑ ancestry   Ⓒ sign   Ⓓ future

3. imperative : necessary :: distinctive : _____

   Ⓐ ordinary   Ⓑ optional   Ⓒ notable   Ⓓ suspicious

4. jostle : shake :: perspire : _____

   Ⓐ sweat   Ⓑ ascend   Ⓒ hesitate   Ⓓ acquire

5. cheating : plagiarism :: lying : _____

   Ⓐ morality   Ⓑ jealousy   Ⓒ fraud   Ⓓ shoplifting

6. peace : harmony :: suffering : _____

   Ⓐ fortune   Ⓑ prosperity   Ⓒ oppression   Ⓓ equality

7. heritage : _____ :: forefathers : ancestors

   Ⓐ education   Ⓑ history   Ⓒ stories   Ⓓ science

8. airplane : runway :: car : _____

   Ⓐ driveway   Ⓑ stop sign   Ⓒ turn lane   Ⓓ traffic

9. duty : responsibility :: knowledge : _____

   Ⓐ environment   Ⓑ awareness   Ⓒ conservation   Ⓓ action

10. groggy : sleepy :: feeble : _____

    Ⓐ weak   Ⓑ suspicious   Ⓒ immature   Ⓓ worried

11. older : ancestor :: younger : _____

    Ⓐ progeny   Ⓑ genealogy   Ⓒ heritage   Ⓓ sibling

12. scribe : writer :: warrior : _____

    Ⓐ fighter   Ⓑ scientist   Ⓒ ruler   Ⓓ teacher

Study the relationship between the first set of words. Pick the word that completes the second pair with this same relationship.

1. mistake : _____ :: success : achievement

    Ⓐ fix   Ⓑ horrible   Ⓒ punishment   Ⓓ error

2. nimble : agile :: wary : _____

    Ⓐ menacing   Ⓑ astonished   Ⓒ cautious   Ⓓ feeble

3. street : driver :: sidewalk : _____

    Ⓐ walking   Ⓑ pedestrian   Ⓒ concrete   Ⓓ traffic

4. Teacher : knowledge :: Judge : _____

    Ⓐ instruction   Ⓑ liberty   Ⓒ freedom   Ⓓ justice

5. _____ : feeble :: quick and coordinated : agile

    Ⓐ weak   Ⓑ immature   Ⓒ suspicious   Ⓓ worried

6. heritage : _____ :: symbol : sign

    Ⓐ future   Ⓑ responsibility   Ⓒ ancestry   Ⓓ sign

7. resolution : a determination :: encounter : _____

    Ⓐ an argument   Ⓑ a meeting   Ⓒ a belief   Ⓓ a choice

8. diminutive : gigantic :: defiant : _____

    Ⓐ feeble   Ⓑ tremulous   Ⓒ obedient   Ⓓ willful

9. duty : responsibility :: knowledge : _____

    Ⓐ action   Ⓑ conservation   Ⓒ environment   Ⓓ awareness

10. encounter : meet :: accomplish : _____

    Ⓐ decide   Ⓑ scare   Ⓒ help   Ⓓ achieve

11. awareness : knowledge :: responsibility : _____

    Ⓐ common occurrence   Ⓑ story   Ⓒ oddity   Ⓓ duty

12. warrior : courage :: storyteller : _____

    Ⓐ love   Ⓑ paint   Ⓒ imagination   Ⓓ listen

Study the relationship between the first set of words. Pick the word that completes the second pair with this same relationship.

1. futile : ineffective :: frugal : _____

    A thrifty   **B** efficient   **C** obvious   **D** isolated

2. uncover : dig :: cover : _____

    A treasure   **B** shovel   **C** dirt   **D** bury

3. genuine : authentic :: counterfeit : _____

    A real   **B** money   **C** valuable   **D** unreliable

4. treasured : beloved :: pleasing : _____

    A hopeful   **B** unruly   **C** overwhelming   **D** attractive

5. winged : moth :: wingless : _____

    A wasp   **B** ant   **C** butterfly   **D** grasshopper

6. day : rotation :: year : _____

    A spin   **B** tilt   **C** phase   **D** revolution

7. to search : look for :: to bundle : _____

    A hide   **B** wrap   **C** spoon   **D** spin

8. uncomfortable : uneasy :: kind : _____

    A courteous   **B** cultured   **C** somber   humorous

9. _____ : honesty :: transgression : righteousness

    A character   **B** wrath   **C** deceit   **D** vengeance

10. debate : argue :: invert : _____

    A spin   **B** turn over   **C** resist   **D** fold

11. a right : privilege :: a condition : _____

    A sovereign   **B** provision   **C** debt   **D** writ

12. bad behavior : discipline :: good behavior : _____

    A test   **B** reward   **C** teacher   **D** attitude

Study the relationship between the first set of words. Pick the word that completes the second pair with this same relationship.

1. _____ : suitcase :: money : wallet

   Ⓐ airport   Ⓑ clothes   Ⓒ telephone   Ⓓ furniture

2. Relax : unwind :: Labor : _____

   Ⓐ employ   Ⓑ work   Ⓒ retire   Ⓓ job

3. debt : money owed to a creditor :: capital : _____

   Ⓐ profit   Ⓑ something of value   Ⓒ tariff   Ⓓ standard of living

4. hateful : odious :: unmannered : _____

   Ⓐ boorish   Ⓑ swarthy   Ⓒ somber   Ⓓ docile

5. bury : cover :: dig : _____

   Ⓐ dirt   Ⓑ treasure   Ⓒ uncover   Ⓓ shovel

6. hard to find : _____ :: treasured : precious

   Ⓐ none   Ⓑ scarce   Ⓒ lazy   Ⓓ taunt

7. tax : tariff :: trade : _____

   Ⓐ barter   Ⓑ output   Ⓒ debt   Ⓓ risk

8. futile : ineffective :: frugal : _____

   Ⓐ efficient   Ⓑ isolated   Ⓒ thrifty   Ⓓ obvious

9. moth : light :: butterfly : _____

   Ⓐ darkness   Ⓑ taste   Ⓒ texture   Ⓓ color

10. secret : _____ :: mystery : unexplained

    Ⓐ dark   Ⓑ hidden   Ⓒ small   Ⓓ hard to remember

11. worthless : valuable :: wicked : _____

    Ⓐ naughty   Ⓑ expensive   Ⓒ cheap   Ⓓ virtuous

12. red and swollen : inflamed :: nervous : _____

    Ⓐ edgy   Ⓑ viable   Ⓒ somber   Ⓓ placid

Study the relationship between the first set of words. Pick the word that completes the second pair with this same relationship.

1. uncomfortable : uneasy :: kind : _____

   Ⓐ courteous   Ⓑ humorous   Ⓒ cultured   Ⓓ somber

2. trade : barter :: tax : _____

   Ⓐ debt   Ⓑ tariff   Ⓒ output   Ⓓ risk

3. _____ : suitcase :: money : wallet

   Ⓐ telephone   Ⓑ furniture   Ⓒ airport   Ⓓ clothes

4. library : books :: bank : _____

   Ⓐ money   Ⓑ medicine   Ⓒ park   Ⓓ help

5. honor roll : reward :: lose recess : _____

   Ⓐ punish   Ⓑ reward   Ⓒ detain   Ⓓ dream

6. winged : moth :: wingless : _____

   Ⓐ wasp   Ⓑ ant   Ⓒ butterfly   Ⓓ grasshopper

7. worthless : valuable :: wicked : _____

   Ⓐ expensive   Ⓑ naughty   Ⓒ virtuous   Ⓓ cheap

8. treasured : beloved :: pleasing : _____

   Ⓐ overwhelming   Ⓑ hopeful   Ⓒ attractive   Ⓓ unruly

9. _____ : flower :: moth : light

   Ⓐ math   Ⓑ report   Ⓒ words   Ⓓ bee

10. hard to find : _____ :: treasured : precious

    Ⓐ lazy   Ⓑ taunt   Ⓒ scarce   Ⓓ none

11. trade : barter :: tax : _____

    Ⓐ tariff   Ⓑ debt   Ⓒ output   Ⓓ risk

12. bank : money :: _____ : books

    Ⓐ hospital   Ⓑ teacher   Ⓒ library   Ⓓ gas station

Study the relationship between the first set of words. Pick the word that completes the second pair with this same relationship.

1. secret : hidden :: mystery : _____

   (A) clue (B) understood (C) unexplained (D) crime

2. song : carol :: folklore : _____

   (A) artisan (B) legend (C) trouble (D) tradition

3. strength : weakness :: _____ : impartial

   (A) civility (B) prejudice (C) persistence (D) equality

4. _____ : broom :: scrub : sponge

   (A) wash (B) sweep (C) cool (D) fold

5. wizened : shriveled :: tremulous : _____

   (A) shaking (B) amazing (C) terrifying (D) enormous

6. tongue : taste :: _____ : see.

   (A) sight (B) eye (C) light (D) seeing

7. antiquity : ancientness :: obstinacy : _____

   (A) strength (B) massiveness (C) stubbornness (D) openness

8. night : dark :: _____ : light.

   (A) day (B) week (C) month (D) awake

9. secret : unknown :: admirer : _____

   (A) flowers (B) suitor (C) delivery (D) gift

10. pen : write :: _____ : sweep

    (A) full moon (B) bat (C) pumpkin (D) broom

11. tend : _____ :: train : teach

    (A) build (B) give (C) care for (D) play

12. deserted : abandoned :: inhabited by ghosts : _____

    (A) bedraggled (B) terrified (C) spooked (D) haunted

Name _____ **LESSON 101** Date _____

Study the relationship between the first set of words. Pick the word that completes the second pair with this same relationship.

1. apprehension : fear :: wrath : _____

   Ⓐ anger   Ⓑ deceit   Ⓒ humor   Ⓓ joy

2. train : teach :: tend : _____

   Ⓐ care for   Ⓑ build   Ⓒ play   Ⓓ give

3. instruct : _____ :: confess : admit

   Ⓐ play   Ⓑ give   Ⓒ teach   Ⓓ change

4. pledge : promise :: homage : _____

   Ⓐ labor   Ⓑ loyalty   Ⓒ tax   Ⓓ power

5. devotion : dedication :: compassion : _____

   Ⓐ hardworking   Ⓑ helpful   Ⓒ sympathy   Ⓓ attitude

6. _____ : help :: problems : trouble

   Ⓐ tower   Ⓑ basement   Ⓒ support   Ⓓ stage

7. begrudge : envy :: inform : _____

   Ⓐ tell   Ⓑ trouble   Ⓒ reward   Ⓓ admire

8. _____ : dirt :: furniture : dust

   Ⓐ roof   Ⓑ walls   Ⓒ door   Ⓓ floor

9. bee : flower :: moth : _____

   Ⓐ grass   Ⓑ light   Ⓒ fly   Ⓓ wings

10. _____ : mercy :: sorrow : pity

    Ⓐ donation   Ⓑ kindness   Ⓒ begging   Ⓓ reproach

11. fire : smoke :: energy : _____

    Ⓐ power   Ⓑ smog   Ⓒ machine   Ⓓ flames

12. sympathy for the misfortunes of others : compassion :: giving to those in need : _____

    Ⓐ sympathy   Ⓑ commiseration   Ⓒ camaraderie   Ⓓ charity

Name _____   **LESSON 102**   Date _____

Study the relationship between the first set of words. Pick the word that completes the
second pair with this same relationship.

1. watch : _____ :: calendar : days

   Ⓐ twelve   Ⓑ hours   Ⓒ hands   Ⓓ weeks

2. teach : educate :: beckon : _____

   Ⓐ summon   Ⓑ communicate   Ⓒ understand   Ⓓ process

3. sight : _____ :: hearing : hearing aid

   Ⓐ pants   Ⓑ keys   Ⓒ glasses   Ⓓ gloves

4. fortune : luck :: misfortune : _____

   Ⓐ trouble   Ⓑ blessing   Ⓒ tradition   Ⓓ mystery

5. book : read :: TV : _____

   Ⓐ show   Ⓑ VCR   Ⓒ watch   Ⓓ record

6. to eat : consume :: to use a tool : _____

   Ⓐ wield   Ⓑ devise   Ⓒ emulate   Ⓓ grapple

7. devotion : dedication :: compassion : _____

   Ⓐ helpful   Ⓑ attitude   Ⓒ hardworking   Ⓓ sympathy

8. secret : unknown :: admirer : _____

   Ⓐ gift   Ⓑ suitor   Ⓒ flowers   Ⓓ delivery

9. clandestine : secret :: torrid : _____

   Ⓐ punishing   Ⓑ great   Ⓒ deep   Ⓓ hot

10. devour : consume :: _____ : stroll

   Ⓐ teeter   Ⓑ trudge   Ⓒ scamper   Ⓓ amble

11. sun : light :: Nile River : _____

   Ⓐ blankets   Ⓑ green   Ⓒ money   Ⓓ water

12. safe : secure :: danger : _____

   Ⓐ stability   Ⓑ trouble   Ⓒ stories   Ⓓ chance

Study the relationship between the first set of words. Pick the word that completes the second pair with this same relationship.

1. Washington, D.C. : United States :: London : _____

   (A) Italy   (B) Germany   (C) Africa   (D) England

2. New York : New Amsterdam :: Mexico City : _____

   (A) Tenochtitlan   (B) Puebla   (C) Cuidad de Mexico   (D) Mazatlan

3. Abraham Lincoln : Illinois :: John F. Kennedy : _____

   (A) New York   (B) California   (C) Massachusetts   (D) Ohio

4. Pearl Harbor : Hawaii :: Arlington : _____

   (A) Pennsylvania   (B) Virginia   (C) New York   (D) Florida

5. mummy : Egypt :: vampire : _____

   (A) coffin   (B) Transylvania   (C) Pennsylvania   (D) full moon

6. Sforza family : Milan :: Medici family : _____

   (A) Paris   (B) Rome   (C) Athens   (D) Florence

7. Grimmauld Place : London :: Shrieking Shack : _____

   (A) Surrey   (B) Hogwarts   (C) Hogsmeade   (D) Godric's Hollow

8. Coliseum : Rome :: Taj Mahal : _____

   (A) London   (B) Agra   (C) Delhi   (D) Cairo

9. France : Europe :: Ghana : _____

   (A) Australia   (B) Africa   (C) Asia   (D) South America

10. Egypt : hieroglyphics :: Mesopotamia : _____

    (A) agriculture   (B) cuneiform   (C) sanskrit   (D) ashipo

11. _____ : calf :: ewe : lamb

    (A) pig   (B) cow   (C) horse   (D) dog

12. Egypt : Africa :: Russia : _____

    (A) North America   (B) Antarctica   (C) Asia   (D) Australia

Name _____ **LESSON 104** Date _____

Study the relationship between the first set of words. Pick the word that completes the second pair with this same relationship.

1. Sforza family : Milan :: Medici family : _____

   ⒜ Athens ⒝ Paris ⒞ Florence ⒟ Rome

2. Egypt : hieroglyphics :: Mesopotamia : _____

   ⒜ cuneiform ⒝ agriculture ⒞ sanskrit ⒟ ashipo

3. Egypt : Africa :: Russia : _____

   ⒜ Europe ⒝ Australia ⒞ North America ⒟ Antarctica

4. New York : New Amsterdam :: Mexico City : _____

   ⒜ Tenochtitlan ⒝ Puebla ⒞ Mazatlan ⒟ Cuidad de Mexico

5. London : _____ :: Paris : France

   ⒜ England ⒝ Germany ⒞ Europe ⒟ Africa

6. Free State : New York :: Border State : _____

   ⒜ Missouri ⒝ South Carolina ⒞ New Hampshire ⒟ Montana

7. Pearl Harbor : Hawaii :: Arlington : _____

   ⒜ Florida ⒝ Virginia ⒞ New York ⒟ Pennsylvania

8. cow : calf :: ewe : _____

   ⒜ baby ⒝ mother ⒞ lamb ⒟ horse

9. Alaska : cold :: Egypt : _____
   ⒜ water ⒝ good ⒞ hot ⒟ deep

10. earn : urn :: ewes : _____

    ⒜ use ⒝ unit ⒞ turn ⒟ tweeze

11. United States : Statue of Liberty :: Egypt : _____

    ⒜ Eiffel Tower ⒝ Mount Rushmore ⒞ The Great Wall ⒟ The Pyramids

12. California : west :: New York : _____

    ⒜ city ⒝ Europe ⒞ east ⒟ north

109

Name _____ **LESSON 105** Date _____

Study the relationship between the first set of words. Pick the word that completes the second pair with this same relationship.

1. New York : New Amsterdam :: Mexico City : _____

    Ⓐ Cuidad de Mexico   Ⓑ Tenochtitlan   Ⓒ Puebla   Ⓓ Mazatlan

2. England : London :: _____ : Dublin

    Ⓐ United States   Ⓑ Denmark   Ⓒ England   Ⓓ Ireland

3. Paris : Eiffel Tower :: _____ : The Sphinx

    Ⓐ king   Ⓑ pyramid   Ⓒ Egypt   Europe

4. United States : Statue of Liberty :: Egypt : _____

    Ⓐ The Great Wall   Ⓑ Mount Rushmore   Ⓒ The Pyramids   Ⓓ Eiffel Tower

5. Washington, D.C. : United States :: London : _____

    Ⓐ England   Ⓑ Africa   Ⓒ Germany   Ⓓ Italy

6. _____ : ewe :: offspring : lamb

    Ⓐ grandfather   Ⓑ sister   Ⓒ old   Ⓓ mother

7. Eiffel Tower : Paris :: London Bridge : _____

    Ⓐ site seeing   Ⓑ Lake Havasu City   Ⓒ is falling down   Ⓓ London, England

8. mummy : Egypt :: vampire : _____

    Ⓐ full moon   Ⓑ Pennsylvania   Ⓒ coffin   Ⓓ Transylvania

9. earn : urn :: ewes : _____
    Ⓐ tweeze   Ⓑ turn   use   Ⓓ unit

10. Egypt : Africa :: Russia : _____

    Ⓐ Australia   Ⓑ Asia   Antarctica   Ⓓ North America

11. Egypt : hieroglyphics :: Mesopotamia : _____

    Ⓐ agriculture   Ⓑ sanskrit   Ⓒ ashipo   Ⓓ cuneiform

12. Pearl Harbor : Hawaii :: Arlington : _____

    Ⓐ New York   Ⓑ Pennsylvania   Ⓒ Virginia   Ⓓ Florida

Study the relationship between the first set of words. Pick the word that completes the second pair with this same relationship.

1. faithful : loyal :: dedicated : _____

   (A) anxious   (B) hard-working   (C) sober   (D) keen

2. tolerance : acceptance :: charity : _____

   (A) inspiration   (B) praise   (C) patience   (D) generosity

3. war : peace :: slave : _____

   (A) free   (B) master   (C) servant   (D) owned

4. massive : _____ :: ferocious : gentle

   (A) many   (B) giant   (C) tiny   (D) huge

5. Confucianism : _____ :: Taoism : simplicity

   (A) donation   (B) kindness   (C) begging   (D) reproach

6. dedicated : hard-working :: faithful : _____

   (A) anxious   (B) keen   (C) sober   (D) loyal

7. fair : unjust :: _____ : violence

   (A) honesty   (B) peace   (C) trust   (D) freedom

8. chagrin : disappointment :: wrath : _____

   (A) anger   (B) fright   (C) humiliation   (D) joy

9. candy : food :: love : _____

   (A) heart   (B) romance   (C) emotion   (D) Cupid

10. resourceful : creativity :: _____ : goodness

    (A) attitude   (B) optimism   (C) aptitude   (D) virtue

11. hard : soft :: _____ : gentle

    (A) rough   (B) stair   (C) enough   (D) muff

12. alacrity : willingness :: modesty : _____

    (A) opulence   (B) faithfulness   (C) honesty   (D) decency

Name _____   **LESSON 107**   Date _____

Study the relationship between the first set of words. Pick the word that completes the second pair with this same relationship.

1. kind : angry :: gentle : _____

    Ⓐ croquette   Ⓑ vicious   Ⓒ distant   Ⓓ special

2. _____ : happiness :: agony : pain

    Ⓐ joy   Ⓑ rage   Ⓒ curiosity   Ⓓ shame

3. treason : loyalty :: divided : _____

    Ⓐ faithful   Ⓑ promised   Ⓒ apart   Ⓓ united

4. dedicated : hard-working :: faithful : _____

    Ⓐ anxious   Ⓑ sober   Ⓒ keen   Ⓓ loyal

5. treasonous : loyal :: divided : _____

    Ⓐ separated   promised   Ⓒ faithful   Ⓓ united

6. massive : _____ :: ferocious : gentle

    Ⓐ tiny   Ⓑ many   Ⓒ huge   Ⓓ giant

7. candy : food :: love : _____

    Ⓐ Cupid   Ⓑ heart   Ⓒ romance   Ⓓ emotion

8. Confucianism : _____ :: Taoism : simplicity

    Ⓐ begging   Ⓑ kindness   Ⓒ reproach   Ⓓ donation

9. alacrity : willingness :: modesty : _____

    Ⓐ decency   Ⓑ honesty   Ⓒ opulence   Ⓓ faithfulness

10. freedom : Independence Day :: love : _____

    Ⓐ Valentine's Day Ⓑ love   Ⓒ February   Ⓓ St. Patrick's Day

11. yellow rose : _____ :: red rose : love

    Ⓐ jealousy   Ⓑ infatuation   Ⓒ emotion   Ⓓ friendship

12. peace : harmony :: suffering : _____

    Ⓐ oppression   Ⓑ equality   Ⓒ prosperity   Ⓓ fortune

Study the relationship between the first set of words. Pick the word that completes the second pair with this same relationship.

1. kind : angry :: gentle : _____

    Ⓐ distant   Ⓑ special   Ⓒ croquette   Ⓓ vicious

2. inquisitiveness : curiosity :: kindness : _____

    Ⓐ courtesy   Ⓑ practicality   Ⓒ humility   Ⓓ generosity

3. alacrity : willingness :: modesty : _____

    Ⓐ faithfulness   Ⓑ opulence   Ⓒ honesty   Ⓓ decency

4. treasonous : loyal :: divided : _____

    Ⓐ separated   Ⓑ united   Ⓒ faithful   Ⓓ promised

5. effrontery : boldness :: elation : _____

    Ⓐ shame   Ⓑ joy   Ⓒ rage   Ⓓ curiosity

6. fair : unjust :: _____ : violence

    Ⓐ honesty   Ⓑ freedom   Ⓒ peace   Ⓓ trust

7. adoration : love :: gratitude : _____

    Ⓐ thankfulness   Ⓑ restlessness   Ⓒ friendliness   Ⓓ sympathy

8. gingerly : gently :: fleeting : _____

    Ⓐ enduring   Ⓑ brief   Ⓒ diligent   Ⓓ helpful

9. fortification : reinforcement :: benevolence : _____

    Ⓐ decoration   Ⓑ kindness   Ⓒ begging   Ⓓ donation

10. faithful : loyal :: dedicated : _____

    Ⓐ sober   Ⓑ anxious   Ⓒ keen   Ⓓ hard-working

11. exuberance : joy :: supplication : _____

    Ⓐ anger   Ⓑ advice   Ⓒ betrayal   Ⓓ prayer

12. massive : _____ :: ferocious : gentle

    Ⓐ huge   Ⓑ tiny   Ⓒ many   Ⓓ giant

Study the relationship between the first set of words. Pick the word that completes the second pair with this same relationship.

1. auditorium : public place for holding lectures or performances :: bungalow : _____

    A small house   **B** soft blanket   **C** bed   **D** tree house

2. romance : _____ :: camaraderie : friendship

    A purity   **B** door   **C** anger   **D** love

3. chapter : book :: _____ : song

    A rhyme   **B** paragraph   **C** verse   **D** haiku

4. oldest : first-born :: youngest : _____

    A middle   **B** son   **C** baby   **D** sibling

5. night : dark :: _____ : light.

    A awake   **B** day   **C** week   **D** month

6. never : always :: none : _____

    A ever   **B** all   **C** funeral   **D** rarely

7. book : _____ :: puzzle : think

    A read   **B** felt   **C** seen   **D** understood

8. mother : ewe :: offspring : _____

    A lamb   **B** mother   **C** sheep   **D** calf

9. niece : aunt :: nephew : _____

    A uncle   **B** son   **C** grandson   **D** father

10. restaurant : eat :: motel : _____

    A night   **B** bed   **C** sleep   **D** travel

11. boy : son :: girl : _____

    A cousin   **B** sibling   **C** daughter   **D** uncle

12. day : night :: feminine : _____

    A poignant   **B** masculine   **C** sanguine   **D** feline

Name _____   **LESSON 110**   Date _____

Study the relationship between the first set of words. Pick the word that completes the second pair with this same relationship.

1. spider : web :: bird : _____

    (A) fly   (B) bed   (C) nest   (D) den

2. utensil : tool :: almanac : _____

    (A) book   (B) speech   (C) machine   (D) vegetable

3. romance : _____ :: camaraderie : friendship

    (A) purity   (B) anger   (C) door   (D) love

4. happy : sad :: _____ : hate

    (A) love   (B) purity   (C) dislike   (D) door

5. desk : work :: bed : _____

    (A) sleep   (B) play   (C) stand   (D) bed

6. oldest : first-born :: youngest : _____

    (A) middle   (B) baby   (C) son   (D) sibling

7. madre : mother :: padre : _____

    (A) teacher   (B) doctor   (C) father   (D) dentist

8. eat : dining room :: _____ : bedroom

    (A) sleep   (B) travel   (C) play   (D) night

9. always : never :: frequent : _____

    (A) idyllic   (B) staccato   (C) reliable   (D) seldom

10. mother : ewe :: offspring : _____

    (A) sheep   (B) mother   (C) calf   (D) lamb

11. sleep : doze :: awaken : _____

    (A) wince   (B) rouse   (C) mystify   (D) fluster

12. bed : sleep :: table : _____

    (A) eat   (B) read   (C) watch football   (D) sing

115

Study the relationship between the first set of words. Pick the word that completes the second pair with this same relationship.

1. _____ : cloth :: bed : bedspread

   Ⓐ bed   Ⓑ table   Ⓒ oven   Ⓓ television

2. mother : ewe :: offspring : _____

   Ⓐ sheep   Ⓑ lamb   Ⓒ calf   Ⓓ mother

3. cup : _____ :: bed : bassinet

   Ⓐ lid   Ⓑ spoon   Ⓒ fire   Ⓓ bottle

4. day : sun :: night : _____

   Ⓐ Saturn   Ⓑ dreams   Ⓒ light   Ⓓ stars

5. Stride Toward Freedom : book :: "I Have A Dream" : _____

   Ⓐ speech   Ⓑ diplomat   Ⓒ inaugurate   Ⓓ song

6. Christianity : Bible :: Buddhism : _____

   Ⓐ Avesta   Ⓑ Torah   Ⓒ Koran   Ⓓ Sutras

7. day : night :: feminine : _____

   Ⓐ masculine   Ⓑ poignant   Ⓒ feline   Ⓓ sanguine

8. boy : son :: girl : _____

   Ⓐ sibling   Ⓑ daughter   Ⓒ uncle   Ⓓ cousin

9. chapter : book :: _____ : unit

   Ⓐ lesson   Ⓑ minister   Ⓒ book   Ⓓ holiday

10. night : dark :: _____ : light.

   Ⓐ month   Ⓑ week   Ⓒ day   Ⓓ awake

11. always : never :: frequent : _____

   Ⓐ reliable   Ⓑ seldom   Ⓒ staccato   Ⓓ idyllic

12. bed : sleep :: table : _____

   Ⓐ watch football Ⓑ eat   Ⓒ sing   Ⓓ read

Study the relationship between the first set of words. Pick the word that completes the second pair with this same relationship.

1. Shakespeare : England :: Faulkner : _____

    A Sweden   **B** Soviet Union   **C** United States   **D** Germany

2. Adolf Hitler : Germany :: Saddam Hussein : _____

    A Iraq   **B** India   **C** Egypt   **D** Italy

3. Francois I : France :: Henry VIII : _____

    A Germany   **B** Italy   **C** England   **D** Spain

4. verde : green :: rojo : _____

    A white   **B** red   **C** black   **D** blue

5. Germany : German shepherd :: _____ : Chihuahua

    A China   **B** England   **C** Columbia   **D** Mexico

6. London : England :: Paris : _____

    A Germany   **B** France   **C** Europe   **D** Italy

7. Normans : France :: Vikings : _____

    A China   **B** Spain   **C** Germany   **D** Scandinavia

8. France : _____ :: Ghana : Africa

    A Europe   **B** Africa   **C** North America   **D** Spanish

9. Kenya : Africa :: Germany : _____

    A Antarctica   **B** Europe   **C** Spanish   **D** Asia

10. Munich : Germany :: Calcutta : _____

    A Albania   **B** Spain   **C** India   **D** Pakistan

11. United States : England :: Mexico : _____

    A Germany   **B** Cuba   **C** England   **D** France

12. red : rojo :: _____ : verde

    A green   **B** red   **C** maroon   **D** black

Name _____   **LESSON 113**   Date _____

Study the relationship between the first set of words. Pick the word that completes the second pair with this same relationship.

1. Germany : German shepherd :: _____ : Chihuahua

   Ⓐ China   Ⓑ England   Ⓒ Columbia   Ⓓ Mexico

2. Francois I : France :: Henry VIII : _____

   Ⓐ Germany   Ⓑ England   Ⓒ Spain   Ⓓ Italy

3. red : rojo :: _____ : verde

   Ⓐ green   Ⓑ black   Ⓒ maroon   Ⓓ red

4. Adolf Hitler : Germany :: Saddam Hussein : _____

   Ⓐ Iraq   Ⓑ Egypt   Ⓒ India   Ⓓ Italy

5. Shakespeare : England :: Faulkner : _____

   Ⓐ Germany   Ⓑ United States   Ⓒ Soviet Union   Ⓓ Sweden

6. Munich : Germany :: Calcutta : _____

   Ⓐ Spain   Ⓑ India   Ⓒ Pakistan   Ⓓ Albania

7. Kenya : Africa :: Germany : _____

   Ⓐ Antarctica   Ⓑ Asia   Ⓒ Europe   Ⓓ Spanish

8. verde : green :: rojo : _____

   Ⓐ blue   Ⓑ white   Ⓒ black   Ⓓ red

9. London : England :: Paris : _____

   Ⓐ Italy   Ⓑ France   Ⓒ Germany   Ⓓ Europe

10. Normans : France :: Vikings : _____

   Ⓐ Spain   Ⓑ China   Ⓒ Scandinavia   Ⓓ Germany

11. France : _____ :: Ghana : Africa

   Ⓐ Africa   Ⓑ Europe   Ⓒ North America   Ⓓ Spanish

12. United States : England :: Mexico : _____

   Ⓐ Germany   Ⓑ England   Ⓒ Cuba   Ⓓ France

Name _____   **LESSON 114**   Date _____

Study the relationship between the first set of words. Pick the word that completes the second pair with this same relationship.

1. Normans : France :: Vikings : _____

    ⒶScandinavia   ⒷSpain   ⒸGermany   ⒹChina

2. Kenya : Africa :: Germany : _____

    ⒶAsia   ⒷSpanish   ⒸAntarctica   ⒹEurope

3. France : _____ :: Ghana : Africa

    ⒶSpanish   ⒷEurope   ⒸAfrica   ⒹNorth America

4. Germany : German shepherd :: _____ : Chihuahua

    ⒶEngland   ⒷColumbia   ⒸChina   ⒹMexico

5. United States : England :: Mexico : _____

    ⒶGermany   ⒷCuba   ⒸFrance   ⒹEngland

6. Shakespeare : England :: Faulkner : _____

    ⒶSweden   ⒷGermany   ⒸSoviet Union   ⒹUnited States

7. Francois I : France :: Henry VIII : _____

    ⒶSpain   ⒷEngland   ⒸItaly   ⒹGermany

8. Adolf Hitler : Germany :: Saddam Hussein : _____

    ⒶItaly   ⒷIraq   ⒸIndia   ⒹEgypt

9. verde : green :: rojo : _____

    Ⓐred   Ⓑwhite   Ⓒblue   Ⓓblack

10. red : rojo :: _____ : verde

    Ⓐgreen   Ⓑred   Ⓒblack   Ⓓmaroon

11. London : England :: Paris : _____

    ⒶGermany   ⒷFrance   ⒸItaly   ⒹEurope

12. Munich : Germany :: Calcutta : _____

    ⒶAlbania   ⒷSpain   ⒸIndia   ⒹPakistan

Study the relationship between the first set of words. Pick the word that completes the second pair with this same relationship.

1. Mexico : south :: Canada : _____

    Ⓐ cold   Ⓑ east   Ⓒ north   Ⓓ west

2. Athens : Greece :: Rome : _____

    Ⓐ France   Ⓑ England   Ⓒ Spain   Ⓓ Italy

3. Greece : _____ :: Sweden : North Sea

    Ⓐ Black Sea   Ⓑ Red Sea   Ⓒ Mediterranean Sea   Ⓓ North Sea

4. France : Bastille Day :: United States : _____

    Ⓐ Flag Day   Ⓑ Independence Day   Ⓒ Presidents Day   Ⓓ Memorial Day

5. United Nations : New York City :: Catholic Church : _____

    Ⓐ Paris   Ⓑ Athens   Ⓒ Vatican City   Ⓓ Rome

6. Adolf Hitler : Germany :: Saddam Hussein : _____

    Ⓐ Iraq   Ⓑ Indonesia   Ⓒ Iran   Ⓓ Italy

7. France : _____ :: Greece : east

    Ⓐ south   Ⓑ northeast   Ⓒ west   Ⓓ California

8. American Independence : England :: Mexican Independence : _____

    Ⓐ Aztecs   Ⓑ Spain   Ⓒ Portugal   Ⓓ United States

9. Old World : Eastern Hemisphere :: New World : _____

    Ⓐ North America Ⓑ Mexico   Ⓒ India   Ⓓ China

10. Germany : German shepherd :: Mexico : _____

    Ⓐ wolfhound   Ⓑ Chihuahua   Ⓒ poodle   Ⓓ beagle

11. Inglés : English :: Español : _____

    Ⓐ United States Ⓑ French   Ⓒ Spanish   Ⓓ Mexico

12. Christopher Columbus : Spain :: Leif Eriksson : _____

    Ⓐ Italy   Ⓑ England   Ⓒ Norway   Ⓓ France

Name _____   **LESSON 116**   Date _____

Study the relationship between the first set of words. Pick the word that completes the second pair with this same relationship.

1. fork : United States :: chopsticks : _____

   (A) spoon   (B) Egypt   (C) England   (D) China

2. Lewis and Clark : American west :: Hernando De Soto : _____

   (A) American southeast   (B) Canada   (C) American southwest   (D) Mexico

3. Adolf Hitler : Germany :: Saddam Hussein : _____

   (A) Iraq   (B) Iran   (C) Italy   (D) Indonesia

4. Old World : Eastern Hemisphere :: New World : _____

   (A) China   (B) India   (C) Mexico   (D) North America

5. Stonehenge : England :: Loch Ness : _____

   (A) Ireland   (B) Scotland   (C) Denmark   (D) Wales

6. Normandy : France :: Bay of Pigs : _____
   (A) England   (B) Vietnam   (C) Cuba   (D) Korea

7. hieroglyphics : Egypt :: cuneiform : _____

   (A) Mesopotamia   (B) Rome   (C) India   (D) Greece

8. Athens : Greece :: Rome : _____

   (A) Italy   (B) Spain   (C) England   (D) France

9. Eiffel Tower : Paris :: London Bridge : _____

   (A) is falling down   (B) Lake Havasu City   (C) London, England   (D) site seeing

10. _____ : horses :: Egypt : camels

    (A) Germany   (B) England   (C) Italy   (D) Spain

11. India : Indian Ocean :: _____ : Mediterranean Sea

    (A) France   (B) Italy   (C) China   (D) Egypt

12. Shakespeare : England :: Faulkner : _____

    (A) Sweden   (B) Soviet Union   (C) Germany   (D) United States

121

Name _____   **LESSON 117**   Date _____

Study the relationship between the first set of words. Pick the word that completes the second pair with this same relationship.

1. Old World : Eastern Hemisphere :: New World : _____

   Ⓐ India   Ⓑ North America   Ⓒ Mexico   Ⓓ China

2. Adolf Hitler : Germany :: Saddam Hussein : _____

   Ⓐ Iran   Ⓑ Italy   Ⓒ Iraq   Ⓓ Indonesia

3. American Independence : England :: Mexican Independence : _____

   Ⓐ United States   Ⓑ Portugal   Ⓒ Spain   Ⓓ Aztecs

4. Thailand : Asia :: Morocco : _____

   Ⓐ Africa   Ⓑ South America   Ⓒ Australia   Ⓓ Japan

5. España : Spain :: Los Estados Unidos : _____
   Ⓐ Australia   Ⓑ United States   Ⓒ France   Ⓓ Mexico

6. _____ : London :: Poland : Warsaw

   Ⓐ Italy   Ⓑ England   Ⓒ Europe   Ⓓ Spain

7. Southern Ocean : Antarctica :: Indian Ocean : _____

   Ⓐ Japan   Ⓑ Kenya   Ⓒ Chile   Ⓓ Morocco

8. Grimmauld Place : London :: Shrieking Shack : _____

   Ⓐ Hogwarts   Ⓑ Godric's Hollow   Ⓒ Surrey   Ⓓ Hogsmeade

9. Mexico : south :: Canada : _____

   Ⓐ west   Ⓑ north   Ⓒ east   Ⓓ cold

10. fork : United States :: chopsticks : _____

    Ⓐ Egypt   Ⓑ spoon   Ⓒ England   Ⓓ China

11. Inglés : English :: Español : _____

    Ⓐ Mexico   Ⓑ French   Ⓒ United States   Ⓓ Spanish

12. World War I : Germany, Austria, Hungary :: WWII : _____

    Ⓐ Germany   Ⓑ Iraq   Ⓒ Germany, Japan, and Italy   Ⓓ Germany and Japan

Study the relationship between the first set of words. Pick the word that completes the second pair with this same relationship.

1. desert : Sahara :: rainforest : _____

   Ⓐ Seattle   Ⓑ Nile   Ⓒ Amazon   Ⓓ Mexican

2. Sahara : _____ :: Amazon : rainforest

   Ⓐ desert   Ⓑ Amazon   Ⓒ Mojave   Ⓓ wet

3. Mediterranean : Sea :: Amazon : _____

   Ⓐ country   Ⓑ river   Ⓒ ocean   Ⓓ lake

4. Arctic : polar bear :: Amazon : _____

   Ⓐ capybara   Ⓑ beaver   Ⓒ grizzly bear   Ⓓ whale

5. mountain : valley :: rainforest : _____

   Ⓐ jungle   Ⓑ Amazon   Ⓒ desert   Ⓓ wet

6. _____ : Nile :: Brazil : Amazon

   Ⓐ India   Ⓑ pyramid   Ⓒ France   Ⓓ Egypt

7. encumber : burden :: belittle : _____

   Ⓐ survey   Ⓑ insult   Ⓒ mutter   Ⓓ praise

8. birth : birth announcement :: death : _____

   Ⓐ disclosure   Ⓑ memorandum   Ⓒ chorale   Ⓓ obituary

9. section of the newspaper that lists the names of people in the community who have died : Obituaries :: section of the newspaper where you will find advertisements : _____

   Ⓐ Community   Ⓑ Editorials   Ⓒ Classifieds   Ⓓ World News

Name _____ **LESSON 119** Date _____

Study the relationship between the first set of words. Pick the word that completes the second pair with this same relationship.

1. birth : birth announcement :: death : _____

    A memorandum **B** chorale **C** disclosure **D** obituary

2. Sahara : _____ :: Amazon : rainforest

    A desert **B** wet **C** Amazon **D** Mojave

3. desert : Sahara :: rainforest : _____

    A Amazon **B** Mexican **C** Nile **D** Seattle

4. Arctic : polar bear :: Amazon : _____

    A beaver **B** grizzly bear **C** whale **D** capybara

5. mountain : valley :: rainforest : _____

    A desert **B** wet **C** jungle **D** Amazon

6. _____ : Nile :: Brazil : Amazon

    A France **B** pyramid **C** India **D** Egypt

7. Mediterranean : Sea :: Amazon : _____

    A river **B** lake **C** ocean **D** country

8. encumber : burden :: belittle : _____

    A survey **B** praise **C** insult **D** mutter

9. Section of the newspaper that lists the names of people in the community who have died : Obituaries :: section of the newspaper where you will find advertisements : _____

    A Community **B** Editorials **C** World News **D** Classifieds

124

Name _____   **LESSON 120**   Date _____

Study the relationship between the first set of words. Pick the word that completes the second pair with this same relationship.

1. _____ : Nile :: Brazil : Amazon

   A India   **B** France   **C** Egypt   **D** pyramid

2. Sahara : _____ :: Amazon : rainforest

   A desert   **B** Mojave   **C** wet   **D** Amazon

3. Arctic : polar bear :: Amazon : _____

   A beaver   **B** grizzly bear   **C** whale   **D** capybara

4. desert : Sahara :: rainforest : _____

   A Mexican   **B** Seattle   **C** Nile   **D** Amazon

5. mountain : valley :: rainforest : _____

   A Amazon   **B** desert   **C** wet   **D** jungle

6. encumber : burden :: belittle : _____

   A mutter   **B** survey   **C** praise   **D** insult

7. section of the newspaper that lists the names of people in the community who have died : Obituaries :: section of the newspaper where you will find advertisements : _____

   A Editorials   **B** Community   **C** World News   **D** Classifieds

8. birth : birth announcement :: death : _____

   A chorale   **B** memorandum   **C** disclosure   **D** obituary

9. Mediterranean : Sea :: Amazon : _____

   A ocean   **B** river   **C** lake   **D** country

Study the relationship between the first set of words. Pick the word that completes the second pair with this same relationship.

1.   desert : Sahara :: rainforest : _____

   A Seattle   **B** Nile   **C** Amazon   **D** Mexican

2.   Sahara : _____ :: Amazon : rainforest

   A desert   **B** Amazon   **C** Mojave   **D** wet

3.   Mediterranean : Sea :: Amazon : _____

   A country   **B** river   **C** ocean   **D** lake

4.   Arctic : polar bear :: Amazon : _____

   A capybara   **B** beaver   **C** grizzly bear   **D** whale

5.   mountain : valley :: rainforest : _____

   A jungle   **B** Amazon   **C** desert   **D** wet

6.   _____ : Nile :: Brazil : Amazon

   A India   **B** pyramid   **C** France   **D** Egypt

7.   encumber : burden :: belittle : _____

   A survey   **B** insult   **C** mutter   **D** praise

8.   birth : birth announcement :: death : _____

   A disclosure   **B** memorandum   **C** chorale   **D** obituary

9.   section of the newspaper that lists the names of people in the community who have died : Obituaries :: section of the newspaper where you will find advertisements : _____

   A Community   **B** Editorials   **C** Classifieds   **D** World News

Name _____ **LESSON 122** Date _____

Study the relationship between the first set of words. Pick the word that completes the second pair with this same relationship.

1. birth : birth announcement :: death : _____

   Ⓐ memorandum Ⓑ chorale Ⓒ disclosure Ⓓ obituary

2. Sahara : _____ :: Amazon : rainforest

   Ⓐ desert Ⓑ wet Ⓒ Amazon Ⓓ Mojave

3. desert : Sahara :: rainforest : _____

   Ⓐ Amazon Ⓑ Mexican Ⓒ Nile Ⓓ Seattle

4. Arctic : polar bear :: Amazon : _____

   Ⓐ beaver Ⓑ grizzly bear Ⓒ whale Ⓓ capybara

5. mountain : valley :: rainforest : _____

   Ⓐ desert Ⓑ wet Ⓒ jungle Ⓓ Amazon

6. _____ : Nile :: Brazil : Amazon

   Ⓐ France Ⓑ pyramid Ⓒ India Ⓓ Egypt

7. Mediterranean : Sea :: Amazon : _____

   Ⓐ river Ⓑ lake Ⓒ ocean Ⓓ country

8. encumber : burden :: belittle : _____

   Ⓐ survey Ⓑ praise Ⓒ insult Ⓓ mutter

9. section of the newspaper that lists the names of people in the community who have died : Obituaries :: section of the newspaper where you will find advertisements : _____

   Ⓐ Community Ⓑ Editorials Ⓒ World News Ⓓ Classifieds

127

Name _____ **LESSON 123** Date _____

Study the relationship between the first set of words. Pick the word that completes the second pair with this same relationship.

1. _____ : Nile :: Brazil : Amazon

   Ⓐ India   Ⓑ France   Ⓒ Egypt   Ⓓ pyramid

2. Sahara : _____ :: Amazon : rainforest

   Ⓐ desert   Ⓑ Mojave   Ⓒ wet   Ⓓ Amazon

3. Arctic : polar bear :: Amazon : _____

   Ⓐ beaver   Ⓑ grizzly bear   Ⓒ whale   Ⓓ capybara

4. desert : Sahara :: rainforest : _____

   Ⓐ Mexican   Ⓑ Seattle   Ⓒ Nile   Ⓓ Amazon

5. mountain : valley :: rainforest : _____

   Ⓐ Amazon   Ⓑ desert   Ⓒ wet   Ⓓ jungle

6. encumber : burden :: belittle : _____

   Ⓐ mutter   Ⓑ survey   Ⓒ praise   Ⓓ insult

7. section of the newspaper that lists the names of people in the community who have died : Obituaries :: section of the newspaper where you will find advertisements : _____

   Ⓐ Editorials   Ⓑ Community   Ⓒ World News   Ⓓ Classifieds

8. birth : birth announcement :: death : _____

   Ⓐ chorale   Ⓑ memorandum   Ⓒ disclosure   Ⓓ obituary

9. Mediterranean : Sea :: Amazon : _____

   Ⓐ ocean   Ⓑ river   Ⓒ lake   Ⓓ country

Name _____   **LESSON 124**   Date _____

Study the relationship between the first set of words. Pick the word that completes the second pair with this same relationship.

1. assimilated : conformed :: abridged : _____

   (A) lengthened   (B) shortened   (C) surrounded   (D) disclosed

2. penguin : bird :: dolphin : _____

   (A) fish   (B) crustacean   (C) insect   (D) mammal

3. imperious : overbearing :: obstinate : _____

   (A) stubborn   (B) dirty   (C) focused   (D) civil

4. piranha : fish :: tarantula : _____

   (A) crustacean   (B) amphibian   (C) spider   (D) insect

5. extravagant : _____ :: preposterous : absurd

   (A) famous   (B) luxurious   (C) humble   (D) knowledgeable

6. penguin : bird :: dolphin : _____

   (A) mammal   (B) crustacean   (C) insect   (D) fish

7. spider : arachnid :: crab : _____

   (A) avian   (B) amphibian   (C) mammalian   (D) crustacean

8. of deep meaning : profound :: few words : _____

   (A) benign   (B) succinct   (C) benevolent   (D) sumptuous

9. _____ : myth :: allegory : fable

   (A) artisan   (B) legend   (C) tradition   (D) trouble

10. earnest : _____ :: preposterous : absurd

    (A) serious   (B) confused   (C) courageous   (D) tiring

11. whale : mammal :: lobster : _____

    (A) crustacean   (B) amphibian   (C) mammalian   (D) fish

12. legend : myth :: allegory : _____

    (A) fable   (B) drama   (C) fallacy   (D) fortune

Study the relationship between the first set of words. Pick the word that completes the second pair with this same relationship.

1. piranha : fish :: tarantula : _____

   (A) spider   (B) crustacean   (C) amphibian   (D) insect

2. whale : mammal :: lobster : _____

   (A) crustacean   (B) amphibian   (C) fish   (D) mammalian

3. imperious : overbearing :: obstinate : _____

   (A) dirty   (B) focused   (C) civil   (D) stubborn

4. penguin : bird :: dolphin : _____

   (A) mammal   (B) fish   (C) insect   (D) crustacean

5. legend : myth :: allegory : _____

   (A) fortune   (B) drama   (C) fallacy   (D) fable

6. of deep meaning : profound :: few words : _____

   (A) sumptuous   (B) succinct   (C) benevolent   (D) benign

7. earnest : _____ :: preposterous : absurd

   (A) confused   (B) serious   (C) tiring   (D) courageous

8. assimilated : conformed :: abridged : _____

   (A) disclosed   (B) shortened   (C) surrounded   (D) lengthened

9. spider : arachnid :: crab : _____

   (A) amphibian   (B) avian   (C) crustacean   (D) mammalian

10. extravagant : _____ :: preposterous : absurd

    (A) humble   (B) famous   (C) luxurious   (D) knowledgeable

11. _____ : myth :: allegory : fable

    (A) tradition   (B) legend   (C) trouble   (D) artisan

12. penguin : bird :: dolphin : _____

    (A) fish   (B) insect   (C) mammal   (D) crustacean

Name _____   **LESSON 126**   Date _____

Study the relationship between the first set of words. Pick the word that completes the second pair with this same relationship.

1. whale : mammal :: lobster : _____

    Ⓐ amphibian   Ⓑ fish   Ⓒ crustacean   Ⓓ mammalian

2. spider : arachnid :: crab : _____

    Ⓐ avian   Ⓑ amphibian   Ⓒ mammalian   Ⓓ crustacean

3. _____ : myth :: allegory : fable

    Ⓐ trouble   Ⓑ artisan   Ⓒ tradition   Ⓓ legend

4. imperious : overbearing :: obstinate : _____

    Ⓐ stubborn   Ⓑ focused   Ⓒ dirty   Ⓓ civil

5. penguin : bird :: dolphin : _____

    Ⓐ insect   Ⓑ fish   Ⓒ mammal   Ⓓ crustacean

6. piranha : fish :: tarantula : _____

    Ⓐ insect   Ⓑ amphibian   Ⓒ crustacean   Ⓓ spider

7. earnest : _____ :: preposterous : absurd

    Ⓐ serious   Ⓑ courageous   Ⓒ tiring   Ⓓ confused

8. assimilated : conformed :: abridged : _____

    Ⓐ lengthened   Ⓑ surrounded   Ⓒ disclosed   Ⓓ shortened

9. legend : myth :: allegory : _____

    Ⓐ fallacy   Ⓑ fable   Ⓒ fortune   Ⓓ drama

10. penguin : bird :: dolphin : _____

    Ⓐ mammal   Ⓑ fish   Ⓒ crustacean   Ⓓ insect

11. of deep meaning : profound :: few words : _____

    Ⓐ sumptuous   Ⓑ benign   Ⓒ benevolent   Ⓓ succinct

12. extravagant : _____ :: preposterous : absurd

    Ⓐ famous   Ⓑ luxurious   Ⓒ knowledgeable   Ⓓ humble

Study the relationship between the first set of words. Pick the word that completes the second pair with this same relationship.

1. coward : cowered :: sneakers : _____

   Ⓐ shabby   Ⓑ shoes   Ⓒ ran   Ⓓ peekers

2. Renaissance : culture :: _____ : religion

   Ⓐ Reformation   Ⓑ Restoration   Ⓒ Protestant   Ⓓ Reclamation

3. period before the Middle Ages : Dark Ages :: period after the Middle Ages : _____

   Ⓐ Renaissance   Ⓑ Imperialism   Ⓒ Industrial Revolution   Ⓓ Crusades

4. Industrial Revolution : technological advances :: Renaissance : _____

   Ⓐ cultural rebirth   Ⓑ political unrest   Ⓒ increased faith in the Catholic Church   Ⓓ educational decline

5. wizened : shriveled :: dithering : _____

   Ⓐ muttering   Ⓑ trembling   Ⓒ stumbling   Ⓓ laughing

6. stand tall : confident :: cower : _____
   Ⓐ angry   Ⓑ scared   Ⓒ sleepy   Ⓓ happy

7. shriveled : wizened :: _____ : bemused

   Ⓐ contained   Ⓑ confused   Ⓒ appalled   Ⓓ indulgent

8. cultural : Renaissance :: religious : _____

   Ⓐ Reformation   Ⓑ Reclamation   Ⓒ Restoration   Ⓓ Protestant

9. car : parked :: ship : _____

   Ⓐ cowered   Ⓑ moored   Ⓒ sodden   Ⓓ landed

10. Romeo and Juliet : Renaissance :: Canterbury Tales : _____

    Ⓐ Industrial Revolution   Ⓑ Middle Ages   Ⓒ Roman Empire   Ⓓ Bronze Age

11. cower : cringe :: traipse : _____

    Ⓐ loiter   Ⓑ arbor   Ⓒ veer   Ⓓ meander

12. remunerate : pay :: augment : _____

    Ⓐ cover   Ⓑ steal   Ⓒ cheat   Ⓓ add to

Name _____ **LESSON 128** Date _____

Study the relationship between the first set of words. Pick the word that completes the second pair with this same relationship.

1. swill : swirl :: expel : _____

    Ⓐ fold up   Ⓑ pry   Ⓒ swing   Ⓓ force out

2. fray : unravel :: whorl : _____

    Ⓐ tighten   Ⓑ swirl   Ⓒ pool   Ⓓ snap

3. stand tall : confident :: cower : _____

    Ⓐ angry   Ⓑ sleepy   Ⓒ scared   Ⓓ happy

4. cower : cringe :: traipse : _____

    Ⓐ meander   Ⓑ veer   Ⓒ arbor   Ⓓ loiter

5. wizened : shriveled :: dithering : _____

    Ⓐ muttering   Ⓑ trembling   Ⓒ laughing   Ⓓ stumbling

6. wizened : shriveled :: tremulous : _____

    Ⓐ terrifying   Ⓑ falling   Ⓒ enormous   Ⓓ shaking

7. Renaissance : culture :: _____ : religion

    Ⓐ Restoration   Ⓑ Reclamation   Ⓒ Protestant   Ⓓ Reformation

8. cultural : Renaissance :: religious : _____

    Ⓐ Reclamation   Ⓑ Reformation   Ⓒ Protestant   Ⓓ Restoration

9. coward : cowered :: sneakers : _____

    Ⓐ ran   Ⓑ shabby   Ⓒ shoes   Ⓓ peekers

10. cower : cringe :: grimace : _____

    Ⓐ blush   Ⓑ wink   Ⓒ scowl   Ⓓ shrug

11. period before the Middle Ages : Dark Ages :: period after the Middle Ages : _____

    Ⓐ Imperialism   Ⓑ Crusades   Ⓒ Renaissance   Ⓓ Industrial Revolution

12. remunerate : pay :: augment : _____

    Ⓐ add to   Ⓑ cover   Ⓒ cheat   Ⓓ steal

Name _____   **LESSON 129**   Date _____

Study the relationship between the first set of words. Pick the word that completes the second pair with this same relationship.

1. Renaissance : culture :: _____ : religion

    Ⓐ Reclamation   Ⓑ Protestant   Ⓒ Reformation   Ⓓ Restoration

2. stand tall : confident :: cower : _____

    Ⓐ happy   Ⓑ sleepy   Ⓒ scared   Ⓓ angry

3. swill : swirl :: expel : _____

    Ⓐ force out   Ⓑ pry   Ⓒ fold up   Ⓓ swing

4. coward : cowered :: sneakers : _____

    Ⓐ shoes   Ⓑ peekers   Ⓒ ran   Ⓓ shabby

5. remunerate : pay :: augment : _____

    Ⓐ add to   Ⓑ cover   Ⓒ cheat   Ⓓ steal

6. wizened : shriveled :: tremulous : _____

    Ⓐ shaking   Ⓑ falling   Ⓒ enormous   Ⓓ terrifying

7. fray : unravel :: whorl : _____

    Ⓐ snap   Ⓑ pool   Ⓒ swirl   Ⓓ tighten

8. cower : crouch :: traipse : _____

    Ⓐ loiter   Ⓑ loom   Ⓒ cobble   Ⓓ meander

9. car : parked :: ship : _____

    Ⓐ sodden   Ⓑ moored   Ⓒ cowered   Ⓓ landed

10. cower : cringe :: traipse : _____

    Ⓐ meander   Ⓑ veer   Ⓒ loiter   Ⓓ arbor

11. wizened : shriveled :: dithering : _____

    Ⓐ laughing   Ⓑ stumbling   Ⓒ muttering   Ⓓ trembling

12. Romeo and Juliet : Renaissance :: Canterbury Tales : _____

    Ⓐ Bronze Age   Ⓑ Middle Ages   Ⓒ Roman Empire   Ⓓ Industrial Revolution

stealthily	artifacts and remains
proposal	certain
insulting	theology
elusive	

Study the relationship between the first set of words. Pick one word from the word bank that completes the second pair with this same relationship.

1.
   imbecilically : foolishly :: furtively : _____

2.
   plan : strategy :: suggestion : _____

3.
   the study of humans and their cultures : anthropology :: the study of religion :

   _____

4.
   anthropology : culture of humankind :: archaeology : _____

5.
   humble : modest :: definite : _____

6.
   derisive : _____ :: furtive : sneaky

7.
   sneaky : stealthy :: difficult to catch : _____

artifacts and remains	stealthily
proposal	elusive
insulting	theology
certain	

Study the relationship between the first set of words. Pick one word from the word bank that completes the second pair with this same relationship.

1.
    sneaky : stealthy :: difficult to catch : _____

2.
    anthropology : culture of humankind :: archaeology : _____

3.
    the study of humans and their cultures : anthropology :: the study of religion :

    _____

4.
    plan : strategy :: suggestion : _____

5.
    humble : modest :: definite : _____

6.
    imbecilically : foolishly :: furtively : _____

7.
    derisive : _____ :: furtive : sneaky

insulting	certain
proposal	stealthily
theology	elusive
artifacts and remains	

Study the relationship between the first set of words. Pick one word from the word bank that completes the second pair with this same relationship.

1.	derisive : _____ :: furtive : sneaky
2.	the study of humans and their cultures : anthropology :: the study of religion : _____
3.	humble : modest :: definite : _____
4.	anthropology : culture of humankind :: archaeology : _____
5.	plan : strategy :: suggestion : _____
6.	sneaky : stealthy :: difficult to catch : _____
7.	imbecilically : foolishly :: furtively : _____

Study the relationship between the first set of words. Pick the word that completes the second pair with this same relationship.

1. relenting : surrendering :: intricate : _____

   Ⓐ perfect   Ⓑ complex   Ⓒ wary   Ⓓ slow

2. entertain : regale :: collect : _____

   Ⓐ adorn   Ⓑ accumulate   Ⓒ imbue   Ⓓ intimidate

3. articulate : eloquent :: intricate : _____

   Ⓐ perfect   Ⓑ slow   Ⓒ complex   Ⓓ delicate

4. encouraging : intimidating :: _____ : stingy

   Ⓐ angry   Ⓑ jealous   Ⓒ generous   Ⓓ honesty

5. impudent : rude :: indolent : _____

   Ⓐ lazy   Ⓑ happy   Ⓒ kind   Ⓓ silly

6. allure : attraction :: aversion : _____

   Ⓐ restitution   Ⓑ antipathy   Ⓒ sympathy   Ⓓ diversion

7. to show prejudice : discriminate :: to cause fear : _____

   Ⓐ alleviate   Ⓑ appropriate   Ⓒ disengage   Ⓓ intimidate

8. relenting : forgiving :: intricate : _____

   Ⓐ wary   Ⓑ perfect   Ⓒ complex   Ⓓ slow

Name _____   **LESSON 134**   Date _____

Study the relationship between the first set of words. Pick the word that completes the second pair with this same relationship.

1. to show prejudice : discriminate :: to cause fear : _____

    (A) intimidate   (B) disengage   (C) appropriate   (D) alleviate

2. entertain : regale :: collect : _____

    (A) adorn   (B) accumulate   (C) intimidate   (D) imbue

3. encouraging : intimidating :: _____ : stingy

    (A) generous   (B) jealous   (C) angry   (D) honesty

4. relenting : forgiving :: intricate : _____

    (A) wary   (B) complex   (C) slow   (D) perfect

5. relenting : surrendering :: intricate : _____

    (A) complex   (B) slow   (C) wary   (D) perfect

6. allure : attraction :: aversion : _____

    (A) restitution   (B) antipathy   (C) sympathy   (D) diversion

7. impudent : rude :: indolent : _____

    (A) happy   (B) kind   (C) lazy   (D) silly

8. articulate : eloquent :: intricate : _____

    (A) delicate   (B) slow   (C) perfect   (D) complex

Name _____   **LESSON 135**   Date _____

Study the relationship between the first set of words. Pick the word that completes the second pair with this same relationship.

1. impudent : rude :: indolent : _____

    A kind   **B** lazy   **C** silly   **D** happy

2. relenting : surrendering :: intricate : _____

    A perfect   **B** complex   **C** slow   **D** wary

3. articulate : eloquent :: intricate : _____

    A delicate   **B** complex   **C** perfect   **D** slow

4. entertain : regale :: collect : _____

    A accumulate   **B** adorn   **C** intimidate   **D** imbue

5. allure : attraction :: aversion : _____

    A antipathy   **B** sympathy   **C** restitution   **D** diversion

6. encouraging : intimidating :: _____ : stingy

    A generous   **B** honesty   **C** angry   **D** jealous

7. relenting : forgiving :: intricate : _____

    A complex   **B** slow   **C** wary   **D** perfect

8. to show prejudice : discriminate :: to cause fear : _____

    A intimidate   **B** disengage   **C** alleviate   **D** appropriate

Study the relationship between the first set of words. Pick the word that completes the second pair with this same relationship.

1. solitude : seclusion :: majesty : _____

    Ⓐ grandeur   Ⓑ forgery   Ⓒ entourage   Ⓓ mayhem

2. hopeful : optimistic :: sentimental : _____

    Ⓐ pessimistic   Ⓑ nostalgic   Ⓒ centrifugal   Ⓓ sad

3. atrocious : _____ :: intrepid : fearless

    Ⓐ quiet   Ⓑ beautiful   Ⓒ dreadful   Ⓓ scary

4. Australia : Aborigines :: Italy : _____

    Ⓐ Vikings   Ⓑ Gauls   Ⓒ Etruscans   Ⓓ Huns

5. fable : tells a story :: metaphor : _____

    Ⓐ corrects a   Ⓑ makes a   Ⓓ makes a
       mistake   connection   Ⓒ teaches a lesson   comparison

6. bears : hibernate :: birds : _____

    Ⓐ metamorphosis   Ⓑ insect   Ⓒ migrate   Ⓓ winter

7. bewildered : confused :: intrepid : _____

    Ⓐ traveling   Ⓑ hidden   Ⓒ prominent   Ⓓ fearless

8. tadpole : toad :: _____ : butterfly

    Ⓐ cocoon   Ⓑ chrysalis   Ⓒ metamorphosis   Ⓓ egg

9. butterfly : caterpillar :: damselfly : _____

    Ⓐ insects   Ⓑ nymph   Ⓒ metamorphosis   Ⓓ cocoon

10. _____ : Aborigines :: North America : Native Americans

    Ⓐ South America   Ⓑ Europe   Ⓒ Mexico   Ⓓ Australia

11. fly : decomposition :: bee : _____

    Ⓐ metamorphosis   Ⓑ pollination   Ⓒ pollution   Ⓓ chrysalis

12. Australia : Aborigines :: North America : _____

    Ⓐ Vikings   Ⓑ Native   Ⓒ Pilgrims   Ⓓ Incas
                         Americans

Study the relationship between the first set of words. Pick the word that completes the second pair with this same relationship.

1. Francisco Pizarro : Incas :: Hernando Cortez : _____

   Ⓐ Cherokees   Ⓑ Navajos   Ⓒ Aztecs   Ⓓ Aborigines

2. Australia : Aborigines :: North America : _____

   Ⓐ Vikings   Ⓑ Pilgrims   Ⓒ Native Americans   Ⓓ Incas

3. bears : hibernate :: birds : _____

   Ⓐ migrate   Ⓑ insect   Ⓒ winter   Ⓓ metamorphosis

4. solitude : seclusion :: majesty : _____

   Ⓐ mayhem   Ⓑ forgery   Ⓒ grandeur   Ⓓ entourage

5. atrocious : _____ :: intrepid : fearless

   Ⓐ quiet   Ⓑ beautiful   Ⓒ dreadful   Ⓓ scary

6. _____ : Aborigines :: North America : Native Americans

   Ⓐ Mexico   Ⓑ Australia   Ⓒ South America   Ⓓ Europe

7. fly : decomposition :: bee : _____

   Ⓐ metamorphosis   Ⓑ pollination   Ⓒ pollution   Ⓓ chrysalis

8. fable : tells a story :: metaphor : _____

   Ⓐ corrects a mistake   Ⓑ makes a comparison   Ⓒ makes a connection   Ⓓ teaches a lesson

9. butterfly : caterpillar :: damselfly : _____

   Ⓐ metamorphosis   Ⓑ nymph   Ⓒ cocoon   Ⓓ insects

10. tadpole : toad :: _____ : butterfly

    Ⓐ metamorphosis   Ⓑ cocoon   Ⓒ egg   Ⓓ chrysalis

11. bewildered : confused :: intrepid : _____

    Ⓐ prominent   Ⓑ traveling   Ⓒ fearless   Ⓓ hidden

12. Australia : Aborigines :: Italy : _____

    Ⓐ Gauls   Ⓑ Vikings   Ⓒ Etruscans   Ⓓ Huns

Name _____ **LESSON 138** Date _____

Study the relationship between the first set of words. Pick the word that completes the second pair with this same relationship.

1. bears : hibernate :: birds : _____

   (A) migrate   (B) insect   (C) winter   (D) metamorphosis

2. tadpole : toad :: _____ : butterfly

   (A) cocoon   (B) egg   (C) metamorphosis   (D) chrysalis

3. Australia : Aborigines :: North America : _____

   (A) Pilgrims   (B) Incas   (C) Native Americans   (D) Vikings

4. _____ : Aborigines :: North America : Native Americans

   (A) Australia   (B) Mexico   (C) Europe   (D) South America

5. Francisco Pizarro : Incas :: Hernando Cortez : _____

   (A) Aztecs   (B) Navajos   (C) Cherokees   (D) Aborigines

6. fly : decomposition :: bee : _____

   (A) chrysalis   (B) pollination   (C) metamorphosis   (D) pollution

7. atrocious : _____ :: intrepid : fearless

   (A) beautiful   (B) dreadful   (C) scary   (D) quiet

8. solitude : seclusion :: majesty : _____

   (A) grandeur   (B) entourage   (C) forgery   (D) mayhem

9. Australia : Aborigines :: Italy : _____

   (A) Huns   (B) Vikings   (C) Gauls   (D) Etruscans

10. bewildered : confused :: intrepid : _____

    (A) hidden   (B) traveling   (C) fearless   (D) prominent

11. hopeful : optimistic :: sentimental : _____

    (A) pessimistic   (B) sad   (C) centrifugal   (D) nostalgic

12. fable : tells a story :: metaphor : _____

    (A) corrects a mistake   (B) teaches a lesson   (C) makes a comparison   (D) makes a connection

Study the relationship between the first set of words. Pick the word that completes the second pair with this same relationship.

1. truth : confession :: lie : _____

   Ⓐ perjury   Ⓑ obstruction   Ⓒ interrogation   Ⓓ innocence

2. deft : _____ :: diligent : persistent

   Ⓐ childish   Ⓑ clever   Ⓒ annoying   Ⓓ dexterity

3. new : original :: repetitive : _____

   Ⓐ old   Ⓑ transparent   Ⓒ redundant   Ⓓ required

4. conspicuous : noteworthy :: deft : _____

   Ⓐ foolish   Ⓑ skillful   Ⓒ generous   Ⓓ conspicuous

5. very large : massive :: harsh : _____

   Ⓐ deft   Ⓑ lanky   Ⓒ strident   Ⓓ ideal

6. _____ : protect :: virus : corrupts

   Ⓐ firewall   Ⓑ memory   Ⓒ ethernet   Ⓓ breach

7. humans : physician :: animals : _____

   ․ equestrian   Ⓑ biologist   Ⓒ mammalian   Ⓓ veterinarian

8. truth : confession :: lie : _____

   Ⓐ innocence   Ⓑ obstruction   Ⓒ interrogation   Ⓓ perjury

9. worm : tunnel :: virus : _____

   Ⓐ infects   Ⓑ encrypts   Ⓒ conducts   Ⓓ tracks

10. humans : physician :: animals : _____

   Ⓐ equestrian   Ⓑ biologist   Ⓒ veterinarian   Ⓓ mammalian

Name _____   **LESSON 140**   Date _____

Study the relationship between the first set of words. Pick the word that completes the second pair with this same relationship.

1. deft : _____ :: diligent : persistent

   (A) childish   (B) clever   (C) annoying   (D) dexterity

2. conspicuous : noteworthy :: deft : _____

   (A) conspicuous   (B) foolish   (C) skillful   (D) generous

3. worm : tunnel :: virus : _____

   (A) infects   (B) encrypts   (C) tracks   (D) conducts

4. humans : physician :: animals : _____

   (A) biologist   (B) mammalian   (C) equestrian   (D) veterinarian

5. _____ : protect :: virus : corrupts

   (A) breach   (B) memory   (C) ethernet   (D) firewall

6. truth : confession :: lie : _____

   (A) perjury   (B) innocence   (C) interrogation   (D) obstruction

7. truth : confession :: lie : _____

   (A) innocence   (B) perjury   (C) interrogation   (D) obstruction

8. very large : massive :: harsh : _____

   (A) deft   (B) strident   (C) lanky   (D) ideal

9. new : original :: repetitive : _____

   (A) transparent   (B) redundant   (C) required   (D) old

10. humans : physician :: animals : _____

   (A) mammalian   (B) veterinarian   (C) equestrian   (D) biologist

Name _____   **LESSON 141**   Date _____

Study the relationship between the first set of words. Pick the word that completes the second pair with this same relationship.

1. truth : confession :: lie : _____

    A obstruction   **B** perjury   **C** innocence   **D** interrogation

2. humans : physician :: animals : _____

    A mammalian   **B** biologist   **C** equestrian   **D** veterinarian

3. worm : tunnel :: virus : _____

    A infects   **B** conducts   **C** encrypts   **D** tracks

4. very large : massive :: harsh : _____

    A lanky   **B** ideal   **C** strident   **D** deft

5. _____ : protect :: virus : corrupts

    A ethernet   **B** breach   **C** firewall   **D** memory

6. new : original :: repetitive : _____

    A old   **B** required   **C** transparent   **D** redundant

7. humans : physician :: animals : _____

    A veterinarian   **B** biologist   **C** equestrian   **D** mammalian

8. conspicuous : noteworthy :: deft : _____

    A conspicuous   **B** skillful   **C** generous   **D** foolish

9. truth : confession :: lie : _____

    A obstruction   **B** interrogation   **C** perjury   **D** innocence

10. deft : _____ :: diligent : persistent

    A childish   **B** dexterity   **C** clever   **D** annoying

146

Study the relationship between the first set of words. Pick the word that completes the second pair with this same relationship.

1. anthropology : culture of humankind :: archaeology : _____

    (A) artifacts and remains   (B) dinosaurs   (C) dirt   (D) architecture

2. expedition : journey :: ramification : _____

    (A) consequence   (B) barrier   (C) plan   (D) choice

3. sneaky : stealthy :: difficult to catch : _____

    (A) furtive   (B) poignant   (C) elusive   (D) servile

4. imbecilically : foolishly :: furtively : _____

    (A) elaborately   (B) stealthily   (C) thoughtfully   (D) remotely

5. plan : strategy :: suggestion : _____

    (A) rationalization   (B) execution   (C) corroboration   (D) proposal

6. tribulations : hardships :: ramifications : _____

    (A) consequences   (B) accidents   (C) reviews   (D) agreements

7. derisive : _____ :: furtive : sneaky

    (A) frightening   (B) pleasing   (C) insulting   (D) encouraging

8. humble : modest :: definite : _____

    (A) furtive   (B) surly   (C) certain   (D) loping

9. The study of humans and their cultures : anthropology :: the study of religion : _____

    (A) psychology   (B) theology   (C) astronomy   (D) economics

Name _____   **LESSON 143**   Date _____

Study the relationship between the first set of words. Pick the word that completes the second pair with this same relationship.

1.   The study of humans and their cultures : anthropology :: the study of religion : _____

   Ⓐ psychology   Ⓑ astronomy   Ⓒ theology   Ⓓ economics

2.   humble : modest :: definite : _____

   Ⓐ certain   Ⓑ furtive   Ⓒ loping   Ⓓ surly

3.   derisive : _____ :: furtive : sneaky

   Ⓐ frightening   Ⓑ pleasing   Ⓒ encouraging   Ⓓ insulting

4.   anthropology : culture of humankind :: archaeology : _____

   Ⓐ dirt   Ⓑ dinosaurs   Ⓒ artifacts and remains   Ⓓ architecture

5.   expedition : journey :: ramification : _____

   Ⓐ consequence   Ⓑ plan   Ⓒ barrier   Ⓓ choice

6.   plan : strategy :: suggestion : _____

   Ⓐ proposal   Ⓑ rationalization   Ⓒ corroboration   Ⓓ execution

7.   imbecilically : foolishly :: furtively : _____

   Ⓐ remotely   Ⓑ thoughtfully   Ⓒ stealthily   Ⓓ elaborately

8.   tribulations : hardships :: ramifications : _____

   Ⓐ consequences   Ⓑ accidents   Ⓒ agreements   Ⓓ reviews

9.   sneaky : stealthy :: difficult to catch : _____

   Ⓐ furtive   Ⓑ poignant   Ⓒ elusive   Ⓓ servile

Study the relationship between the first set of words. Pick the word that completes the second pair with this same relationship.

1. derisive : _____ :: furtive : sneaky

    A pleasing **B** encouraging **C** frightening **D** insulting

2. sneaky : stealthy :: difficult to catch : _____

    A poignant **B** furtive **C** elusive **D** servile

3. imbecilically : foolishly :: furtively : _____

    A thoughtfully **B** elaborately **C** remotely **D** stealthily

4. tribulations : hardships :: ramifications : _____

    A reviews **B** agreements **C** accidents **D** consequences

5. plan : strategy :: suggestion : _____

    A rationalization **B** execution **C** proposal **D** corroboration

6. anthropology : culture of humankind :: archaeology : _____

    A artifacts and remains **B** dirt **C** architecture **D** dinosaurs

7. the study of humans and their cultures : anthropology :: the study of religion : _____

    A astronomy **B** economics **C** theology **D** psychology

8. expedition : journey :: ramification : _____

    A choice **B** consequence **C** plan **D** barrier

9. humble : modest :: definite : _____

    A surly **B** certain **C** loping **D** furtive

Study the relationship between the first set of words. Pick the word that completes the second pair with this same relationship.

1. wagon : cart :: cottage : _____

    A mansion   **B** tent   **C** carriage   **D** cabin

2. boat : skiff :: _____ : carriage

    A bray   **B** cart   **C** saddle   **D** pull

3. cherry tree : Washington :: honesty : _____

    A Oregon   **B** trustworthy   **C** dishonesty   **D** Lincoln

4. Johnson : Kennedy :: Roosevelt : _____

    A Wilson   **B** McKinley   **C** Truman   **D** Hoover

5. procession : line :: sheath : _____

    A cover   **B** cart   **C** field   **D** ring

6. _____ : hauling :: plow : digging

    A bray   **B** cart   **C** pull   **D** saddle

7. cart : push :: ladder : _____

    A lift   **B** roll   **C** climb   **D** slide

8. tugboat : barge :: mule : _____

    A bray   **B** cart   **C** pull   **D** saddle

Study the relationship between the first set of words. Pick the word that completes the second pair with this same relationship.

1. boat : skiff :: _____ : carriage

   Ⓐ saddle   Ⓑ bray   Ⓒ cart   Ⓓ pull

2. tugboat : barge :: mule : _____

   Ⓐ pull   Ⓑ cart   Ⓒ bray   Ⓓ saddle

3. _____ : hauling :: plow : digging

   Ⓐ bray   Ⓑ pull   Ⓒ cart   Ⓓ saddle

4. wagon : cart :: cottage : _____

   Ⓐ tent   Ⓑ mansion   Ⓒ cabin   Ⓓ carriage

5. Johnson : Kennedy :: Roosevelt : _____

   Ⓐ McKinley   Ⓑ Truman   Ⓒ Hoover   Ⓓ Wilson

6. cart : push :: ladder : _____

   Ⓐ lift   Ⓑ climb   Ⓒ slide   Ⓓ roll

7. cherry tree : Washington :: honesty : _____

   Ⓐ dishonesty   Ⓑ Oregon   Ⓒ Lincoln   Ⓓ trustworthy

8. procession : line :: sheath : _____

   Ⓐ cart   Ⓑ field   Ⓒ ring   Ⓓ cover

Name _____ **LESSON 147** Date _____

Study the relationship between the first set of words. Pick the word that completes the second pair with this same relationship.

1.	cart : push :: ladder : _____
	(A) slide **(B)** climb **(C)** roll **(D)** lift
2.	cherry tree : Washington :: honesty : _____
	(A) Lincoln **(B)** trustworthy **(C)** dishonesty **(D)** Oregon
3.	Johnson : Kennedy :: Roosevelt : _____
	(A) Truman **(B)** Wilson **(C)** Hoover **(D)** McKinley
4.	tugboat : barge :: mule : _____
	(A) cart **(B)** pull **(C)** saddle **(D)** bray
5.	procession : line :: sheath : _____
	(A) cart **(B)** ring **(C)** field **(D)** cover
6.	_____ : hauling :: plow : digging
	(A) pull **(B)** cart **(C)** saddle **(D)** bray
7.	boat : skiff :: _____ : carriage
	(A) bray **(B)** cart **(C)** pull **(D)** saddle
8.	wagon : cart :: cottage : _____
	(A) tent **(B)** mansion **(C)** carriage **(D)** cabin

**Study the relationship between the first set of words. Pick the word th[at]
second pair with this same relationship.**

1. temporary : pencil :: permanent : _____

   (A) eraser   (B) ink   (C) watercolor

2. bones : skeletal system :: heart : _____

   (A) air   (B) digestive system   (C) respiratory system   (D) skeletal system

3. create : make :: concept : _____

   (A) tool   (B) team   (C) idea   (D) change

4. harmony : peace :: adversity : _____

   (A) prosperity   (B) fortune   (C) suffering   (D) same

5. cowardice : courage :: shame : _____

   (A) fear   (B) kindness   (C) glory   (D) pride

6. team : players :: choir : _____

   (A) singers   (B) composers   (C) band   (D) instruments

7. dislike : like :: loathe : _____

   (A) attentive   (B) apathy   (C) adore   (D) animosity

8. excusable : unforgivable :: _____ : honorable

   (A) generous   (B) difficult   (C) despicable   (D) unbelievable

9. independence : freedom :: _____ : fairness

   (A) justice   (B) honor   (C) nurse   (D) liberty

10. awareness : knowledge :: responsibility : _____

    (A) authority   (B) common occurrence   (C) duty   (D) altruism

11. Christianity : Bible :: Buddhism : _____

    (A) Sutras   (B) Koran   (C) Avesta   (D) Torah

12. amendment : alteration :: petition : _____

    (A) request   (B) scandal   (C) deadline   (D) ballot

Name _____ **LESSON 149** Date _____

Study the relationship between the first set of words. Pick the word that completes the second pair with this same relationship.

1. mile : smiles :: pear : _____

   (A) peach   (B) dear   (C) kumquats   (D) spears

2. smirk : smile :: glare : _____

   (A) magnify   (B) plan   (C) stare   (D) cover

3. voice : melody :: piano : _____

   (A) harmony   (B) pitch   (C) key   (D) accompaniment

4. heritage : ancestry :: symbol : _____

   (A) future   (B) sign   (C) address   (D) responsibility

5. chapel : steeple :: _____ : monuments

   (A) cemetery   (B) church   (C) towering   (D) famous

6. humble : arrogant :: willing : _____

   (A) honorable   (B) stubborn   (C) haughty   (D) decadent

7. prevent opponent from scoring : defense :: score points : _____

   (A) team   (B) umpire   (C) offense   (D) coach

8. finish line : race :: pot of gold : _____

   (A) ocean   (B) rainbow   (C) tornado   (D) clouds

9. harmony : peace :: adversity : _____

   (A) same   (B) prosperity   (C) suffering   (D) fortune

10. instantaneous : only a second :: eternal : _____

    (A) days   (B) until the end of the day   (C) forever   (D) years

11. natural : pure :: harmony : _____

    (A) hostility   (B) cleanness   (C) courtesy   (D) balance

12. happy : smile :: sad : _____

    (A) correct   (B) fight   (C) cry   (D) sad

Study the relationship between the first set of words. Pick the word that completes the second pair with this same relationship. [*Hint: American Presidents & Politics*]

1. president : George Washington :: inventor : _____
   - Ⓐ Walt Whitman
   - Ⓑ John Adams
   - Ⓒ Charlie Chaplin
   - Ⓓ Benjamin Franklin

2. founder of the Red Cross : _____ :: Union President : Abraham Lincoln
   - Ⓐ Eleanor Roosevelt
   - Ⓑ Susan B. Anthony
   - Ⓒ Jeanette Rankin
   - Ⓓ Clara Barton

3. $50 bill : Ulysses S. Grant :: $20 bill : _____
   - Ⓐ Andrew Jackson
   - Ⓑ Thomas Jefferson
   - Ⓒ Abraham Lincoln
   - Ⓓ Benjamin Franklin

4. penny : Abraham Lincoln :: nickel : _____
   - Ⓐ Thomas Jefferson
   - Ⓑ John F. Kennedy
   - Ⓒ George Washington
   - Ⓓ Benjamin Franklin

5. 16th President : Abraham Lincoln :: 1st President : _____
   - Ⓐ Bill Clinton
   - Ⓑ George Washington
   - Ⓒ John Adams
   - Ⓓ Theodore Roosevelt

6. _____ : Illinois :: John F. Kennedy : Massachusetts
   - Ⓐ Robert E. Lee
   - Ⓑ George Washington
   - Ⓒ Ulysses S Grant
   - Ⓓ Abraham Lincoln

7. George Washington : Mount Vernon :: Thomas Jefferson : _____
   - Ⓐ The Hermitage
   - Ⓑ Monticello
   - Ⓒ Montpelier
   - Ⓓ Sagamore Hill

8. "Old Hickory" : Andrew Jackson :: "Father of the Constitution" : _____
   - Ⓐ Zachary Taylor
   - Ⓑ James Madison
   - Ⓒ George Washington
   - Ⓓ Ulysses S. Grant

9. _____ : American history :: Mark Twain : American literature
   - Ⓐ Abraham Lincoln
   - Ⓑ Ulysses S Grant
   - Ⓒ George Washington
   - Ⓓ James Madison

10. James Madison : Dolley Madison :: George Washington : _____
   - Ⓐ Jane Washington
   - Ⓑ Molly Washington
   - Ⓒ Ellen Washington
   - Ⓓ Martha Washington

11. _____ : president :: Christopher Columbus : explorer
   - Ⓐ Theodore Roosevelt
   - Ⓑ Abraham Lincoln
   - Ⓒ Robert E. Lee
   - Ⓓ Ulysses S Grant

12. "The Little Magician" : Martin Van Buren :: "Honest Abe" : _____
   - Ⓐ Robert E. Lee
   - Ⓑ George Washington
   - Ⓒ Abraham Lincoln
   - Ⓓ Ulysses S Grant

Name _____   **LESSON 151**   Date _____

Study the relationship between the first set of words. Pick the word that completes the second pair with this same relationship. *[Hint: American Presidents & Politics]*

1.	Richard Nixon : impeached :: _____ : assassinated
	Ⓐ James Madison Ⓑ Theodore Roosevelt Ⓒ Abraham Lincoln Ⓓ Ulysses S Grant
2.	_____ : Illinois :: John F. Kennedy : Massachusetts
	Ⓐ George Washington Ⓑ Ulysses S Grant Ⓒ Robert E. Lee Ⓓ Abraham Lincoln
3.	founder of the Red Cross : _____ :: Union President : Abraham Lincoln
	Ⓐ Jeanette Rankin Ⓑ Eleanor Roosevelt Ⓒ Susan B. Anthony Ⓓ Clara Barton
4.	Monticello : Thomas Jefferson :: Mount Vernon : _____
	Ⓐ John F. Kennedy Ⓑ John Adams Ⓒ Abraham Lincoln Ⓓ George Washington
5.	"Old Hickory" : Andrew Jackson :: "Father of the Constitution" : _____
	Ⓐ George Washington Ⓑ James Madison Ⓒ Zachary Taylor Ⓓ Ulysses S. Grant
6.	16th President : Abraham Lincoln :: 1st President : _____
	Ⓐ Bill Clinton Ⓑ John Adams Ⓒ George Washington Ⓓ Theodore Roosevelt
7.	_____ : president :: Christopher Columbus : explorer
	Ⓐ Ulysses S Grant Ⓑ Robert E. Lee Ⓒ Abraham Lincoln Ⓓ Theodore Roosevelt
8.	"The Little Magician" : Martin Van Buren :: "Honest Abe" : _____
	Ⓐ Ulysses S Grant Ⓑ Abraham Lincoln Ⓒ George Washington Ⓓ Robert E. Lee
9.	$50 bill : Ulysses S. Grant :: $20 bill : _____
	Ⓐ Benjamin Franklin Ⓑ Andrew Jackson Ⓒ Abraham Lincoln Ⓓ Thomas Jefferson
10.	president : George Washington :: inventor : _____
	Ⓐ John Adams Ⓑ Benjamin Franklin Ⓒ Charlie Chaplin Ⓓ Walt Whitman
11.	James Madison : Dolley Madison :: George Washington : _____
	Ⓐ Ellen Washington Ⓑ Martha Washington Jane Washington Ⓓ Molly Washington
12.	George Washington : Mount Vernon :: Thomas Jefferson : _____
	Ⓐ Sagamore Hill Ⓑ Montpelier Ⓒ Monticello Ⓓ The Hermitage

Name _____ **LESSON 152** Date _____

Study the relationship between the first set of words. Pick the word that completes the second pair with this same relationship. [*Hint: American Presidents &Politics*]

1. _____ : Illinois :: John F. Kennedy : Massachusetts
   - **A** Robert E. Lee
   - **B** Abraham Lincoln
   - **C** George Washington
   - **D** Ulysses S Grant

2. _____ : president :: Christopher Columbus : explorer
   - **A** Ulysses S Grant
   - **B** Theodore Roosevelt
   - **C** Abraham Lincoln
   - **D** Robert E. Lee

3. "Old Hickory" : Andrew Jackson :: "Father of the Constitution" : _____
   - **A** James Madison
   - **B** George Washington
   - **C** Ulysses S. Grant
   - **D** Zachary Taylor

4. penny : Abraham Lincoln :: nickel : _____
   - **A** George Washington
   - **B** Benjamin Franklin
   - **C** Thomas Jefferson
   - **D** John F. Kennedy

5. "The Little Magician" : Martin Van Buren :: "Honest Abe" : _____
   - **A** Robert E. Lee
   - **B** Ulysses S Grant
   - **C** Abraham Lincoln
   - **D** George Washington

6. _____ : American history :: Mark Twain : American literature
   - **A** Ulysses S Grant
   - **B** James Madison
   - **C** George Washington
   - **D** Abraham Lincoln

7. $50 bill : Ulysses S. Grant :: $20 bill : _____
   - **A** Andrew Jackson
   - **B** Benjamin Franklin
   - **C** Abraham Lincoln
   - **D** Thomas Jefferson

8. James Madison : Dolley Madison :: George Washington : _____
   - **A** Ellen Washington
   - **B** Martha Washington
   - **C** Jane Washington
   - **D** Molly Washington

9. founder of the Red Cross : _____ :: Union President : Abraham Lincoln
   - **A** Susan B. Anthony
   - **B** Jeanette Rankin
   - **C** Eleanor Roosevelt
   - . Clara Barton

10. Richard Nixon : impeached :: _____ : assassinated
    - **A** Ulysses S Grant
    - **B** Abraham Lincoln
    - **C** Theodore Roosevelt
    - **D** James Madison

11. Monticello : Thomas Jefferson :: Mount Vernon : _____
    - **A** John F. Kennedy
    - **B** Abraham Lincoln
    - **C** John Adams
    - **D** George Washington

12. 16th President : Abraham Lincoln :: 1st President : _____
    - **A** Theodore Roosevelt
    - **B** George Washington
    - **C** Bill Clinton
    - **D** John Adams

Name _____   **LESSON 153**   Date _____

Study the relationship between the first set of words. Pick the word that completes the second pair with this same relationship. *[Hint: American Presidents & Politics]*

1. 16th President : Abraham Lincoln :: 1st President : _____
    - **A** George Washington
    - **B** Bill Clinton
    - **C** Theodore Roosevelt
    - **D** John Adams

2. Entrepreneur : Bill Gates :: Virtuoso : _____
    - **A** Britney Spears
    - **B** Harry Potter
    - **C** George Bush
    - **D** Luciano Pavarotti

3. George W. Bush : Texas :: Bill Clinton : _____
    - **A** Arkansas
    - **B** Missouri
    - **C** Atlanta
    - **D** Georgia

4. "The Little Magician" : Martin Van Buren :: "Honest Abe" : _____
    - **A** James Madison
    - **B** Theodore Roosevelt
    - **C** Abraham Lincoln
    - **D** George Washington

5. Theodore Roosevelt : president :: _____ : astronaut
    - **A** Francis Drake
    - **B** George Washington
    - **C** Neil Armstrong
    - **D** John Glenn

6. United States of America : George W. Bush :: al Qaeda : _____
    - **A** Fidel Castro
    - **B** Osama bin Laden
    - **C** Kim Jong Il
    - **D** Saddam Hussein

7. Pearl Harbor : Franklin D. Roosevelt :: September 11 : _____
    - **A** George W. Bush
    - **B** Colin Powell
    - **C** Bill Clinton
    - **D** Dick Cheney

8. United States : George W. Bush :: Mexico : _____
    - **A** Lopez-Portillo
    - **B** Vincente Fox
    - **C** Carlos Salinas
    - **D** Poncho Villa

9. Spanish American War : Theodore Roosevelt :: _____ : George Washington
    - **A** Civil War
    - **B** World War I
    - **C** Revolutionary War
    - **D** Vietnam War

10. Democrat : John F. Kennedy :: Republican : _____
    - **A** Jimmy Carter
    - **B** Bill Clinton
    - **C** Ronald Reagan
    - **D** Lyndon Johnson

11. Jimmy Carter : peanut farmer :: Ronald Reagan : _____
    - **A** lawyer
    - **B** actor
    - **C** teacher
    - **D** doctor

Name _____ **LESSON 154** Date _____

**Study the relationship between the first set of words. Pick the word that completes the
second pair with this same relationship.** *[Hint: American Presidents & Politics]*

1. Pearl Harbor : Franklin D. Roosevelt :: September 11 : _____

    Ⓐ Dick Cheney Ⓑ Colin Powell Ⓒ George W. Bush Ⓓ Bill Clinton

2. George W. Bush : Texas :: Bill Clinton : _____

    Ⓐ Atlanta Ⓑ Georgia Ⓒ Arkansas Ⓓ Missouri

3. United States of America : George W. Bush :: al Qaeda : _____

    Ⓐ Kim Jong Il Ⓑ Osama bin Laden Ⓒ Saddam Hussein Ⓓ Fidel Castro

4. "The Little Magician" : Martin Van Buren :: "Honest Abe" : _____

    Ⓐ Theodore Roosevelt Ⓑ Abraham Lincoln Ⓒ George Washington Ⓓ James Madison

5. Theodore Roosevelt : president :: _____ : astronaut

    Ⓐ Neil Armstrong Ⓑ John Glenn Ⓒ George Washington Ⓓ Francis Drake

6. United States : George W. Bush :: Mexico : _____

    Ⓐ Poncho Villa Ⓑ Lopez-Portillo Ⓒ Carlos Salinas Ⓓ Vincente Fox

7. Democrat : John F. Kennedy :: Republican : _____

    Ⓐ Jimmy Carter Ⓑ Bill Clinton Ⓒ Ronald Reagan Ⓓ Lyndon Johnson

8. Entrepreneur : Bill Gates :: Virtuoso : _____

    Ⓐ Britney Spears Ⓑ George Bush Ⓒ Luciano Pavarotti Ⓓ Harry Potter

9. 16th President : Abraham Lincoln :: 1st President : _____

    Ⓐ Theodore Roosevelt Ⓑ John Adams Ⓒ George Washington Ⓓ Bill Clinton

10. Jimmy Carter : peanut farmer :: Ronald Reagan : _____

    Ⓐ lawyer Ⓑ actor Ⓒ teacher Ⓓ doctor

11. Spanish American War : Theodore Roosevelt :: _____ : George Washington

    Ⓐ Revolutionary War Ⓑ Vietnam War Ⓒ Civil War Ⓓ World War I

Name _____ **LESSON 155** Date _____

Study the relationship between the first set of words. Pick the word that completes the second pair with this same relationship. [*Hint: American Presidents & Politics*]

1. Jimmy Carter : peanut farmer :: Ronald Reagan : _____

   Ⓐ doctor   Ⓑ teacher   Ⓒ actor   Ⓓ lawyer

2. United States : George W. Bush :: Mexico : _____

   Ⓐ Carlos Salinas   Ⓑ Poncho Villa   Ⓒ Vincente Fox   Ⓓ Lopez-Portillo

3. 16th President : Abraham Lincoln :: 1st President : _____

   Ⓐ George Washington   Ⓑ Theodore Roosevelt   Ⓒ John Adams   Ⓓ Bill Clinton

4. Democrat : John F. Kennedy :: Republican : _____

   Ⓐ Bill Clinton   Ⓑ Ronald Reagan   Ⓒ Lyndon Johnson   Ⓓ Jimmy Carter

5. Entrepreneur : Bill Gates :: Virtuoso : _____

   Ⓐ Britney Spears   Ⓑ Luciano Pavarotti   Ⓒ Harry Potter   Ⓓ George Bush

6. United States of America : George W. Bush :: al Qaeda : _____

   Ⓐ Osama bin Laden   Ⓑ Saddam Hussein   Ⓒ Fidel Castro   Ⓓ Kim Jong Il

7. Pearl Harbor : Franklin D. Roosevelt :: September 11 : _____

   Ⓐ George W. Bush   Ⓑ Bill Clinton   Ⓒ Colin Powell   Ⓓ Dick Cheney

8. Spanish American War : Theodore Roosevelt :: _____ : George Washington

   Ⓐ Revolutionary War   Ⓑ Vietnam War   Ⓒ World War I   Ⓓ Civil War

9. "The Little Magician" : Martin Van Buren :: "Honest Abe" : _____

   Ⓐ George Washington   Ⓑ Theodore Roosevelt   Ⓒ Abraham Lincoln   Ⓓ James Madison

10. George W. Bush : Texas :: Bill Clinton : _____

   Ⓐ Arkansas   Ⓑ Missouri   Ⓒ Georgia   Ⓓ Atlanta

11. Theodore Roosevelt : president :: _____ : astronaut

   Ⓐ Neil Armstrong   Ⓑ John Glenn   Ⓒ Francis Drake   Ⓓ George Washington

Name _____   **LESSON 156**   Date _____

Study the relationship between the first set of words. Pick the word that completes the second pair with this same relationship. *[Hint: American states & Politics]*

1.	New Mexico : USA :: Coolidge : _____ Ⓐ Chief Justice of the Supreme Court Ⓑ president Ⓒ country Ⓓ Vice President
2.	Montgomery : Alabama :: Memphis : _____ Ⓐ Tennessee Ⓑ Georgia Ⓒ Mississippi Ⓓ Virginia
3.	Indianapolis : Indiana :: Salem : _____ Ⓐ USA Ⓑ Massachusetts Ⓒ Virginia Ⓓ Oregon
4.	Chicago : Illinois :: Boston : _____ Ⓐ Maine Ⓑ New York Ⓒ Massachusetts Ⓓ Ohio
5.	Gulf of Mexico : Texas :: Gulf of California : _____ Ⓐ Yucatan Ⓑ Baja California Ⓒ Louisiana Ⓓ Florida
6.	President : Washington, DC :: Santa Claus : _____ Ⓐ North Pole Ⓑ South Pole Ⓒ Canada Ⓓ Florida
7.	New Mexico : Santa Fe :: Texas : _____ Ⓐ Dallas Ⓑ Galveston Ⓒ Austin Ⓓ Brownsville
8.	California : gold :: Mexico : _____ Ⓐ copper Ⓑ silver Ⓒ gold Ⓓ diamonds
9.	state : Alabama :: city : _____ Ⓐ Montgomery Ⓑ montgomery Ⓒ capital Ⓓ town
10.	Hawaii : island :: Florida : _____ Ⓐ reef Ⓑ beach Ⓒ peninsula Ⓓ atoll
11.	Cartier : St. Lawrence River :: Cabrillo : _____ Ⓐ Quebec Ⓑ Mt. Whitney Ⓒ California Ⓓ Mississippi River
12.	Pacific Ocean : Oregon :: Atlantic Ocean : _____ Ⓐ North Carolina Ⓑ Michigan Ⓒ Texas Ⓓ California

161

Name _____ **LESSON 157** Date _____

Study the relationship between the first set of words. Pick the word that completes the second pair with this same relationship. *[Hint: American states & Politics]*

1. James Cook : Hawaii :: Eric the Red : _____

    Ⓐ Antarctica   Ⓑ India   Ⓒ Greenland   Ⓓ Africa

2. Egypt : Nile :: Brazil : _____

    Ⓐ Mississippi   Ⓑ Yangtze   Ⓒ Amazon   Ⓓ Tiber

3. Hurricane Katrina : Louisiana :: Galveston Hurricane : _____

    Ⓐ Alabama   Ⓑ Texas   Ⓒ Mississippi   Ⓓ Florida

4. smallest state : Rhode Island :: largest state : _____

    Ⓐ Hawaii   Ⓑ Alaska   Ⓒ California   Ⓓ Missouri

5. New York : New Amsterdam :: _____ : Tenochtitlan

    Ⓐ Mexico City   Ⓑ Acapulco   Ⓒ Baja California   Ⓓ Los Angeles

6. sister : family :: state : _____

    Ⓐ president   Ⓑ city   Ⓒ Delaware   Ⓓ nation

7. Indianapolis : Indiana :: Salem : _____

    Ⓐ Massachusetts   Ⓑ Virginia   Ⓒ USA   Ⓓ Oregon

8. Pearl Harbor : Hawaii :: Arlington : _____

    Ⓐ Florida   Ⓑ New York   Ⓒ Pennsylvania   Ⓓ Virginia

9. George W. Bush : Texas :: Bill Clinton : _____

    Ⓐ Alabama   Ⓑ Missouri   Ⓒ Arkansas   Ⓓ Georgia

10. New Mexico : Santa Fe :: Texas : _____

    Ⓐ Brownsville   Ⓑ Austin   Ⓒ Dallas   Ⓓ Galveston

11. Cartier : St. Lawrence River :: Cabrillo : _____

    Ⓐ Mt. Whitney   Ⓑ Mississippi River   Ⓒ California   Ⓓ Quebec

12. Chicago : Illinois :: Boston : _____

    Ⓐ Maine   Ⓑ Ohio   Ⓒ Massachusetts   Ⓓ New York

Name _____ **LESSON 158** Date _____

Study the relationship between the first set of words. Pick the word that completes the second pair with this same relationship. *[Hint: American states & Politics]*

1. "The Garden State" : New Jersey :: "The Land of Lincoln" : _____

   Ⓐ Nebraska   Ⓑ Pennsylvania   Ⓒ Missouri   Ⓓ Illinois

2. New York City : Eastern Standard Time :: Chicago : _____

   Ⓐ Mountain Standard Time   Ⓑ Pacific Standard Time   Ⓒ Central Standard Time   Ⓓ Illinois

3. Indianapolis : Indiana :: Salem : _____

   Ⓐ Virginia   Ⓑ Oregon   Ⓒ USA   Ⓓ Massachusetts

4. Honolulu : Hawaii :: Juneau : _____

   Ⓐ Wyoming   Ⓑ Alaska   Ⓒ Missouri   Ⓓ California

5. California : _____ :: New York : east

   Ⓐ walk   Ⓑ west   Ⓒ south   Ⓓ northeast

6. state : Alabama :: city : _____

   Ⓐ capital   Ⓑ Montgomery   Ⓒ town   Ⓓ montgomery

7. New Mexico : Santa Fe :: Texas : _____

   Ⓐ Austin   Ⓑ Brownsville   Ⓒ Galveston   Ⓓ Dallas

8. _____ : cold :: Egypt : hot

   Ⓐ California   Ⓑ Hawaii   Ⓒ Alaska   Ⓓ Idaho

9. Free State : New York :: Border State : _____

   Ⓐ Georgia   Ⓑ New Hampshire   Ⓒ Missouri   Ⓓ South Carolina

10. Hurricane Katrina : Louisiana :: Galveston Hurricane : _____

    Ⓐ Alabama   Ⓑ Florida   Ⓒ Mississippi   Ⓓ Texas

11. Chicago : Illinois :: Boston : _____

    Ⓐ Maine   Ⓑ Ohio   Ⓒ Massachusetts   Ⓓ New York

12. _____ : Atlantic Ocean :: California : Pacific Ocean

    Ⓐ California   Ⓑ North Carolina   Ⓒ Michigan   Ⓓ Texas

Name _____   **LESSON 159**   Date _____

Study the relationship between the first set of words. Pick the word that completes the second pair with this same relationship. *[Hint: American states & Politics]*

1. Utah : Salt Lake City :: Missouri : _____

    Ⓐ Branson   Ⓑ Jefferson City   Ⓒ St. Louis   Ⓓ Carson City

2. Gettysburg : Pennsylvania :: Shiloh : _____

    Ⓐ Mississippi   Ⓑ Tennessee   Ⓒ Virginia   Ⓓ Missouri

3. "The Garden State" : New Jersey :: "The Land of Lincoln" : _____

    Ⓐ Illinois   Ⓑ Pennsylvania   Ⓒ Missouri   Ⓓ Nebraska

4. South Dakota : Pierre :: North Dakota : _____

    Ⓐ Ontario   Ⓑ Jean-Luc   Ⓒ Bismarck   Ⓓ borders

5. Chicago : Illinois :: Boston : _____

    Ⓐ Maine   Ⓑ Massachusetts   Ⓒ Colorado   Ⓓ New York

6. Honolulu : Hawaii :: Juneau : _____

    Ⓐ Wyoming   Ⓑ California   Ⓒ Alaska   Ⓓ Missouri

7. Texas : state :: America : _____

    Ⓐ beautiful   Ⓑ continent   Ⓒ North America   Ⓓ country

8. mummy : Egypt :: vampire : _____

    Ⓐ full moon   Ⓑ Pennsylvania   Ⓒ coffin   Ⓓ Transylvania

9. Pacific Ocean : Oregon :: _____ : North Carolina

    Ⓐ Pacific Ocean   Ⓑ Atlantic Ocean   Ⓒ Arctic Ocean   Ⓓ English Ocean

10. _____ : TN :: Kentucky : KY

    Ⓐ Tennessee   Ⓑ Georgia   Ⓒ Arkansas   Ⓓ Virginia

11. colonies : England :: states : _____

    Ⓐ King George   Ⓑ United States of America   Ⓒ Virginia   Ⓓ president

12. "The Aloha State" : Hawaii :: "The Grand Canyon State" : _____

    Ⓐ New Mexico   Ⓑ Arizona   Ⓒ Colorado   Ⓓ Utah

Name _____ **LESSON 160** Date _____

Study the relationship between the first set of words. Pick the word that completes the second pair with this same relationship. *[Hint: American states & Politics]*

1. Texas : Oklahoma :: California : _____

   Ⓐ Arkansas   Ⓑ Oregon   Ⓒ Maine   Ⓓ Colorado

2. Gettysburg : Pennsylvania :: Shiloh : _____

   Ⓐ Missouri   Ⓑ Mississippi   Ⓒ Virginia   Ⓓ Tennessee

3. Chicago : Illinois :: Boston : _____

   Ⓐ New York   Ⓑ Massachusetts   Ⓒ Colorado   Ⓓ Maine

4. _____ : TN :: Kentucky : KY

   Ⓐ Arkansas   Ⓑ Virginia   Ⓒ Tennessee   Ⓓ Georgia

5. South Dakota : Pierre :: North Dakota : _____

   Ⓐ Jean-Luc   Ⓑ Bismarck   Ⓒ borders   Ⓓ Ontario

6. Rio Grande River : _____ :: Mississippi River : Louisiana

   Ⓐ Mississippi   Ⓑ Texas   Ⓒ Alabama   Ⓓ Florida

7. Baton Rouge : Louisiana :: Cheyenne : _____

   Ⓐ Kansas   Ⓑ Nebraska   Ⓒ Idaho   Ⓓ Wyoming

8. Pacific Ocean : Oregon :: _____ : North Carolina

   Ⓐ Atlantic Ocean   Ⓑ Pacific Ocean   Ⓒ Arctic Ocean   Ⓓ English Ocean

9. Yellowstone National Park : Wyoming :: Yosemite National Park : _____

   Ⓐ California   Ⓑ Ohio   Ⓒ Oregon   Ⓓ Kentucky

10. Honolulu : Hawaii :: Juneau : _____

    Ⓐ Wyoming   Ⓑ Missouri   Ⓒ California   Ⓓ Alaska

11. Mount Rushmore : South Dakota :: Lincoln Memorial : _____

    Ⓐ New York City, NY   Ⓑ Washington, DC   Ⓒ Philadelphia, PA   Ⓓ Chicago, IL

12. "The Garden State" : New Jersey :: "The Land of Lincoln" : _____

    Ⓐ Missouri   Ⓑ Illinois   Ⓒ Nebraska   Ⓓ Pennsylvania

Name _____   **LESSON 161**   Date _____

Study the relationship between the first set of words. Pick the word that completes the second pair with this same relationship. *[Hint: American states & Politics]*

1. Baton Rouge : Louisiana :: Cheyenne : _____

   Ⓐ Idaho   Ⓑ Wyoming   Ⓒ Kansas   Ⓓ Nebraska

2. Pearl Harbor : Hawaii :: Arlington : _____

   Ⓐ Virginia   Ⓑ Florida   Ⓒ Pennsylvania   Ⓓ New York

3. Inuit : Alaska :: Seminole : _____

   Ⓐ Oklahoma   Ⓑ Florida   Ⓒ South Dakota   Ⓓ Arizona

4. South Dakota : Pierre :: North Dakota : _____

   Ⓐ Ontario   Ⓑ Jean-Luc   Ⓒ borders   Ⓓ Bismarck

5. Gettysburg : Pennsylvania :: Shiloh : _____

   Ⓐ Virginia   Ⓑ Mississippi   Ⓒ Tennessee   Ⓓ Missouri

6. Utah : Salt Lake City :: Missouri : _____

   Ⓐ Carson City   Ⓑ St. Louis   Ⓒ Jefferson City Ⓓ Branson

7. mummy : Egypt :: vampire : _____

   Ⓐ coffin   Ⓑ Transylvania   Ⓒ Pennsylvania   Ⓓ full moon

8. smallest state : Rhode Island :: largest state : _____

   Ⓐ Hawaii   Ⓑ Idaho   Ⓒ Wyoming   Ⓓ Alaska

9. _____ : TN :: Kentucky : KY

   Ⓐ Georgia   Ⓑ Arkansas   Ⓒ Virginia   Ⓓ Tennessee

10. cherry tree : Washington :: honesty : _____

    Ⓐ Oregon   Ⓑ trustworthy   Ⓒ Lincoln   Ⓓ dishonesty

11. Texas : Oklahoma :: California : _____

    Ⓐ Oregon   Ⓑ Colorado   Ⓒ Arkansas   Ⓓ Maine

12. Gulf of Mexico : Texas :: Gulf of California : _____

    Ⓐ Florida   Ⓑ Louisiana   Ⓒ Baja California Ⓓ Yucatan

Name_____ **LESSON 162** Date_____

Study the relationship between the first set of words. Pick the word that completes the second pair with this same relationship. *[Hint: American states & Politics]*

1. Yellowstone National Park : Wyoming :: Yosemite National Park : _____

   Ⓐ Oregon   Ⓑ California   Ⓒ Kentucky   Ⓓ Ohio

2. Texas : Oklahoma :: _____ : Oregon

   Ⓐ Mt. Whitney   Ⓑ Quebec   Ⓒ Kentucky   Ⓓ California

3. mummy : Egypt :: vampire : _____

   Ⓐ coffin   Ⓑ Pennsylvania   Ⓒ Transylvania   Ⓓ full moon

4. Rio Grande River : Texas :: Mississippi River : _____

   Ⓐ Wyoming   Ⓑ Ohio   Ⓒ Florida   Ⓓ Louisiana

5. smallest state : Rhode Island :: largest state : _____

   Ⓐ Alaska   Ⓑ Wyoming   Ⓒ California   Ⓓ Idaho

6. California : Sacramento :: Utah : _____

   Ⓐ Moab   Ⓑ Austin   Ⓒ Salt Lake City   Ⓓ Denver

7. Chicago : Illinois :: Boston : _____

   Ⓐ Colorado   Ⓑ New York   Ⓒ Maine   Ⓓ Massachusetts

8. Gettysburg : Pennsylvania :: Shiloh : _____

   Ⓐ Arkansas   Ⓑ Mississippi   Ⓒ Tennessee   Ⓓ Georgia

9. California : _____ :: Texas : Gulf of Mexico

   Ⓐ Atlantic Ocean   Ⓑ Panama   Ⓒ Red Sea   Ⓓ Pacific Ocean

10. South Dakota : Pierre :: North Dakota : _____

    Ⓐ Ontario   Ⓑ Bismarck   Ⓒ Jean-Luc   Ⓓ borders

11. Utah : Salt Lake City :: Missouri : _____

    Ⓐ Branson   Ⓑ Carson City   Ⓒ Jefferson City   Ⓓ St. Louis

12. colonies : England :: states : _____

    Ⓐ president   Ⓑ United States of America   Ⓒ Virginia   Ⓓ King George

Name _____   **LESSON 163**   Date _____

Study the relationship between the first set of words. Pick the word that completes the second pair with this same relationship. *[Hint: American states & Politics]*

1. Utah : Salt Lake City :: Missouri : _____

    (A) St. Louis   (B) Carson City   (C) Branson   (D) Jefferson City

2. Honolulu : Hawaii :: Juneau : _____

    (A) Alaska   (B) California   (C) Missouri   (D) Wyoming

3. "The Aloha State" : Hawaii :: "The Grand Canyon State" : _____

    (A) Arizona   (B) New Mexico   (C) Colorado   (D) Utah

4. Indianapolis : Indiana :: Salem : _____

    (A) Virginia   (B) Massachusetts   (C) Oregon   (D) USA

5. South Dakota : Pierre :: North Dakota : _____

    (A) borders   (B) Jean-Luc   (C) Ontario   (D) Bismarck

6. "The Garden State" : New Jersey :: "The Land of Lincoln" : _____

    (A) Missouri   (B) Pennsylvania   (C) Nebraska   (D) Illinois

7. Free State : New York :: Border State : _____

    (A) Georgia   (B) South Carolina   (C) Missouri   (D) New Hampshire

8. smallest state : Rhode Island :: largest state : _____

    (A) Idaho   (B) California   (C) Alaska   (D) Wyoming

9. California : _____ :: Texas : Gulf of Mexico

    (A) Red Sea   (B) Panama   (C) Pacific Ocean   (D) Atlantic Ocean

10. Texas : Oklahoma :: _____ : Oregon

    (A) Quebec   (B) Mt. Whitney   (C) California   (D) Kentucky

11. Mount Rushmore : South Dakota :: Lincoln Memorial : _____

    (A) New York City, NY   (B) Philadelphia, PA   (C) Washington, DC   (D) Chicago, IL

12. George W. Bush : Texas :: Bill Clinton : _____

    (A) Arkansas   (B) Georgia   (C) Missouri   (D) Alabama

Name _____   **LESSON 164**   Date _____

Study the relationship between the first set of words. Pick the word that completes the second pair with this same relationship. *[Hint: American states & Politics]*

1. Texas : Oklahoma :: _____ : Oregon

   A Quebec   **B** California   **C** Kentucky   **D** Mt. Whitney

2. colonies : England :: states : _____

   A Virginia   **B** United States of America   **C** King George   **D** president

3. George W. Bush : Texas :: Bill Clinton : _____

   A Alabama   **B** Arkansas   **C** Georgia   **D** Missouri

4. Mount Rushmore : South Dakota :: Lincoln Memorial : _____

   A New York City, NY   **B** Philadelphia, PA   **C** Chicago, IL   **D** Washington, DC

5. Yellowstone National Park : Wyoming :: Yosemite National Park : _____

   A Oregon   **B** California   **C** Kentucky   **D** Ohio

6. Inuit : Alaska :: Seminole : _____

   A Arizona   **B** Oklahoma   **C** Florida   **D** South Dakota

7. Indianapolis : Indiana :: Salem : _____

   A USA   **B** Oregon   **C** Virginia   **D** Massachusetts

8. Gulf of Mexico : Texas :: Gulf of California : _____

   A Baja California   **B** Yucatan   **C** Florida   **D** Louisiana

9. Hurricane Katrina : _____ :: Galveston Hurricane : Texas

   A Florida   **B** Louisiana   **C** Ohio   **D** Wyoming

10. Baton Rouge : Louisiana :: Cheyenne : _____

    A Kansas   **B** Nebraska   **C** Idaho   **D** Wyoming

11. California : Sacramento :: Utah : _____

    A Denver   **B** Salt Lake City   **C** Moab   **D** Austin

12. Pacific Ocean : Oregon :: Atlantic Ocean : _____

    A California   **B** Michigan   **C** Texas   **D** North Carolina

169

Name _____   **LESSON 165**   Date _____

Study the relationship between the first set of words. Pick the word that completes the second pair with this same relationship.

1. flat : lower pitch :: sharp : _____

    A note   **B** on pitch   **C** higher pitch   **D** stanza

2. speak : words :: hum : _____

    A notes   **B** whistle   **C** sing   **D** musicians

3. snack : _____ :: feast : large

    A ugly   **B** many   **C** small   **D** nice

4. land : tornado :: ocean : _____

    A hurricane   **B** flood   **C** waves   **D** snow

5. baseball : bat :: cricket : _____

    A stick   **B** insect   **C** club   **D** wicket

6. dry : land :: wet : _____

    A ocean   **B** land   **C** mountain   **D** ice

7. morning : breakfast :: evening : _____

    A eat   **B** dinner   **C** snack   **D** lunch

8. bike : ride :: ball : _____

    A hike   **B** sand   **C** buy   **D** throw

9. apple : snack :: oatmeal : _____

    A lunch   **B** dinner   **C** breakfast   **D** milk

10. sip : drink :: munch : _____

    A snack   **B** crush   **C** view   **D** wash

11. bulletins : messages :: refreshments : _____

    A replacements   **B** snacks   **C** gifts   **D** reminders

12. breakfast : morning :: _____ : noon

    A lunch   **B** dinner   **C** snack   **D** sandwich

170

Name _____ **LESSON 166** Date _____

Study the relationship between the first set of words. Pick the word that completes the second pair with this same relationship.

1. baseball : bat :: cricket : _____

   (A) wicket   (B) club   (C) stick   (D) insect

2. bacon and eggs : breakfast :: meat and potatoes : _____

   (A) dessert   (B) dinner   (C) snack   (D) kitchen

3. pitch a ball : throw :: pitch a tent : _____

   (A) set up   (B) carry   (C) pack   (D) sleep

4. morning : breakfast :: evening : _____

   (A) eat   (B) dinner   (C) lunch   (D) snack

5. bill : paper :: coin : _____

   (A) metal   (B) cloth   (C) plastic   (D) wood

6. sip : drink :: munch : _____

   (A) view   (B) wash   (C) snack   (D) crush

7. dry : land :: wet : _____

   (A) land   (B) mountain   (C) ocean   (D) ice

8. essay : words :: concerto : _____

   (A) musicians   (B) whistle   (C) sing   (D) notes

9. flat : lower pitch :: sharp : _____

   (A) note   (B) higher pitch   (C) stanza   (D) on pitch

10. land : tyrannosaurus :: _____ : ichthyosaurus

    (A) deserts   (B) water   (C) blankets   (D) trunk

11. food that provides vitamins, minerals, and energy for your body : nutritious :: food that is high in fat, sugar, and/or salt and provides few nutrients : _____

    (A) calories   (B) artificial   (C) snack   (D) junk food

12. _____ : club :: tennis : racquet

    (A) hockey   (B) golf   (C) ping pong   (D) tennis

Study the relationship between the first set of words. Pick the word that completes the second pair with this same relationship.

1.	bike : ride :: ball : _____
	Ⓐ buy Ⓑ sand Ⓒ throw Ⓓ hike
2.	food that provides vitamins, minerals, and energy for your body : nutritious :: food that is high in fat, sugar, and/or salt and provides few nutrients : _____
	Ⓐ calories Ⓑ artificial Ⓒ snack Ⓓ junk food
3.	bacon and eggs : breakfast :: meat and potatoes : _____
	Ⓐ dinner Ⓑ kitchen Ⓒ dessert Ⓓ snack
4.	_____ : gallons :: land : acres
	Ⓐ light Ⓑ dustpan Ⓒ water Ⓓ milk
5.	club : sandwich :: chowder : _____
	Ⓐ salad Ⓑ seafood Ⓒ soup Ⓓ fruit
6.	matches : matchbook :: cigarettes : _____
	Ⓐ wallet Ⓑ lighter Ⓒ pack Ⓓ deck
7.	letters : words :: notes : _____
	Ⓐ music Ⓑ names Ⓒ paper Ⓓ numbers
8.	speak : words :: hum : _____
	Ⓐ sing Ⓑ notes Ⓒ musicians Ⓓ whistle
9.	person : settler :: land : _____
	Ⓐ bronco Ⓑ corral Ⓒ holster Ⓓ territory
10.	baseball : bat :: golf : _____
	Ⓐ club Ⓑ puck Ⓒ racket Ⓓ hoop
11.	quarter : coin :: twenty dollars : _____
	Ⓐ penny Ⓑ face Ⓒ dime Ⓓ bill
12.	locomotive : _____ :: cab : taxi
	Ⓐ train Ⓑ leash Ⓒ collar Ⓓ heel

Name _____ **LESSON 168** Date _____

Study the relationship between the first set of words. Pick the word that completes the second pair with this same relationship.

1. water : gallons :: land : _____

    Ⓐ plot   Ⓑ acres   Ⓒ feet   Ⓓ ranch

2. golf : club :: _____ : racquet

    Ⓐ tennis   Ⓑ racquetball   Ⓒ golf   Ⓓ bowling

3. apple : core :: cigarette : _____

    Ⓐ butt   Ⓑ filter   Ⓒ lighter   Ⓓ pack

4. _____ : tornado :: ocean : hurricane

    Ⓐ instrument   Ⓑ land   Ⓒ dungeon   Ⓓ weapon

5. bike : ride :: _____ : throw

    Ⓐ triangle   Ⓑ rectangle   Ⓒ golf   Ⓓ ball

6. snack : small :: feast : _____

    Ⓐ turkey   Ⓑ short   Ⓒ slow   Ⓓ large

7. locomotive : train :: cab : _____

    Ⓐ bicycle   Ⓑ taxi   Ⓒ subway   Ⓓ streets

8. bacon and eggs : breakfast :: meat and potatoes : _____

    Ⓐ dessert   Ⓑ dinner   Ⓒ kitchen   Ⓓ snack

9. toss : pitch :: catch : _____

    Ⓐ run   Ⓑ lift   Ⓒ jump   Ⓓ grab

10. bill : _____ :: coin : circle

    Ⓐ rectangle   Ⓑ geometry   Ⓒ circle   Ⓓ perimeter

11. sip : drink :: munch : _____

    Ⓐ crush   Ⓑ snack   Ⓒ view   Ⓓ wash

12. club : sandwich :: chowder : _____

    Ⓐ salad   Ⓑ fruit   Ⓒ seafood   Ⓓ soup

Study the relationship between the first set of words. Pick the word that completes the second pair with this same relationship.

1. bill : paper :: coin : _____

   Ⓐ wood   Ⓑ plastic   Ⓒ cloth   Ⓓ metal

2. calendar : date :: wristwatch : _____

   Ⓐ appointments   Ⓑ address   Ⓒ time   Ⓓ notes

3. birds : flock :: fish : _____

   Ⓐ school   Ⓑ pack   Ⓒ herd   Ⓓ family

4. locomotive : train :: cab : _____

   Ⓐ streets   Ⓑ subway   Ⓒ bicycle   Ⓓ taxi

5. kettle : pot :: company : _____

   Ⓐ snacks   Ⓑ visitors   Ⓒ pets   Ⓓ music

6. baseball : bat :: cricket : _____

   Ⓐ stick   Ⓑ insect   Ⓒ wicket   Ⓓ club

7. apple : snack :: oatmeal : _____

   Ⓐ dinner   Ⓑ breakfast   Ⓒ lunch   Ⓓ milk

8. sip : drink :: munch : _____

   Ⓐ view   Ⓑ wash   Ⓒ snack   Ⓓ crush

9. bike : ride :: _____ : throw

   Ⓐ rectangle   Ⓑ golf   Ⓒ triangle   Ⓓ ball

10. supper : dinner :: hearty : _____

   Ⓐ snack   Ⓑ filling   Ⓒ warm   Ⓓ sweet

11. toss : pitch :: catch : _____

   Ⓐ jump   Ⓑ lift   Ⓒ run   Ⓓ grab

12. letters : words :: notes : _____

   Ⓐ numbers   Ⓑ names   Ⓒ music   Ⓓ paper

Study the relationship between the first set of words. Pick the word that completes the second pair with this same relationship.

1. to lie in wait : lurk :: to try hard to avoid something : _____

    (A) amble   (B) lope   (C) shun   (D) retreat

2. dislike : like :: loathe : _____

    (A) adore   (B) attentive   (C) apathy   (D) animosity

3. tardy : late :: truant : _____

    (A) on time   (B) absent   (C) present   (D) early

4. absent : present :: tardy : _____

    (A) on-time   (B) missing   (C) late   (D) past

5. absent : _____ :: tardy : early

    (A) present   (B) ancient   (C) prehistoric   (D) future

6. allure : attraction :: aversion : _____

    (A) diversion   (B) sympathy   (C) antipathy   (D) restitution

7. antibiotics : meat and milk :: pesticides : _____

    (A) cheese   (B) organic   (C) insects   (D) fruits and vegetables

8. not at school : absent :: late : _____

    (A) missing   (B) tardy   (C) student   (D) suspended

9. not at school : absent :: late : _____

    (A) student   (B) suspended   (C) tardy   (D) missing

10. dislike : like :: loathe : _____

    (A) apathy   (B) animosity   (C) adore   (D) attentive

11. police officers : police car :: paramedic : _____

    (A) fire truck   (B) ambulance   (C) patrol car   (D) taxi

12. unanimous : in complete agreement :: anonymous : _____

    (A) professional   (B) nickname   (C) proper   (D) unnamed

Study the relationship between the first set of words. Pick the word that completes the second pair with this same relationship.

1. absent : _____ :: tardy : early

   Ⓐ prehistoric   Ⓑ future   Ⓒ ancient   Ⓓ present

2. amble : walk :: oblige : _____

   Ⓐ help   Ⓑ stop   Ⓒ write   Ⓓ hinder

3. allure : attraction :: aversion : _____

   Ⓐ antipathy   Ⓑ diversion   Ⓒ sympathy   Ⓓ restitution

4. absent : present :: tardy : _____

   Ⓐ past   Ⓑ on-time   Ⓒ late   Ⓓ missing

5. school : school bus :: hospital : _____

   Ⓐ doctor   Ⓑ patrol car   Ⓒ tractor   Ⓓ ambulance

6. not at school : absent :: late : _____

   Ⓐ suspended   Ⓑ student   Ⓒ missing   Ⓓ tardy

7. tardy : late :: truant : _____

   Ⓐ absent   Ⓑ present   Ⓒ early   Ⓓ on time

8. to lie in wait : lurk :: to try hard to avoid something : _____

   Ⓐ retreat   Ⓑ lope   Ⓒ amble   Ⓓ shun

9. dislike : like :: loathe : _____

   Ⓐ attentive   Ⓑ apathy   Ⓒ adore   Ⓓ animosity

10. inquisitiveness : curiosity :: perseverance : _____

    Ⓐ persistence   Ⓑ apathy   Ⓒ insecurity   Ⓓ successful

11. devour : consume :: _____ : stroll

    Ⓐ trudge   Ⓑ amble   Ⓒ scamper   Ⓓ teeter

12. antibiotics : meat and milk :: pesticides : _____

    Ⓐ cheese   Ⓑ fruits and vegetables   Ⓒ organic   Ⓓ insects

Study the relationship between the first set of words. Pick the word that completes the second pair with this same relationship.

1. _____ : struggles :: green : good fortunes

   Ⓐ rough   Ⓑ sharp   Ⓒ red   Ⓓ tan

2. vacation : trip :: photographs : _____

   Ⓐ snapshots   Ⓑ copies   Ⓒ tent   Ⓓ camera

3. puny : weak :: peevish : _____

   Ⓐ dirty   Ⓑ kind   Ⓒ bashful   Ⓓ irritable

4. plains : buffalo :: rivers : _____

   Ⓐ amphibian   Ⓑ fish   Ⓒ crab   Ⓓ bird

5. crescendo : louder :: decrescendo : _____

   Ⓐ lower   Ⓑ longer   Ⓒ softer   Ⓓ slower

6. inert : non-reactive :: ornate : _____

   Ⓐ troublesome   Ⓑ decorated   Ⓒ plain   Ⓓ volatile

7. tacitly : silently :: sagely : _____

   Ⓐ discretely   Ⓑ loudly   Ⓒ controlled   Ⓓ wisely

8. melancholy : sad :: boisterous : _____

   Ⓐ loud   Ⓑ silent   Ⓒ happy   Ⓓ dreamlike

9. boisterous : noisy :: melancholy : _____

   Ⓐ silent   Ⓑ happy   Ⓒ dreamlike   Ⓓ sad

10. photographs : _____ :: vacation : trip

    Ⓐ snapshots   Ⓑ remember   Ⓒ copies   Ⓓ camera

11. mottled : spotted :: frail : _____

    Ⓐ broken   Ⓑ troublesome   Ⓒ plain   Ⓓ delicate

12. solitary : alone :: idle : _____

    Ⓐ dull   Ⓑ still   Ⓒ warm   Ⓓ silent

Study the relationship between the first set of words. Pick the word that completes the second pair with this same relationship.

1. cantelope : melon :: romaine : _____

   A apple   **B** lettuce   **C** green   **D** watermelon

2. idle : still :: nonplused : _____

   A busy   **B** confused   **C** silent   **D** lazy

3. boisterous : noisy :: melancholy : _____

   A sad   **B** dreamlike   **C** silent   **D** happy

4. always : never :: frequent : _____

   A circumspectly   **B** seldom   **C** reliable   **D** often

5. mottled : spotted :: frail : _____

   A broken   **B** delicate   **C** troublesome   **D** plain

6. carrot : _____ :: celery : green

   A green   **B** knife   **C** purple   **D** orange

7. timorous : fearful :: mute : _____

   A ignorant   **B** silent   **C** loud   **D** careful

8. cannot be heard : silent :: cannot be seen : _____

   A invisible   **B** carsick   **C** incredible   **D** scolded

9. inert : non-reactive :: ornate : _____

   A troublesome   **B** plain   **C** volatile   **D** decorated

10. _____ : green :: bark : brown

    A smog   **B** water   **C** streams   **D** leaves

11. weak : speak :: hour : _____

    A flower   **B** zodiac   **C** leaf   **D** candy

12. intent : focused :: insolent : _____

    A generous   **B** devoted   **C** rude   **D** plain

Study the relationship between the first set of words. Pick the word that completes the second pair with this same relationship.

1. head : _____ :: gift : bow

   A food   **B** socks   **C** hat   **D** shirt

2. entwine : disentangle :: _____ : explain

   A console   **B** confuse   **C** funny   **D** dry

3. cower : cringe :: grimace : _____

   A wink   **B** shrug   **C** scowl   **D** nod

4. gift : box :: _____ : envelope

   A envelope   **B** hug   **C** card   **D** February

5. card : envelope :: gift : _____

   A lights   **B** wrapping paper   **C** tape   **D** stamp

6. uncomplicated : simple :: _____ : nice

   A kind   **B** terrible   **C** genuine   **D** person

7. ammonia : smelly :: tar : _____

   A gas   **B** healthy   **C** clear   **D** sticky

8. to get rid of something : discard :: to share a secret with someone : _____

   A scold   **B** confide   **C** dismay   **D** boast

9. clean : spotless :: dirty : _____

   A dark   **B** scrub   **C** clear   **D** filthy

10. complicated : _____ :: jumbled : orderly

    A dignified   **B** simple   **C** dirty   **D** elegant

11. address : speech :: vote : _____

    A poll   **B** choose   **C** nation   **D** veto

12. ask : question :: define : _____

    A intrude   **B** preempt   **C** explain   **D** devise

Name _____   LESSON 175   Date _____

Study the relationship between the first set of words. Pick the word that completes the second pair with this same relationship.

1. to get rid of something : discard :: to share a secret with someone : _____

    Ⓐ scold   Ⓑ dismay   Ⓒ boast   Ⓓ confide

2. blurry : clear :: flexible : _____

    Ⓐ bumpy   Ⓑ smooth   Ⓒ fuzzy   Ⓓ rigid

3. take charge : lead :: choose : _____

    Ⓐ empire   Ⓑ dictator   Ⓒ veto   Ⓓ elect

4. Rubeus Hagrid : Fang :: Argus Filch : _____

    Ⓐ Hedwig   Ⓑ Fluffy   Ⓒ Trevor   Ⓓ Mrs. Norris

5. pudgy : puny :: muddled : _____

    Ⓐ smart   Ⓑ curvy   Ⓒ clear   Ⓓ loved

6. ask : question :: define : _____

    Ⓐ preempt   Ⓑ intrude   Ⓒ devise   Ⓓ explain

7. clean : spotless :: dirty : _____

    Ⓐ scrub   Ⓑ clear   Ⓒ filthy   Ⓓ dark

8. boast : roast :: trick : _____

    Ⓐ pick   Ⓑ magic   Ⓒ cards   Ⓓ treat

9. _____ : stream :: clearing : meadow

    Ⓐ tower   Ⓑ ancient city   Ⓒ river   Ⓓ dream

10. fury : anger :: boasting : _____

    Ⓐ encouraging   Ⓑ insulting   Ⓒ bragging   Ⓓ rude

11. card : envelope :: gift : _____

    Ⓐ stamp   Ⓑ lights   Ⓒ wrapping paper Ⓓ tape

12. cower : cringe :: grimace : _____

    Ⓐ shrug   Ⓑ scowl   Ⓒ wink   Ⓓ nod

180

Study the relationship between the first set of words. Pick the word that completes the second pair with this same relationship.

1. tailor : clothing :: blacksmith : _____

   (A) lumber   (B) food   (C) saddles   (D) horseshoes

2. to stir together : mix :: to determine the correct amount : _____

   (A) measure   (B) boil   (C) stir   (D) chop

3. English : letters :: Chinese : _____

   (A) numbers   (B) French   (C) characters   (D) cartoons

4. chop : cut :: bake : _____

   (A) cook   (B) pour   (C) slice   (D) measure

5. land : tornado :: ocean : _____

   (A) float   (B) waves   (C) hurricane   (D) storm

6. slow : stir :: fast : _____

   (A) measure   (B) pour   (C) fold   (D) beat

7. wrench : turn :: saw : _____

   (A) cut   (B) fasten   (C) clean   (D) measure

8. spring : tornadoes :: winter : _____

   (A) snowstorm   (B) hurricane   (C) sunburn   (D) heat wave

9. cool : chilly :: fall : _____

   (A) winter   (B) autumn   (C) school   (D) leaves

10. topple : fall :: cease : _____

    (A) sprint   (B) gnaw   (C) stop   (D) escape

11. rain : shower :: tornado : _____

    (A) wind   (B) twister   (C) drizzle   (D) hail

12. evade : escape :: topple : _____

    (A) punish   (B) trick   (C) catch   (D) fall

Study the relationship between the first set of words. Pick the word that completes the second pair with this same relationship.

1. slow : stir :: fast : _____

   A beat   B pour   C fold   D measure

2. portrait : realistic :: caricature : _____

   A cartoon   B art   C personal   D drawing

3. price : fare :: boarding pass : _____

   A tank   B measure   C costume   D ticket

4. human resource : education :: capital resource : _____

   A skill   B tools   C lumber   D water

5. chop : cut :: bake : _____

   A pour   B slice   C measure   D cook

6. rain : shower :: tornado : _____

   A hail   B twister   C drizzle   D wind

7. cool : chilly :: fall : _____

   A autumn   B school   C winter   D leaves

8. English : letters :: Chinese : _____

   A cartoons   B characters   C numbers   D French

9. to stir together : mix :: to determine the correct amount : _____

   A measure   B stir   C chop   D boil

10. brave : afraid :: proud : _____

   A ashamed   B angry   C glad   D shy

11. obey : _____ :: escape : get away

   A sit   B hope   C follow   D change

12. tailor : clothing :: blacksmith : _____

   A food   B horseshoes   C saddles   D lumber

Study the relationship between the first set of words. Pick the word that completes the second pair with this same relationship.

1. not at school : absent :: late : _____

    A tardy   **B** suspended   **C** student   **D** missing

2. artist : brush :: harvester : _____

    A wrench   **B** scythe   **C** protractor   **D** computer

3. wrench : turn :: saw : _____

    A cut   **B** clean   **C** measure   **D** fasten

4. nurse : Clara Barton :: abolitionist : _____

    A Jefferson Davis   **B** Eli Whitney   **C** Robert E. Lee   **D** Frederick Douglass

5. absent : present :: tardy : _____

    A past   **B** on-time   **C** late   **D** missing

6. slowly run : jog :: gently throw : _____

    A march   **B** toss   **C** leap   **D** grab

7. Robert E. Lee : Confederate general :: Clara Barton : _____

    A singer   **B** First Lady   **C** slave   **D** nurse

8. _____ : jump :: shimmy : shake

    A throw   **B** march   **C** leap   **D** grab

9. moccasins : _____ :: muskets : weapons

    A shoes   **B** gloves   **C** coat   **D** hat

10. leap : jump :: scamper : _____

    A toss   **B** run   **C** talk   **D** race

11. _____ : library :: nurse : hospital

    A cook   **B** headmaster   **C** gardener   **D** librarian

12. screwdriver : screw :: hammer : _____

    A nail   **B** iron   **C** wrench   **D** drill

Study the relationship between the first set of words. Pick the word that completes the second pair with this same relationship.

1. gold : metal :: granite : _____

    (A) rock   (B) gem   (C) plant   (D) insect

2. cold : _____ :: heat : oppressive

    (A) hot   (B) bitter   (C) sugar   (D) brown

3. top : leaves :: bottom : _____

    (A) bird   (B) trunk   (C) branches   (D) green

4. _____ : taste :: music : sound

    (A) brown   (B) bitter   (C) hot   (D) sugar

5. baseball : bat :: hockey : _____

    (A) goal   (B) puck   (C) racquet   (D) stick

6. diamond : hard :: _____ : soft

    (A) talc   (B) gem   (C) emerald   (D) rock

7. acrid : bitter :: brackish : _____

    (A) crunchy   (B) salty   (C) muddy   (D) sweet

8. _____ : find :: invent : create

    (A) discover   (B) extinct   (C) dinosaurs   (D) mystery

9. writer : stories :: jester : _____

    (A) rules   (B) history   (C) lullabies   (D) jokes

10. football : cleats :: hockey : _____

    (A) skis   (B) ice skates   (C) boots   (D) tennis shoes

11. rainforest : sunlight :: desert : _____

    (A) rainfall   (B) branches   (C) sand   (D) canopy

12. twig : branch :: brambles : _____

    (A) thorns   (B) leaves   (C) trees   (D) rocks

Study the relationship between the first set of words. Pick the word that completes the second pair with this same relationship.

1. decoy : look-alike :: disguise : _____

   (A) crime   (B) clue   (C) costume   (D) hide-out

2. missing : lost :: seek : _____

   (A) found   (B) search   (C) clue   (D) trail

3. plummet : fall :: fret : _____

   (A) tangle   (B) slide   (C) worry   (D) soothe

4. attitude : outlook :: aptitude : _____

   (A) ability   (B) intelligence   (C) morals   (D) compassion

5. genuine : real :: _____ : fake

   (A) fresh   (B) artificial   (C) nutritious   (D) healthy

6. aptitude : _____ :: attitude : outlook

   (A) morals   (B) ability   (C) intelligence   (D) compassion

7. lost : found :: lie : _____

   (A) jail   (B) truth   (C) hide   (D) clue

8. plunder : rob :: fret : _____

   (A) gossip   (B) destroy   (C) worry   (D) conceal

9. clue : written note :: trail : _____

   (A) missing   (B) shirt   (C) wallet   (D) footprints

10. wrong : incorrect :: accurate : _____

    (A) results   (B) answer   (C) right   (D) flawed

11. when : time :: where : _____

    (A) victim   (B) clue   (C) scene   (D) weapon

12. prod : poke :: fret : _____

    (A) worry   (B) slide   (C) conceal   (D) hit

Study the relationship between the first set of words. Pick the word that completes the second pair with this same relationship.

1. divine : godly :: miraculous : _____

   Ⓐ charitable   Ⓑ phenomenal   Ⓒ ordinary   Ⓓ eternal

2. marvelous : wonderful :: hideous : _____

   Ⓐ sad   Ⓑ unsure   Ⓒ confused   Ⓓ ugly

3. _____ : rare :: ordinary : legendary

   Ⓐ secret   Ⓑ common   Ⓒ antique   Ⓓ hidden

4. _____ : imagine :: convince : persuade

   Ⓐ create   Ⓑ pretend   Ⓒ jump   Ⓓ forgive

5. blame : accuse :: confess : _____

   Ⓐ allow   Ⓑ blame   Ⓒ admit   Ⓓ trust

6. to tell your name to someone you do not know : introduce :: to make believe : _____

   Ⓐ forgive   Ⓑ sing   Ⓒ jump   Ⓓ pretend

7. instruct : _____ :: confess : admit

   Ⓐ play   Ⓑ teach   Ⓒ give   Ⓓ change

8. view : see :: visualize : _____

   Ⓐ imagine   Ⓑ discuss   Ⓒ hear   Ⓓ touch

9. think back : _____ :: dream : imagine

   Ⓐ hide   Ⓑ remember   Ⓒ replenish   Ⓓ give

10. peer : look :: transport : _____

    Ⓐ cut   Ⓑ near   Ⓒ move   Ⓓ cover

11. convince : persuade :: pretend : _____

    Ⓐ imagine   Ⓑ ignore   Ⓒ understand   Ⓓ count

12. something anticipated : expectation :: something dreamed up : _____

    Ⓐ conditional   Ⓑ projected   Ⓒ imagined   Ⓓ deceived

| man | pride | solve | ridicule |
| languid | decision | give | |

Complete the analogies.

1. decision : judgment :: derision : _____

2. heave : pull :: bestow : _____

3. sonic : symphonic :: vision : _____

4. girl : woman :: boy : _____

5. cowardice : courage :: shame : _____

6. active : energetic :: inactive : _____

7. code : decipher :: puzzle : _____

8. massive : tiny :: ferocious : _____

   Ⓐ frightened   Ⓑ active   Ⓒ fierce   Ⓓ gentle

9. effrontery : boldness :: treachery : _____

   Ⓐ obedience   Ⓑ silliness   Ⓒ bravery   Ⓓ betrayal

10. brave : coward :: _____ : reckless

    Ⓐ together   Ⓑ hidden   Ⓒ quiet   Ⓓ careful

11. patriotism : _____ :: terrorism : fear

    Ⓐ fear   Ⓑ herd   Ⓒ pride   Ⓓ glory

12. swell : shrink :: insult : _____

    Ⓐ bawl   Ⓑ smear   Ⓒ resist   Ⓓ compliment

13. active : energetic :: inactive : _____

    Ⓐ languid   Ⓑ judicious   Ⓒ placid   Ⓓ charismatic

| inherit | dormant | demonstrate | scrape |
| miss | dried up | approach | |

Complete the analogies.

1. encircle : surround :: move closer : _____

2. tell how to do something : instruct :: show how to do something :

   _____

3. sleek : smooth :: withered : _____

4. partner : help :: heir : _____

5. man : mister :: woman : _____

6. awake : sleeping :: active : _____

7. nick : hit :: scuff : _____

8. decision : resolution :: alteration : _____

   Ⓐ amendment   Ⓑ law   Ⓒ aristocrat   Ⓓ preamble

9. solve : answer :: estimate : _____

   Ⓐ factor   Ⓑ simplify   Ⓒ reason   Ⓓ approximate

10. mingle : mix :: weep : _____

    Ⓐ sad   Ⓑ rustle   Ⓒ swim   Ⓓ cry

11. girl : woman :: boy : _____

    Ⓐ lady   Ⓑ female   Ⓒ miss   Ⓓ man

12. sonic : symphonic :: vision : _____

    Ⓐ sound   Ⓑ decision   Ⓒ friction   Ⓓ sight

13. surround : encircle :: _____ : go along with

    Ⓐ accompany   Ⓑ review   Ⓒ plead   Ⓓ call

investigate	not good enough	complex
necessities	dreadful	evil
relieve	expenses	concentrate
survey	convince	talent
valuable		

Study the relationship between the first set of words. Pick one word from the word bank that completes the second pair with this same relationship.

1. earnings : income :: bills : _____

2. warn : alert :: persuade : _____

3. wheedle : persuade :: assuage : _____

4. worthless : _____ :: wicked : virtuous

5. to hold responsible for a deed : blame :: to examine in detail :

   _____

6. inconceivable : unthinkable :: inadequate : _____

7. pretend : imagine :: _____ : persuade

8. a distinctive quality : characteristic :: an ability : _____

9. splendid : wonderful :: appalling : _____

10. ask forgiveness : apologize :: focus : _____

11. spiteful : mean :: wicked : _____

12. sorrowful : sad :: complicated : _____

13. disapprove : veto :: _____ : poll

14. wants : wishes :: needs : _____

Name _____ LESSON 185 Date _____

messy	pleasant	erect	convince
dreadful	deposit	nonsense	concentrate
necessities	distasteful	remove	valuable

Study the relationship between the first set of words. Pick one word from the word bank that completes the second pair with this same relationship.

1.
take a chance : venture :: put upright : _____

2.
splendid : wonderful :: appalling : _____

3.
raspy : harsh :: unsavory : _____

4.
ask forgiveness : apologize :: focus : _____

5.
pretend : imagine :: _____ : persuade

6.
decorated : fancy :: nice : _____

7.
warn : alert :: persuade : _____

8.
eject : _____ :: substitute : replace

9.
wants : wishes :: needs : _____

10.
take money out of a bank account : withdrawal :: put money into a bank account :

_____

11.
swift : quick :: unkempt : _____

12.
_____ : persuade :: pretend : imagine

13.
worthless : _____ :: wicked : virtuous

14.
astounding : amazing :: balderdash : _____

Study the relationship between the first set of words. Pick the word that completes the second pair with this same relationship.

1. despondent : hopeless :: nefarious : _____

   A wicked   **B** shy   **C** angry   **D** energetic

2. astounding : amazing :: balderdash : _____

   A relief   **B** proper   **C** surprise   **D** nonsense

3. worthless : _____ :: wicked : virtuous

   A valuable   **B** strong   **C** soft   **D** cheap

4. talk : speak :: yell : _____

   A fear   **B** protect   **C** nonsense   **D** holler

5. wheedle : persuade :: assuage : _____

   A convince   **B** control   **C** review   **D** relieve

6. sorrowful : sad :: complicated : _____

   A complete   **B** convinced   **C** capable   **D** complex

7. worthless : _____ :: wicked : virtuous

   A cheap   **B** soft   **C** valuable   **D** strong

8. earnings : income :: bills : _____

   A prices   **B** goods   **C** trade   **D** expenses

9. ask forgiveness : apologize :: focus : _____

   A express   **B** grieve   **C** concentrate   **D** retire

10. enthralled : captivated :: enchanted : _____

    A perplexing   **B** imaginary   **C** magical   **D** wicked

11. warn : alert :: persuade : _____

    A forgive   **B** convince   **C** hide   **D** leave

12. take a chance : venture :: put upright : _____

    A convince   **B** peruse   **C** burnish   **D** erect

191

expenses	profit	clumsily	unharmed
justice	disheartened	competent	unexplained
unfair	awkward	freedom	pension
"who-dun-it"			

Study the relationship between the first set of words. Pick one word from the word bank that completes the second pair with this same relationship.

1.	indifferent : uncaring :: unscathed : _____
2.	romance : love story :: mystery : _____
3.	earnings : income :: bills : _____
4.	graceful : gracefully :: clumsy_____ : _____
5.	lose money : loss :: make money : _____
6.	Teacher : knowledge :: Judge : _____
7.	Employee : salary :: Retiree : _____
8.	mystery : _____ :: secret : unknown
9.	reverence : respect :: liberty : _____
10.	agitated : turbulent :: capable : _____
11.	gruesome : horrific :: unjust : _____
12.	fairness : _____ :: freedom : liberty
13.	derisive : mocking :: dejected : _____
14.	graceful : clumsy :: comfortable : _____

unfair	selfish	mystery
cannot read	freedom	refund
profit	unharmed	William Shakespeare
game	unfairness	unexplained
liberty	slavery	

Study the relationship between the first set of words. Pick one word from the word bank that completes the second pair with this same relationship.

1. reverence : respect :: liberty : _____

2. illegal : against the law :: illiterate : _____

3. _____ : Sonnets :: Agatha Christie : Mysteries

4. justice : injustice :: freedom : _____

5. laws : country :: rules : _____

6. mystery : _____ :: secret : unknown

7. gruesome : horrific :: unjust : _____

8. justice : injustice :: fairness : _____

9. fairness : justice :: freedom : _____

10. to give money in exchange for a good or service : pay :: to have money returned for something that has been paid for : _____

11. known : fact :: unknown : _____

12. indifferent : uncaring :: unscathed : _____

13. lose money : loss :: make money : _____

14. caring : unkind :: selfless : _____

Study the relationship between the first set of words. Pick the word that completes the second pair with this same relationship.

1. fairness : justice :: freedom : _____

   (A) unfairness   (B) slavery   (C) liberty   (D) prison

2. romance : love story :: mystery : _____

   (A) science fiction   (B) drama   (C) non-fiction   (D) "who-dun-it"

3. employee : salary :: retiree : _____

   (A) pension   (B) vacation   (C) income   (D) savings

4. graceful : clumsy :: comfortable : _____

   (A) sarcastic   (B) disgusting   (C) awkward   (D) relaxing

5. graceful : gracefully :: clumsy_____ : _____

   (A) clumsily   (B) awkwardly   (C) clumsyfully   (D) clumsifully

6. lose money : loss :: make money : _____

   (A) profit   (B) income   (C) cost   (D) capital

7. mystery : _____ :: secret : unknown

   (A) clue   (B) unexplained   (C) understood   (D) crime

8. laws : country :: rules : _____

   (A) freedom   (B) game   (C) liberty   (D) flag

9. reverence : respect :: liberty : _____

   (A) honor   (B) freedom   (C) allegiance   (D) duty

10. Employee : salary :: Retiree : _____

    (A) income   (B) vacation   (C) pension   (D) savings

11. _____ : ! :: mystery : ?

    (A) disappointment   (B) envy   (C) superstition   (D) excitement

12. illegal : against the law :: illiterate : _____

    (A) underground   (B) unkind   (C) cannot vote   (D) cannot read

crave	abrupt	modify	journey
reuse	uncertain	disappointed	strum
complex	surprised	courteous	torn
fault	well-being		

Study the relationship between the first set of words. Pick one word from the word bank that completes the second pair with this same relationship.

1.	assist : help :: recycle : _____
2.	voyage : _____ :: colony : settlement
3.	uncomfortable : uneasy :: kind : _____
4.	stop : quit :: desperately want : _____
5.	uncertain : sure :: gradual : _____
6.	pristine : perfect :: tattered : _____
7.	cranky : grouchy :: dumbfounded : _____
8.	habits : regular activities :: health : _____
9.	assist : aid :: alter : _____
10.	key : press :: string : _____
11.	suspicious : _____ :: mysterious : unknown
12.	confident : certain :: dismayed : _____
13.	relenting : surrendering :: intricate : _____
14.	flawless : perfect :: flawed : _____

change	reuse	fault	modify
perfect	abrupt	journey	delighted
register	urge	strum	uncertain
well-being			

Study the relationship between the first set of words. Pick one word from the word bank that completes the second pair with this same relationship.

1. suspicious : _____ :: mysterious : unknown

2. aid : help :: modify : _____

3. embarrassed : uncomfortable :: happy : _____

4. assist : help :: recycle : _____

5. addiction : habit :: craving : _____

6. flawless : perfect :: flawed : _____

7. assist : aid :: alter : _____

8. uncertain : sure :: gradual : _____

9. voyage : _____ :: colony : settlement

10. flaw : fault :: flawless : _____

11. key : press :: string : _____

12. habits : regular activities :: health : _____

13. tattered : torn :: pristine : _____

14. interpret : decipher :: record : _____

Name _____ LESSON 192 Date _____

Study the relationship between the first set of words. Pick the word that completes the second pair with this same relationship.

1. key : press :: string : _____
   - **A** tighten
   - **B** strum
   - **C** tie
   - **D** break

2. voyage : _____ :: colony : settlement
   - **A** journey
   - **B** runaway
   - **C** supply
   - **D** leader

3. a settlement in a new land that is ruled by the home country of the settlers : colony :: a long journey to a distant land : _____
   - **A** tale
   - **B** alley
   - **C** canvas
   - **D** voyage

4. interpret : decipher :: record : _____
   - **A** lyrics
   - **B** register
   - **C** habit
   - **D** oblivion

5. assist : aid :: alter : _____
   - **A** discriminate
   - **B** overcome
   - **C** modify
   - **D** vision

6. tattered : torn :: pristine : _____
   - **A** too little
   - **B** dirty
   - **C** fellow
   - **D** perfect

7. interpret : decipher :: record : _____
   - **A** oblivion
   - **B** register
   - **C** habit
   - **D** lyrics

8. assist : help :: recycle : _____
   - **A** join
   - **B** aid
   - **C** remember
   - **D** reuse

9. suspicious : _____ :: mysterious : unknown
   - **A** decisive
   - **B** gentle
   - **C** direct
   - **D** uncertain

10. flaw : fault :: flawless : _____
   - **A** perfect
   - **B** fellow
   - **C** damaged
   - **D** dirty

11. invigorated : energized :: abashed : _____
   - **A** injured
   - **B** awestruck
   - **C** embarrassed
   - **D** uncertain

12. colony : settlement :: voyage : _____
   - **A** vehicle
   - **B** journey
   - **C** runaway
   - **D** plantation

dungeon	moat	password	angry
worried	shortage	fidgety	screen name
surplus	useful	clean	unimportant
satisfied			

Study the relationship between the first set of words. Pick one word from the word bank that completes the second pair with this same relationship.

1.	_____ : mad :: drowsy : sleepy
2.	drowsy : sleepy :: antsy : _____
3.	school : nickname :: online : _____
4.	useless : practical :: disappointed : _____
5.	vulgar : crude :: petty : _____
6.	home of a king : castle :: water surrounding a castle for protection against intruders : _____
7.	door : key :: email account : _____
8.	tired : drowsy :: frantic : _____
9.	a way for people to enter the castle by going over the moat : drawbridge :: area of the castle where prisoners were kept : _____
10.	excess : surplus :: scarcity : _____
11.	convenient : difficult :: impractical : _____
12.	prevents users from accessing a file without permission : _____ :: prevents programs from accessing the internet or your computer without permission : firewall
13.	immaterial : unimportant :: immaculate : _____
14.	scarcity : shortage :: excess : _____

shortage	castle	sleepy	password
paragaph	land	fidgety	satisfied
useful	dungeon	cross	worried
clean	screen name		

Study the relationship between the first set of words. Pick one word from the word bank that completes the second pair with this same relationship.

1.
tired : drowsy :: frantic : _____

2.
immaterial : unimportant :: immaculate : _____

3.
letters : word :: sentence : _____

4.
door : key :: email account : _____

5.
jousting : sport :: fief : _____

6.
happy : cheerful :: cranky : _____

7.
school : nickname :: online : _____

8.
excess : surplus :: scarcity : _____

9.
useless : practical :: disappointed : _____

10.
convenient : difficult :: impractical : _____

11.
angry : mad :: drowsy : _____

12.
water surrounding a castle for protection against intruders : moat :: home of a king :
_____

13.
provided a way for people to enter the castle by going over the moat : drawbridge ::
area of the castle where prisoners were kept : _____

14.
drowsy : sleepy :: antsy : _____

Study the relationship between the first set of words. Pick the word that completes the second pair with this same relationship.

1. palace : castle :: isle : _____

    Ⓐ moat   Ⓑ island   Ⓒ river   Ⓓ dungeon

2. school : nickname :: online : _____

    Ⓐ screen name   Ⓑ password   Ⓒ program   Ⓓ tag

3. happy : cheerful :: cranky : _____

    Ⓐ funny   Ⓑ cross   Ⓒ drowsy   Ⓓ sad

4. vulgar : crude :: petty : _____

    Ⓐ unimportant   Ⓑ dangerous   Ⓒ attractive   Ⓓ polite

5. home of a king : castle :: water surrounding a castle for protection against intruders : _____

    Ⓐ dungeon   Ⓑ monk   Ⓒ moat   Ⓓ armor

6. convenient : difficult :: impractical : _____

    Ⓐ boring   Ⓑ useful   Ⓒ controlled   Ⓓ useless

7. provided a way for people to enter the castle by going over the moat : drawbridge :: area of the castle where prisoners were kept : _____

    Ⓐ crest   Ⓑ dungeon   Ⓒ fief   Ⓓ gargoyle

8. jousting : sport :: fief : _____

    Ⓐ weapon   Ⓑ instrument   Ⓒ dungeon   Ⓓ land

9. water surrounding a castle for protection against intruders : moat :: home of a king : _____

    Ⓐ dungeon   Ⓑ monk   Ⓒ castle   Ⓓ cathedral

10. grave : serious :: fatal : _____

    Ⓐ immense   Ⓑ generous   Ⓒ unimportant   Ⓓ deadly

11. _____ : mad :: drowsy : sleepy

    Ⓐ angry   Ⓑ difficult   Ⓒ foolish   Ⓓ hard

12. drowsy : sleepy :: antsy : _____

    Ⓐ silly   Ⓑ clumsy   Ⓒ jealous   Ⓓ fidgety

shadow	perfectionist	unearth
magician	right	lantern
symbol	fair	cautiously
lamp	luck	poet
party	early	

Study the relationship between the first set of words. Pick one word from the word bank that completes the second pair with this same relationship.

1.
   siesta : nap :: fiesta : _____

2.
   rangy : slender :: gingerly : _____

3.
   wrong : incorrect :: accurate : _____

4.
   wants to be funny : comedian :: wants everything to be its best :
   _____

5.
   _____ : lamp :: festival : party

6.
   superstition : belief :: fortune : _____

7.
   antidote : remedy :: emblem : _____

8.
   research : study :: excavate : _____

9.
   comedian : tells jokes :: _____ : performs magic tricks

10.
    festival : party :: lantern : _____

11.
    elastic : stretchy :: premature : _____

12.
    Bill Cosby : comedian :: Langston Hughes : _____

13.
    lantern : lamp :: festival : _____

14.
    light : _____ :: sound : echo

perfectionist	lantern	guano
unearth	right	luck
nap	poet	party
lamp	fair	cautiously
shadow	magician	

Study the relationship between the first set of words. Pick one word from the word bank that completes the second pair with this same relationship.

1.
   superstition : belief :: fortune : _____

2.
   perch : roost :: poop : _____

3.
   comedian : tells jokes :: _____ : performs magic tricks

4.
   wrong : incorrect :: accurate : _____

5.
   _____ : lamp :: festival : party

6.
   fiesta : party :: siesta : _____

7.
   light : _____ :: sound : echo

8.
   lantern : lamp :: festival : _____

9.
   festival : party :: lantern : _____

10.
   rangy : slender :: gingerly : _____

11.
   siesta : nap :: fiesta : _____

12.
   wants to be funny : comedian :: wants everything to be its best :
   _____

13.
   Bill Cosby : comedian :: Langston Hughes : _____

14.
   research : study :: excavate : _____

Study the relationship between the first set of words. Pick the word that completes the second pair with this same relationship.

1. siesta : nap :: fiesta : _____

   Ⓐ festival   Ⓑ celebration   Ⓒ piñata   Ⓓ party

2. comedian : tells jokes :: _____ : performs magic tricks

   Ⓐ spy   Ⓑ detective   Ⓒ magician   Ⓓ singer

3. antidote : remedy :: emblem : _____

   Ⓐ cause   Ⓑ symbol   Ⓒ result   Ⓓ clue

4. festival : party :: lantern : _____

   Ⓐ fireworks   Ⓑ monster   Ⓒ lamp   Ⓓ fish

5. fiesta : party :: siesta : _____

   Ⓐ piñata   Ⓑ celebration   Ⓒ festival   Ⓓ nap

6. research : study :: excavate : _____

   Ⓐ replicate   Ⓑ display   Ⓒ unearth   Ⓓ bury

7. superstition : belief :: fortune : _____

   Ⓐ luck   Ⓑ chance   Ⓒ festival   Ⓓ mystery

8. lantern : lamp :: festival : _____

   Ⓐ calendar   Ⓑ fair   Ⓒ story   Ⓓ lesson

9. _____ : lamp :: festival : party

   Ⓐ mane   Ⓑ lantern   Ⓒ stirrup   Ⓓ holster

10. elastic : stretchy :: premature : _____

    Ⓐ truant   Ⓑ early   Ⓒ late   Ⓓ attendance

11. rangy : slender :: gingerly : _____

    Ⓐ harshly   Ⓑ cautiously   Ⓒ perfectly   Ⓓ desperately

12. Bill Cosby : comedian :: Langston Hughes : _____

    Ⓐ poet   Ⓑ actor   Ⓒ athlete   Ⓓ singer

irreverence	move	lamb
infringement	boarding pass	gale
plane	gawk	puzzling
graze	feelings	importance
danger		

Study the relationship between the first set of words. Pick one word from the word bank that completes the second pair with this same relationship.

1.
  mother : ewe :: offspring : _____

2.
  appearance : looks :: mood : _____

3.
  cynical : distrusting :: cryptic : _____

4.
  estimation : guess :: significance : _____

5.
  written material : plagiarism :: patented invention : _____

6.
  rain : downpour :: wind : _____

7.
  price : fare :: ticket : _____

8.
  respect : reverence :: disrespect : _____

9.
  play : frolic :: stare : _____

10.
  chicken : peck :: cow : _____

11.
  disaster : catastrophe :: _____ : peril

12.
  transport : _____ :: peer : look

13.
  peer : look :: transport : _____

14.
  farmer : tractor :: pilot : _____

lamb	graze	importance	danger
wobble	plane	puzzling	feelings
gale	ticket	irreverence	pivot
gawk			

Study the relationship between the first set of words. Pick one word from the word bank that completes the second pair with this same relationship.

1.
   play : frolic :: stare : _____

2.
   price : fare :: boarding pass : _____

3.
   respect : reverence :: disrespect : _____

4.
   _____ : eat :: stampede : run

5.
   cynical : distrusting :: cryptic : _____

6.
   to move smoothly : glide :: to turn on a point : _____

7.
   mother : ewe :: offspring : _____

8.
   disaster : catastrophe :: _____ : peril

9.
   estimation : guess :: significance : _____

10.
    farmer : tractor :: pilot : _____

11.
    rain : downpour :: wind : _____

12.
    _____ : scrape :: arrange : place

13.
    crouch : kneel :: teeter : _____

14.
    appearance : looks :: mood : _____

Study the relationship between the first set of words. Pick the word that completes the second pair with this same relationship.

1. danger : peril :: disaster : _____

    Ⓐ terrorism   Ⓑ catastrophe   Ⓒ rescue   Ⓓ memorial

2. respect : reverence :: disrespect : _____

    Ⓐ distrust   Ⓑ honor   Ⓒ irreverence   Ⓓ displease

3. transport : _____ :: peer : look

    Ⓐ speak   Ⓑ hear   Ⓒ move   Ⓓ eat

4. numerical : number :: chronological : _____

    Ⓐ size   Ⓑ letter   Ⓒ time   Ⓓ importance

5. _____ : scrape :: arrange : place

    Ⓐ bleat   Ⓑ graze   Ⓒ herd   Ⓓ cud

6. crouch : kneel :: teeter : _____

    Ⓐ mix   Ⓑ graze   Ⓒ soar   Ⓓ wobble

7. play : frolic :: stare : _____

    Ⓐ wince   Ⓑ graze   Ⓒ gawk   Ⓓ squall

8. appearance : looks :: mood : _____

    Ⓐ feelings   Ⓑ cards   Ⓒ worry   Ⓓ family

9. estimation : guess :: significance : _____

    Ⓐ knowledge   Ⓑ importance   Ⓒ dependability   Ⓓ precision

10. uncontrollably emotional : hysterical :: disheartened : _____

    Ⓐ disingenuous   Ⓑ disregarded   Ⓒ discouraged   Ⓓ distrusting

11. _____ : eat :: stampede : run

    Ⓐ bleat   Ⓑ graze   Ⓒ mutton   Ⓓ beat

12. cynical : distrusting :: cryptic : _____

    Ⓐ simple   Ⓑ trusting   Ⓒ controlling   Ⓓ puzzling

alert	plan	warning	prevent
poison ivy	give	gloomy	outstanding
sorrowful	required	isolated	Constitution
fear			

Study the relationship between the first set of words. Pick one word from the word bank that completes the second pair with this same relationship.

1.	suggestion : hint :: warning : _____
2.	pleasant : enjoyable :: lonely : _____
3.	game : rules :: United States government : _____
4.	allow : permit :: restrict : _____
5.	suggestion : advice :: caution : _____
6.	trivial : insignificant :: stellar : _____
7.	rueful : sorrowful :: dismal : _____
8.	dismal : gloomy :: rueful : _____
9.	_____ : strategy :: suggestion : proposal
10.	disappear : vanish :: _____ : dread
11.	permitted : allowed :: obliged : _____
12.	venom : rattlesnake :: toxin : _____
13.	_____ : sad :: complicated : complex
14.	clean : dirty :: _____ : take

207

iron	warning	stubborn	fear
emerge	prevent	Constitution	outstanding
encrypt	discouraged	sorrowful	required

Study the relationship between the first set of words. Pick one word from the word bank that completes the second pair with this same relationship.

1.	
	to disappear : vanish :: to come into view : _____

2.	
	suggestion : advice :: caution : _____

3.	
	allow : permit :: restrict : _____

4.	
	permit : allow :: restrict : _____

5.	
	bleach : stains :: _____ : wrinkles

6.	
	contrite : sorrowful :: crestfallen : _____

7.	
	disappear : vanish :: _____ : dread

8.	
	disappear : vanish :: _____ : terrify

9.	
	permitted : allowed :: obliged : _____

10.	
	_____ : sad :: complicated : complex

11.	
	mournful : sorrowful :: obstinate : _____

12.	
	game : rules :: United States government : _____

13.	
	make a file smaller : compress :: make a file unrecognizable without authorization : _____

14.	
	trivial : insignificant :: stellar : _____

Study the relationship between the first set of words. Pick the word that completes the second pair with this same relationship.

1. make a file smaller : compress :: make a file unrecognizable without authorization :

   _____

   Ⓐ transfer   Ⓑ import   Ⓒ scan   Ⓓ encrypt

2. clean : dirty :: _____ : take

   Ⓐ purify   Ⓑ wash   Ⓒ bleach   Ⓓ give

3. dismal : gloomy :: rueful : _____

   Ⓐ scant   Ⓑ jealous   Ⓒ sorrowful   Ⓓ honorable

4. mournful : sorrowful :: obstinate : _____

   Ⓐ stubborn   Ⓑ civil   Ⓒ distressed   Ⓓ lame

5. intelligent : smart :: resourceful : _____

   Ⓐ inventive   Ⓑ forbidden   Ⓒ unsavory   Ⓓ fascinating

6. suggestion : hint :: warning : _____

   Ⓐ teach   Ⓑ alert   Ⓒ guess   Ⓓ imitate

7. bleach : stains :: _____ : wrinkles

   Ⓐ copper   Ⓑ lead   Ⓒ oven   Ⓓ iron

8. to disappear : vanish :: to come into view : _____

   Ⓐ emerge   Ⓑ surprise   Ⓒ impress   Ⓓ divulge

9. permit : allow :: restrict : _____

   Ⓐ prevent   Ⓑ include   Ⓒ help   Ⓓ transfer

10. allow : permit :: restrict : _____

    Ⓐ prevent   Ⓑ help   Ⓒ include   Ⓓ transfer

11. venom : rattlesnake :: toxin : _____

    Ⓐ cyanide   Ⓑ alcohol   Ⓒ bleach   Ⓓ poison ivy

12. game : rules :: United States government : _____

    Ⓐ judges   Ⓑ Constitution   Ⓒ lawyers   Ⓓ penalties

reluctant	unknown	call	plentiful
borrow	truthful	odd	destroy
rude	prayer	difficult	shy

Study the relationship between the first set of words. Pick one word from the word bank that completes the second pair with this same relationship.

1.
  bleak : dreary :: copious : _____

2.
  supervise : oversee :: summon : _____

3.
  exuberance : joy :: supplication : _____

4.
  exit : leave :: ruin : _____

5.
  ornery : difficult :: hesitant : _____

6.
  hardworking : dedicated :: _____ : sincere

7.
  strange : odd :: timid : _____

8.
  irritating : bothersome :: honest : _____

9.
  polite : nice :: impolite : _____

10.
  convenient : _____ :: impractical : useful

11.
  laborious : _____ :: phenomenal : amazing

12.
  to temporarily use something that belongs to someone else : _____
  :: to ask someone's opinion : consult

13.
  timid : shy :: strange : _____

14.
  dangerous : unsafe :: mysterious : _____

difficult	combine	intense
rude	go along with	odd
destroy	truthful	warning
call	dangerous	

Study the relationship between the first set of words. Pick one word from the word bank that completes the second pair with this same relationship.

1.	timid : shy :: strange : _____
2.	laborious : _____ :: phenomenal : amazing
3.	supervise : oversee :: summon : _____
4.	_____ : unsafe :: mysterious : unknown
5.	convenient : _____ :: impractical : useful
6.	surround : encircle :: accompany : _____
7.	inadvertent : accidental :: grueling : _____
8.	kind : nice :: honest : _____
9.	polite : nice :: impolite : _____
10.	dubious : doubtful :: arduous : _____
11.	suggestion : advice :: caution : _____
12.	exit : leave :: ruin : _____
13.	conspire : plot :: consolidate : _____
14.	strange : odd :: fierce : _____

Study the relationship between the first set of words. Pick the word that completes the second pair with this same relationship.

1. integration : combining :: segregation : _____

    A separating   **B** division   **C** discrimination   **D** protest

2. suggestion : advice :: caution : _____

    A warning   **B** apology   **C** law   **D** assignment

3. polite : nice :: impolite : _____

    A cautious   **B** truthful   **C** deceptive   **D** rude

4. integration : combining :: segregation : _____

    A division   **B** separation   **C** discrimination   **D** protest

5. dangerous : unsafe :: mysterious : _____

    A clue   **B** unknown   **C** crime   **D** clues

6. dubious : doubtful :: arduous : _____

    A exciting   **B** difficult   **C** well-planned   **D** helpful

7. timid : shy :: strange : _____

    A loud   **B** normal   **C** odd   **D** quiet

8. inadvertent : accidental :: grueling : _____

    A brave   **B** well-planned   **C** difficult   **D** powerful

9. surround : encircle :: accompany : _____

    A clean up   **B** go along with   **C** make up   **D** combine

10. _____ : unsafe :: mysterious : unknown

    A gifted   **B** spectacular   **C** fun   **D** dangerous

11. polite : nice :: impolite : _____

    A "Thank you."   **B** "Please."   **C** truthful   **D** rude

12. exit : leave :: ruin : _____

    A destroy   **B** hold   **C** shout   **D** notice

apart	flexible	persuade	rude
rigid	calm	greed	close
convince	get smaller	dislike	joking
jealous			

Study the relationship between the first set of words. Pick one word from the word bank that completes the second pair with this same relationship.

1. ferocious : fierce :: envious : _____

2. belly-aching : complaining :: banter : _____

3. lament : mourn :: cajole : _____

4. pretend : imagine :: _____ : persuade

5. _____ : like :: loathe : adore

6. contorted : twisted :: pliant : _____

7. good manners : polite :: bad manners : _____

8. stifle : suppress :: entice : _____

9. blurry : clear :: flexible : _____

10. _____ : minimize :: X : ____

11. generosity : charity :: selfishness : _____

12. get bigger : expand :: _____ : diminish

13. equal : different :: together : _____

14. _____ : anxious :: steady : wavering

reuse	expand	greed
innumerable	turn	different
versatile	cannot remember	rude
negotiates	retreat	disagreeable
ancient	bored	

Study the relationship between the first set of words. Pick one word from the word bank that completes the second pair with this same relationship.

1.	new : modern :: old : _____
2.	offensive : objectionable :: having many uses : _____
3.	blind : cannot see :: amnesia : _____
4.	_____ : distinct :: same : identical
5.	move forward : advance :: move back : _____
6.	all alone : lonely :: nothing to do : _____
7.	lithe : flexible :: myriad : _____
8.	multiply : increase in number :: stretch : _____
9.	assist : help :: recycle : _____
10.	Salesperson : persuades :: Diplomat : _____
11.	coquettish : flirty :: cantankerous : _____
12.	distraught : upset :: surly : _____
13.	generosity : charity :: selfishness : _____
14.	stitch : sew :: crank : _____

Study the relationship between the first set of words. Pick the word that completes the second pair with this same relationship.

1. ferocious : fierce :: envious : _____

   Ⓐ laugh Ⓑ jealous Ⓒ honorable Ⓓ anxious

2. _____ : like :: loathe : adore

   Ⓐ compassion Ⓑ surprise Ⓒ dislike Ⓓ insult

3. flexible : _____ :: obedient : defiant

   Ⓐ smooth Ⓑ fuzzy Ⓒ bumpy Ⓓ rigid

4. convince : persuade :: pretend : _____

   Ⓐ count Ⓑ understand Ⓒ imagine Ⓓ ignore

5. _____ : learn :: vacation : relax

   Ⓐ bus Ⓑ school Ⓒ family Ⓓ students

6. cover : reveal :: repel : _____

   Ⓐ hide Ⓑ detract Ⓒ close Ⓓ attract

7. confounded : confused :: apprehensive : _____

   Ⓐ irritating Ⓑ anxious Ⓒ controlling Ⓓ decisive

8. close : near :: _____ : distant

   Ⓐ making a sound Ⓑ moving Ⓒ hard to find Ⓓ far away

9. offensive : objectionable :: having many uses : _____

   Ⓐ untenable Ⓑ garrulous Ⓒ gullible Ⓓ versatile

10. good manners : polite :: bad manners : _____

    Ⓐ hardworking Ⓑ stubborn Ⓒ rude Ⓓ nice

11. peer : look :: recollect : _____

    Ⓐ give Ⓑ replenish Ⓒ decide Ⓓ remember

12. calm : anxious :: _____ : idle

    Ⓐ closed Ⓑ busy Ⓒ serious Ⓓ in love

Name _____   LESSON 211   Date _____

Study the relationship between the first set of words. Pick the word that completes the second pair with this same relationship.

1. belly-aching : complaining :: banter : _____

    Ⓐ laughing   Ⓑ gossiping   Ⓒ arguing   Ⓓ joking

2. _____ : like :: loathe : adore

    Ⓐ compassion   Ⓑ insult   Ⓒ dislike   Ⓓ surprise

3. lithe : flexible :: myriad : _____

    Ⓐ structured   Ⓑ ordinary   Ⓒ unique   Ⓓ innumerable

4. surprised : shocked :: angry : _____

    Ⓐ disappointed   Ⓑ furious   Ⓒ confused   Ⓓ worried

5. strain : stress :: jeopardize : _____

    Ⓐ relax   Ⓑ risk   Ⓒ close   Ⓓ question

6. bike : ride :: ball : _____

    Ⓐ push   Ⓑ throw   Ⓒ sit   Ⓓ buy

7. good manners : polite :: bad manners : _____

    Ⓐ nice   Ⓑ stubborn   Ⓒ hardworking   Ⓓ rude

8. adult : bed :: _____ : cradle

    Ⓐ son   Ⓑ middle   Ⓒ baby   Ⓓ sibling

9. truth : lie :: equal : _____

    Ⓐ different   Ⓑ careless   Ⓒ justice   Ⓓ identical

10. brilliant : splendid :: giddy : _____

    Ⓐ furious   Ⓑ daring   Ⓒ dizzy   Ⓓ content

11. blurry : clear :: flexible : _____

    Ⓐ rigid   Ⓑ bumpy   Ⓒ fuzzy   Ⓓ smooth

12. be careful : beware :: diminish : _____

    Ⓐ expand   Ⓑ silence   Ⓒ dwindle   Ⓓ increase

entertain	slavery	forever	unruly
put off	phenomenal	grief	anxious
watchfulness	bold	blunder	disfigure
plant			

Study the relationship between the first set of words. Pick one word from the word bank that completes the second pair with this same relationship.

1.
    beckon : call :: amuse : _____

2.
    justice : injustice :: freedom : _____

3.
    quiver : shake :: mangle : _____

4.
    disobedient : _____ :: triumphant : victorious

5.
    vengeance : revenge :: vigilance : _____

6.
    sleep : slumber :: error : _____

7.
    barnacles : animal :: algae : _____

8.
    instantaneous : only a second :: eternal : _____

9.
    divine : godly :: miraculous : _____

10.
    extend : make longer :: postpone : _____

11.
    worshiper : devotion :: mourner : _____

12.
    confounded : confused :: apprehensive : _____

13.
    tears : _____ :: laughter : humor

14.
    brazen : _____ :: baffled : confused

snacks	plentiful	fairness	stop
approximate	blunder	watchfulness	unknown
sad	on-time	slavery	grief
disfigure	plant		

Study the relationship between the first set of words. Pick one word from the word bank that completes the second pair with this same relationship.

1.
   sleep : slumber :: error : _____

2.
   justice : injustice :: freedom : _____

3.
   bulletins : messages :: refreshments : _____

4.
   annoyed : irritated :: glum : _____

5.
   vengeance : revenge :: vigilance : _____

6.
   barnacle : animal :: algae : _____

7.
   worshiper : devotion :: mourner : _____

8.
   quiver : shake :: mangle : _____

9.
   logical : reasonable :: ample : _____

10.
   independence : freedom :: justice : _____

11.
   flight will arrive at the scheduled time : _____ :: flight will be late : delayed

12.
   solve : answer :: estimate : _____

13.
   _____ : prevent :: postpone : delay

14.
   _____ : unfamiliar :: known : familiar

218

Study the relationship between the first set of words. Pick the word that completes the second pair with this same relationship.

1. should : shouldn't :: could : _____

   (A) would   (B) couldn't   (C) can't   (D) mold

2. to seize by force : usurp :: to weaken : _____

   (A) smuggle   (B) fraternize   (C) languish   (D) blunder

3. quiver : shake :: harm : _____

   (A) hurt   (B) timid   (C) heal   (D) stun

4. in control : dominant :: in trouble : _____

   (A) placid   (B) distress   (C) wrack   (D) raucous

5. disobedient : _____ :: triumphant : victorious

   (A) unruly   (B) frightened   (C) loud   (D) worried

6. mistake : error :: success : _____

   (A) achievement   (B) failure   (C) misjudgment   (D) blunder

7. worshiper : devotion :: mourner : _____

   (A) sound   (B) tears   (C) grief   (D) disappointment

8. superfluous : unnecessary :: harrowing : _____

   (A) distressing   (B) skillful   (C) important   (D) brilliant

9. dark : bold :: _____ : pale

   (A) bird   (B) soup   (C) weekend   (D) light

10. accountant : calculator :: candlemaker : _____

    (A) mold   (B) math   (C) gifts   (D) melting

11. record of one person's money in a bank : account :: locked place where banks keep money :

    _____

    (A) safe   (B) loan   (C) credit   (D) exchange

12. intelligent : smart :: handsome : _____

    (A) handy   (B) kind   (C) foolish   (D) good looking

219

disagreement	freedom	honor	interrupt
focus	united	promise	wonderful
courage	communal	protons	agreeable
unearth			

Study the relationship between the first set of words. Pick one word from the word bank that completes the second pair with this same relationship.

1.
    treasonous : loyal :: divided : _____

2.
    shame : honor :: cowardice : _____

3.
    negative : electrons :: positive : _____

4.
    splendid : _____ :: appalling : dreadful

5.
    support : encourage :: fixate : _____

6.
    pledge : _____ :: elect : choose

7.
    private : individual :: collective : _____

8.
    dreadful : alarming :: amiable : _____

9.
    respect : honor :: worship : _____

10.
    allegiance : loyalty :: independence : _____

11.
    research : study :: excavate : _____

12.
    lure : enticement :: objection : _____

13.
    to say something loudly so that many people can hear : announce :: to speak when someone else is talking : _____

14.
    hideous : ugly :: marvelous : _____

Study the relationship between the first set of words. Pick the word that completes the second pair with this same relationship.

1.   soothe : calm :: deprive : _____

    A distinguish   **B** bribe   **C** do without   **D** swig

2.   weary : tired :: meek : _____

    A phony   **B** shy   **C** quiet   **D** complicated

3.   lure : enticement :: objection : _____

    A promise   **B** compromise   **C** disagreement   **D** release

4.   respect : honor :: worship : _____

    A magic   **B** honor   **C** reprieve   **D** mystery

5.   allegiance : loyalty :: independence : _____

    A faith   **B** intelligence   **C** freedom   **D** equal

6.   unnoticeable : inconspicuous :: joyful : _____

    A corrigible   **B** blissful   **C** righteous   **D** melancholy

7.   _____ : unjust :: reward : righteous

    A reward   **B** detain   **C** encourage   **D** punish

8.   allegiance : loyalty :: independence : _____

    A speed   **B** compromise   **C** freedom   **D** equal

9.   private : individual :: collective : _____

    A communal   **B** reliable   **C** righteous   **D** constitutional

10.   glorious : wonderful :: weary : _____

    A bed   **B** thirsty   **C** tired   **D** terrible

11.   a distinctive quality : characteristic :: an ability : _____

    A talent   **B** vocation   **C** accent   **D** procedure

12.   to go along with : agree :: to go against : _____

    A contradict   **B** prose   **C** essay   **D** experiment

Name _____ LESSON 217 Date _____

Study the relationship between the first set of words. Pick the word that completes the second pair with this same relationship.

1. marvelous : wonderful :: hideous : _____

   A. sad   B. confused   C. unsure   D. ugly

2. treasonous : loyal :: divided : _____

   A. promised   B. separated   C. faithful   D. united

3. justice : injustice :: freedom : _____

   A. allegiance   B. slavery   C. irony   D. liberty

4. consign : entrust :: perambulate : _____

   A. hide   B. forgive   C. write   D. walk

5. to say something loudly so that many people can hear : announce :: to speak when someone else is talking : _____

   A. direct   B. question   C. interrupt   D. polite

6. to draw away someone's attention : distract :: to spread out : _____

   A. direct   B. dispense   C. devote   D. disperse

7. loyalty : allegiance :: treason : _____

   A. independence   B. liberty   C. disloyalty   D. faithfulness

8. triumphant : victorious :: jubilant : _____

   A. righteous   B. ludicrous   C. joyous   D. prudish

9. _____ : dedicated :: truthful : sincere

   A. abusive   B. obedient   C. hardworking   D. successful

10. soothe : calm :: deprived : _____

    A. distinguish   B. bribe   C. swig   D. do without

11. justice : fairness :: pledge : _____

    A. punishment   B. vote   C. work   D. promise

12. shame : honor :: cowardice : _____

    A. courage   B. kindness   C. fear   D. glory

all	cinco	his	Dusty's
two	dime	baseball	hymn
we	one	ranch	I
theirs			

Study the relationship between the first set of words. Pick one word from the word bank that completes the second pair with this same relationship.

1.	solo : _____ :: trio : three
2.	one : penny :: ten : _____
3.	cowboy : _____ :: prospector : mine
4.	he : his :: Dusty : _____
5.	allowed : aloud :: him : _____
6.	never : always :: none : _____
7.	duet : two :: solo : _____
8.	yo : I :: nosotros : _____
9.	single : one :: couple : _____
10.	anybody : his :: everybody : _____
11.	one : uno :: five : _____
12.	touchdown : football :: diamond : _____
13.	A : G :: C : _____
14.	I : mine :: they : _____

cinco	dime	Dusty's	I
hymn	one	two	ranch
we	his	baseball	all
theirs			

Study the relationship between the first set of words. Pick one word from the word bank that completes the second pair with this same relationship.

1.	
	I : mine :: they : _____

2.	
	solo : _____ :: trio : three

3.	
	he : his :: Dusty : _____

4.	
	one : penny :: ten : _____

5.	
	yo : I :: nosotros : _____

6.	
	never : always :: none : _____

7.	
	single : one :: couple : _____

8.	
	one : uno :: five : _____

9.	
	cowboy : _____ :: prospector : mine

10.	
	allowed : aloud :: him : _____

11.	
	duet : two :: solo : _____

12.	
	anybody : his :: everybody : _____

13.	
	A : G :: C : _____

14.	
	touchdown : football :: diamond : _____

Study the relationship between the first set of words. Pick the word that completes the second pair with this same relationship.

1. allowed : aloud :: him : _____

   Ⓐ limb   Ⓑ gym   Ⓒ hymn   Ⓓ her

2. A : G :: C : _____

   Ⓐ s   Ⓑ I   Ⓒ i   Ⓓ D

3. solo : _____ :: trio : three

   Ⓐ ten   Ⓑ five   Ⓒ one   Ⓓ two

4. yo : I :: nosotros : _____

   Ⓐ you   Ⓑ she   Ⓒ he   Ⓓ we

5. he : his :: Dusty : _____

   Ⓐ his   Ⓑ Dusty's   Ⓒ Dusties'   Ⓓ him

6. never : always :: none : _____

   Ⓐ ever   Ⓑ rarely   Ⓒ all   Ⓓ funeral

7. duet : two :: solo : _____

   Ⓐ four   Ⓑ three   Ⓒ five   Ⓓ one

8. touchdown : football :: diamond : _____

   Ⓐ mine   Ⓑ field   Ⓒ ring   Ⓓ baseball

9. anybody : his :: everybody : _____

   Ⓐ your   Ⓑ their   Ⓒ ours   Ⓓ his

10. I : mine :: they : _____

   Ⓐ my   Ⓑ theirs   Ⓒ their   Ⓓ them

11. cowboy : _____ :: prospector : mine

   Ⓐ dairy   Ⓑ field   Ⓒ ranch   Ⓓ drive

12. single : one :: couple : _____

   Ⓐ four   Ⓑ two   Ⓒ zero   Ⓓ five

Study the relationship between the first set of words. Pick the word that completes the second pair with this same relationship.

1. duet : two :: solo : _____

   (A) four   (B) three   (C) one   (D) five

2. yo : I :: nosotros : _____

   (A) we   (B) you   (C) he   (D) she

3. anybody : his :: everybody : _____

   (A) ours   (B) their   (C) his   (D) your

4. cowboy : _____ :: prospector : mine

   (A) field   (B) dairy   (C) drive   (D) ranch

5. I : mine :: they : _____

   (A) theirs   (B) my   (C) their   (D) them

6. one : penny :: ten : _____

   (A) dime   (B) 50 cent piece   (C) dollar   (D) quarter

7. touchdown : football :: diamond : _____

   (A) mine   (B) baseball   (C) field   (D) ring

8. single : one :: couple : _____

   (A) five   (B) four   (C) zero   (D) two

9. allowed : aloud :: him : _____

   (A) her   (B) gym   (C) limb   (D) hymn

10. A : G :: C : _____

   (A) D   (B) s   (C) i   (D) I

11. one : uno :: five : _____

   (A) siete   (B) cuatro   (C) seis   (D) cinco

12. solo : _____ :: trio : three

   (A) two   (B) ten   (C) five   (D) one

| still | simple | quiet | waves |
| cautiously | | | |

Study the relationship between the first set of words. Pick one word from the word bank that completes the second pair with this same relationship.

1.	loud : _____ :: restless : still
2.	_____ : motionless :: strong : sturdy
3.	swimming pool : still :: ocean : _____
4.	complicated : _____ :: questionable : undeniable
5.	literally : actually :: gingerly : _____
6.	instantaneous : immediate :: motionless : _____
7.	smoldering : slowly burning :: stagnant : _____

Name _____   LESSON 223   Date _____

Study the relationship between the first set of words. Pick the word that completes the second pair with this same relationship.

1. _____ : motionless :: strong : sturdy

    (A) small   (B) still   (C) silent   (D) busy

2. swimming pool : still :: ocean : _____

    (A) blue   (B) frozen   (C) salt   (D) waves

3. complicated : _____ :: questionable : undeniable

    (A) complex   (B) full   (C) dirty   (D) simple

4. loud : _____ :: restless : still

    (A) sit   (B) play   (C) open   (D) quiet

5. literally : actually :: gingerly : _____

    (A) perfectly   (B) harshly   (C) cautiously   (D) sharply

6. smoldering : slowly burning :: stagnant : _____

    (A) still   (B) rough   (C) smelly   (D) hushed

7. instantaneous : immediate :: motionless : _____

    (A) silent   (B) late   (C) warm   (D) still

Study the relationship between the first set of words. Pick the word that completes the second pair with this same relationship.

1. swimming pool : still :: ocean : _____

   A frozen   **B** blue   **C** salt   **D** waves

2. smoldering : slowly burning :: stagnant : _____

   A rough   **B** smelly   **C** hushed   **D** still

3. _____ : motionless :: strong : sturdy

   A small   **B** busy   **C** silent   **D** still

4. literally : actually :: gingerly : _____

   A harshly   **B** perfectly   **C** cautiously   **D** sharply

5. loud : _____ :: restless : still

   A open   **B** sit   **C** play   **D** quiet

6. instantaneous : immediate :: motionless : _____

   A still   **B** late   **C** warm   **D** silent

7. complicated : _____ :: questionable : undeniable

   A dirty   **B** full   **C** complex   **D** simple

precarious	clammy	blissful	vulnerable
apologize	initiate	sweater	fairness
respect	warning	luck	danger
tremble	find		

Study the relationship between the first set of words. Pick one word from the word bank that completes the second pair with this same relationship.

1. appropriate : felicitous :: unstable : _____

2. grateful : thank :: sorry : _____

3. admiration : _____ :: remorse : regret

4. to end : terminate :: to start : _____

5. unnoticeable : inconspicuous :: joyful : _____

6. fortune : _____ :: misfortune : hardship

7. a loud noise : clamor :: cold and damp : _____

8. stumble : fall :: shake : _____

9. _____ : justice :: freedom : liberty

10. disaster : catastrophe :: _____ : peril

11. gallant : cowardly :: protected : _____

12. spring : T-shirt :: fall : _____

13. discover : _____ :: invent : create

14. suggestion : advice :: caution : _____

promise	feast	anger	comedy
poll	characters	respect	appropriate
unsure	oath	disloyalty	consequences
transform	moral		

Study the relationship between the first set of words. Pick one word from the word bank that completes the second pair with this same relationship.

1. English writing : letters :: Chinese writing : _____

2. doleful : sorrow :: indignation : _____

3. scarcity : famine :: abundance : _____

4. disapprove : veto :: survey : _____

5. tribulations : hardships :: ramifications : _____

6. practical : useful :: suitable : _____

7. run : frightened :: hesitate : _____

8. lead : govern :: promise : _____

9. sad : tragedy :: funny : _____

10. hesitate : pause :: _____ : change

11. loyalty : allegiance :: treason : _____

12. comedy : humor :: fable : _____

13. admiration : _____ :: remorse : regret

14. excuse : explanation :: vow : _____

Study the relationship between the first set of words. Pick the word that completes the second pair with this same relationship.

1. lead : govern :: promise : _____

   Ⓐ elect   Ⓑ veto   Ⓒ oath   Ⓓ campaign

2. admiration : _____ :: remorse : regret

   Ⓐ faith   Ⓑ respect   Ⓒ sympathy   Ⓓ repulsion

3. loyalty : allegiance :: treason : _____

   Ⓐ disloyalty   Ⓑ faithfulness   Ⓒ liberty   Ⓓ independence

4. values : _____ :: virtue : character

   Ⓐ church   Ⓑ facts   Ⓒ beliefs   Ⓓ history

5. misfortune : curse :: good fortune : _____

   Ⓐ prediction   Ⓑ anger   Ⓒ luck   Ⓓ famine

6. sensible : practical :: suitable : _____

   Ⓐ expected   Ⓑ final   Ⓒ helpful   Ⓓ appropriate

7. fracas : fight :: allotment : _____

   Ⓐ plan   Ⓑ agreement   Ⓒ portion   Ⓓ gift

8. Doctor : health :: Judge : _____

   Ⓐ nurse   Ⓑ liberty   Ⓒ prison   Ⓓ justice

9. wishes for the future : hope :: a group with a single goal : _____

   Ⓐ trust   Ⓑ remorse   Ⓒ unity   Ⓓ empathy

10. independence : _____ :: justice : fairness

    Ⓐ compromise   Ⓑ equal   Ⓒ speed   Ⓓ freedom

11. excuse : explanation :: vow : _____

    Ⓐ punishment   Ⓑ promise   Ⓒ equal   Ⓓ vote

12. grimace : pain :: sneer : _____

    Ⓐ remorse   Ⓑ happiness   Ⓒ fear   Ⓓ scorn

Study the relationship between the first set of words. Pick the word that completes the second pair with this same relationship.

1. fortune : luck :: misfortune : _____

    A chance   **B** misery   **C** courtesy   **D** blessing

2. sad : tragedy :: funny : _____

    A poem   **B** play   **C** comedy   **D** plot

3. solitude : seclusion :: exuberance : _____

    A frustration   **B** repentance   **C** dedication   **D** enthusiasm

4. spring : T-shirt :: fall : _____

    A shorts   **B** summer   **C** bathing suit   **D** sweater

5. sensible : practical :: suitable : _____

    A helpful   **B** expected   **C** appropriate   **D** final

6. chef : kitchen :: president : _____

    A oath   **B** ballot   **C** lunch   **D** Oval Office

7. wishes for the future : hope :: a group with a single goal : _____

    A unity   **B** empathy   **C** remorse   **D** trust

8. suggestion : advice :: caution : _____

    A gratitude   **B** request   **C** warning   **D** apology

9. droop : fall :: sway : _____

    A cover   **B** sink   **C** swing   **D** point

10. treason : loyalty :: divided : _____

    A apart   **B** faithful   **C** united   **D** promised

11. comedy : humor :: fable : _____

    A tragedy   **B** moral   **C** death   **D** empathy

12. a penalty given to someone for doing wrong : punishment :: getting back at someone who has done something to hurt you : _____

    A revenge   **B** penance   **C** grievance   **D** munitions

anger	support	dessert	suburbs
menacing	afraid	sand	ending
provision	extinct	scream	resentment
sheep	guess		

Study the relationship between the first set of words. Pick one word from the word bank that completes the second pair with this same relationship.

1.	scared : _____ :: angry : mad
2.	beekeeper : bees :: shepherd : _____
3.	_____ : interminable :: barren : fertile
4.	exert : expert :: desert : _____
5.	tell a joke : laughter :: frighten : _____
6.	a right : privilege :: a condition : _____
7.	doleful : sorrow :: indignation : _____
8.	focus : fixate :: _____ : encourage
9.	Nile River : water :: desert : _____
10.	center : town square :: outskirts : _____
11.	heated : melted :: endangered : _____
12.	fortune : good luck :: grudge : _____
13.	predicament : difficult situation :: hunch : _____
14.	prodigious : extraordinary :: _____ : threatening

Study the relationship between the first set of words. Pick the word that completes the second pair with this same relationship.

1. duel : fight :: slay : _____

   Ⓐ nick   Ⓑ kill   Ⓒ truce   Ⓓ frighten

2. _____ : interminable :: barren : fertile

   Ⓐ ending   Ⓑ coming   Ⓒ sending   Ⓓ detention

3. ominous : threatening :: eccentric : _____

   Ⓐ astonishing   Ⓑ quaint   Ⓒ peculiar   Ⓓ menacing

4. beekeeper : bees :: shepherd : _____

   Ⓐ cows   Ⓑ sheep   Ⓒ chickens   Ⓓ ants

5. depleted : barren :: rich : _____

   Ⓐ fertile   Ⓑ empty   Ⓒ golden   Ⓓ sparse

6. _____ : mad :: scared : afraid

   Ⓐ angry   Ⓑ hard   Ⓒ sad   Ⓓ foolish

7. heated : melted :: endangered : _____

   Ⓐ extinct   Ⓑ crashed   Ⓒ disappear   Ⓓ threatened

8. reassure : calm :: frighten : _____

   Ⓐ flatter   Ⓑ bravery   Ⓒ evaporate   Ⓓ terrify

9. swamp : tundra :: rainforest : _____

   Ⓐ windy   Ⓑ marine   Ⓒ urban   Ⓓ desert

10. Salesperson : persuades :: Diplomat : _____

   Ⓐ dominates   Ⓑ accommodates   Ⓒ negotiates   Ⓓ threatens

11. reassure : calm :: frighten : _____

   Ⓐ ghost   Ⓑ flatter   Ⓒ horrible   Ⓓ terrify

12. deserted : abandoned :: inhabited by ghosts : _____

   Ⓐ bedraggled   Ⓑ terrified   Ⓒ haunted   Ⓓ spooked

Study the relationship between the first set of words. Pick the word that completes the second pair with this same relationship.

1. despondent : discouraging :: scurrilous : _____

    (A) fast   (B) insulting   (C) frightening   (D) encouraging

2. _____ : encourage :: fixate : focus

    (A) stage   (B) tower   (C) basement   (D) support

3. customs : traditions :: sacred : _____

    (A) holy   (B) language   (C) terrifying   (D) battle cry

4. center : mailing address :: top-left corner : _____

    (A) envelope   (B) return address   (C) change of address   (D) stamp

5. wizened : shriveled :: tremulous : _____

    (A) amazing   (B) enormous   (C) shaking   (D) terrifying

6. tell a joke : laughter :: frighten : _____

    (A) journey   (B) scream   (C) peaceful   (D) tatter

7. ask forgiveness : apologize :: _____ : concentrate

    (A) devise   (B) direct   (C) focus   (D) encourage

8. football : quarterback :: basketball : _____

    (A) forward   (B) point guard   (C) center   (D) guard

9. sarcastic : serious :: engrossed : _____

    (A) distracted   (B) sick   (C) curious   (D) focused

10. reassure : calm :: frighten : _____

    (A) horrible   (B) flatter   (C) ghost   (D) terrify

11. complaint : grievance :: disability : _____

    (A) disrespect   (B) illness   (C) advantage   (D) handicap

12. populated : city :: unpopulated : _____

    (A) state   (B) town   (C) herd   (D) wilderness

worship	James	house	iglesia
Jew	Hanukkah	hospital	church
Jewish	Muslim		

Study the relationship between the first set of words. Pick one word from the word bank that completes the second pair with this same relationship.

1.	mosque : Muslim :: synagogue : _____
2.	t : church :: + : _____
3.	_____ : home :: church : chapel
4.	Christmas : Christian :: _____ : Jewish
5.	school : learn :: church : _____
6.	chapel : _____ :: prison : jail
7.	school : escuela :: church : _____
8.	mother : Lily :: father : _____
9.	Christmas : Christian :: Hanukkah : _____
10.	Judaism : Jewish :: Islam : _____
11.	Buddhism : Buddhist :: Islam : _____

worship	James	house	iglesia
Jew	Hanukkah	hospital	church
Jewish	Muslim		

Study the relationship between the first set of words. Pick one word from the word bank that completes the second pair with this same relationship.

1.	mosque : Muslim :: synagogue : _____
2.	t : church :: + : _____
3.	_____ : home :: church : chapel
4.	Christmas : Christian :: _____ : Jewish
5.	school : learn :: church : _____
6.	chapel : _____ :: prison : jail
7.	school : escuela :: church : _____
8.	mother : Lily :: father : _____
9.	Christmas : Christian :: Hanukkah : _____
10.	Judaism : Jewish :: Islam : _____
11.	Buddhism : Buddhist :: Islam : _____

intermittent	community	gratitude	unlearned
Classifieds	evil	greed	fear
skillful	government	guilty	selfish
help	curious		

Study the relationship between the first set of words. Pick one word from the word bank that completes the second pair with this same relationship.

1. charming : delightful :: sinister : _____

2. optimism : hope :: prejudice : _____

3. street : road :: town : _____

4. section of the newspaper that lists the names of people in the community who have died : Obituaries :: section of the newspaper where you will find advertisements : _____

5. history : past events :: politics : _____

6. protect : shield :: assist : _____

7. honest : deceptive :: innocent : _____

8. impolite : rude :: ignorant : _____

9. generosity : charity :: selfishness : _____

10. memorial : tribute :: appreciation : _____

11. regular : consistent :: occasional : _____

12. conspicuous : noteworthy :: deft : _____

13. despondent : disheartened :: inquisitive : _____

14. greed : _____ :: charity : generous

Study the relationship between the first set of words. Pick the word that completes the second pair with this same relationship.

1. street : road :: town : _____

    Ⓐ chapel   Ⓑ community   Ⓒ citizens   Ⓓ council

2. thankfulness : gratefulness :: _____ : generosity

    Ⓐ charity   Ⓑ sympathy   Ⓒ camaraderie   Ⓓ commiseration

3. history : past events :: politics : _____

    Ⓐ legislature   Ⓑ government   Ⓒ Presidents   Ⓓ policy

4. polite : nice :: impolite : _____

    Ⓐ rude   Ⓑ cautious   Ⓒ deceptive   Ⓓ truthful

5. optimism : hope :: prejudice : _____

    Ⓐ dignity   Ⓑ love   Ⓒ respect   Ⓓ fear

6. insolent : rude :: haughty : _____

    Ⓐ charming   Ⓑ arrogant   Ⓒ reclusive   Ⓓ generous

7. charity : generosity :: _____ : happiness

    Ⓐ punish   Ⓑ cheer   Ⓒ dream   Ⓓ inspire

8. offensive : unpleasant :: deceptive : _____

    Ⓐ misleading   Ⓑ dubious   Ⓒ inordinate   Ⓓ persistent

9. average : exceptional :: stingy : _____

    Ⓐ generous   Ⓑ fortunate   Ⓒ thick   Ⓓ dull

10. _____ : bravery :: respect : dignity

    Ⓐ courage   Ⓑ glory   Ⓒ kindness   Ⓓ fear

11. stubborn : determined :: esteemed : _____

    Ⓐ brave   Ⓑ generous   Ⓒ respected   Ⓓ confident

12. section of the newspaper that lists the names of people in the community who have died : Obituaries :: section of the newspaper where you will find advertisements : _____

    Ⓐ Classifieds   Ⓑ Editorials   Ⓒ Community   Ⓓ World News

famine	register	on purpose	snow
diadem	prejudice	ineffective	thoughtfully
truth	arid	stubborn	avalanche
scold	feast		

Study the relationship between the first set of words. Pick one word from the word bank that completes the second pair with this same relationship.

1.	abundance : feast :: scarcity : _____
2.	wet : moist :: dry : _____
3.	ruthlessly : cruelly :: pensively : _____
4.	affirmation : _____ :: lamentation : grief
5.	facile : simple :: futile : _____
6.	deluge : water :: avalanche : _____
7.	ghostly twin : doppelganger :: crown : _____
8.	summon : call :: admonish : _____
9.	freedom : oppression :: tolerance : _____
10.	mud : mudslide :: snow : _____
11.	interpret : decipher :: record : _____
12.	optimum : preferred :: deliberate : _____
13.	humble : arrogant :: willing : _____
14.	scarcity : famine :: abundance : _____

Study the relationship between the first set of words. Pick the word that completes the second pair with this same relationship.

1. interpret : decipher :: record : _____

   (A) lyrics   (B) register   (C) habit   (D) oblivion

2. wet : moist :: dry : _____

   (A) deluge   (B) irrigate   (C) humid   (D) arid

3. freedom : oppression :: tolerance : _____

   (A) civility   (B) equality   (C) prejudice   (D) persistence

4. wet : moist :: dry : _____

   (A) arid   (B) humid   (C) deluge   (D) irrigate

5. optimum : preferred :: deliberate : _____

   (A) simultaneous (B) accidental   (C) simple   (D) on purpose

6. affirmation : _____ :: lamentation : grief

   (A) jail   (B) deceit   (C) truth   (D) admiration

7. in all places at all times : omnipresent :: sees everything : _____

   (A) karma   (B) omniscient   (C) omnipotent   (D) inspired

8. ruthlessly : cruelly :: pensively : _____

   (A) intelligently (B) kindly   (C) sadly   (D) thoughtfully

9. Buddhism : Buddhist :: Islam : _____

   (A) Catholic   (B) Jewish   (C) Christian   (D) Muslim

10. abundance : feast :: scarcity : _____

    (A) plenty   (B) famine   (C) deluge   (D) catastrophe

11. sagacity : cleverness :: anguish : _____

    (A) brooding   (B) relief   (C) suffering   (D) understanding

12. blitz : attack :: maim : _____

    (A) cripple   (B) defeat   (C) truce   (D) surrender

Study the relationship between the first set of words. Pick the word that completes the second pair with this same relationship.

1. in all places at all times : omnipresent :: sees everything : _____

    (A) inspired   (B) omnipotent   (C) omniscient   (D) karma

2. affirmation : _____ :: lamentation : grief

    (A) jail   (B) deceit   (C) truth   (D) admiration

3. shy : timid :: deep in thought : _____

    (A) perplexed   (B) pensive   (C) stolid   (D) stern

4. freedom : oppression :: tolerance : _____

    (A) prejudice   (B) civility   (C) equality   (D) persistence

5. wet : moist :: dry : _____

    (A) arid   (B) irrigate   (C) deluge   (D) humid

6. scarcity : famine :: abundance : _____

    (A) deluge   (B) meager   (C) catastrophe   (D) feast

7. folly : foolishness :: foible : _____

    (A) weakness   (B) bauble   (C) strength   (D) wobble

8. extricated : released :: deluged : _____

    (A) captured   (B) flooded   (C) punished   (D) prodded

9. abundance : feast :: scarcity : _____

    (A) deluge   (B) famine   (C) catastrophe   (D) plenty

10. deluge : water :: avalanche : _____

    (A) snow   (B) mud   (C) wind   (D) cold

11. to free : emancipate :: to give something up : _____

    (A) gesticulate   (B) cajole   (C) admonish   (D) relinquish

12. interpret : decipher :: record : _____

    (A) oblivion   (B) register   (C) habit   (D) lyrics

think	unruly	cat	criticize
vegetable	resuscitate	equine	broken
fabricate	relinquish	cow	coax
feline	mourn		

Study the relationship between the first set of words. Pick one word from the word bank that completes the second pair with this same relationship.

1.	dog : canine :: cat : _____
2.	to join with another in a plot or scheme : conspire :: to revive a person who is not breathing : _____
3.	to free : emancipate :: to give something up : _____
4.	cassock : clothing :: leek : _____
5.	feline : _____ :: bovine : cow
6.	to enjoy greatly : savor :: to create : _____
7.	dog : canine :: _____ : bovine
8.	inconsolable : sad :: incorrigible : _____
9.	incorrigible : unruly :: fractured : _____
10.	to go and bring back something : fetch :: to judge harshly : _____
11.	dog : canine :: horse : _____
12.	abate : diminish :: cajole : _____
13.	cajole : coax :: ruminate : _____
14.	lament : _____ :: cajole : persuade

Study the relationship between the first set of words. Pick the word that completes the second pair with this same relationship.

1. the outer region of an area : periphery :: a narrow opening : _____

   A cavern   **B** fissure   **C** pediment   **D** trestle

2. to join with another in a plot or scheme : conspire :: to revive a person who is not breathing : _____

   A palpitate   **B** respire   **C** hallucinate   **D** resuscitate

3. dog : canine :: horse : _____

   A porcine   **B** equine   **C** feline   **D** bovine

4. abate : diminish :: cajole : _____

   A invoke   **B** increase   **C** coax   **D** vacate

5. to free : emancipate :: to give something up : _____

   A gesticulate   **B** relinquish   **C** admonish   **D** cajole

6. to enjoy greatly : savor :: to create : _____

   A fabricate   **B** distort   **C** palpitate   **D** jostle

7. inconsolable : sad :: incorrigible : _____

   A worried   **B** unruly   **C** loud   **D** frightened

8. dog : canine :: cat : _____

   A bovine   **B** lupine   **C** feline   **D** animal

9. feline : _____ :: bovine : cow

   A cat   **B** eel   **C** dog   **D** tree

10. dog : canine :: _____ : bovine

    A dog   **B** pig   **C** cow   **D** horse

11. incorrigible : unruly :: fractured : _____

    A animated   **B** broken   **C** feisty   **D** controlled

12. to go and bring back something : fetch :: to judge harshly : _____

    A gesticulate   **B** criticize   **C** oppose   **D** vouch

Name _____ LESSON 241 Date _____

Study the relationship between the first set of words. Pick the word that completes the second pair with this same relationship.

1. abate : diminish :: cajole : _____

   (A) coax   (B) increase   (C) vacate   (D) invoke

2. dog : canine :: cat : _____

   (A) bovine   (B) animal   (C) lupine   (D) feline

3. feline : _____ :: bovine : cow

   (A) dog   (B) cat   (C) tree   (D) eel

4. lament : _____ :: cajole : persuade

   (A) mourn   (B) revenge   (C) forgive   (D) forget

5. incorrigible : unruly :: fractured : _____

   (A) animated   (B) controlled   (C) broken   (D) feisty

6. cajole : coax :: ruminate : _____

   (A) mix   (B) think   (C) judge   (D) hurry

7. the outer region of an area : periphery :: a narrow opening : _____

   (A) fissure   (B) trestle   (C) pediment   (D) cavern

8. to join with another in a plot or scheme : conspire :: to revive a person who is not breathing : _____

   (A) resuscitate   (B) palpitate   (C) hallucinate   (D) respire

9. to enjoy greatly : savor :: to create : _____

   (A) fabricate   (B) palpitate   (C) distort   (D) jostle

10. cassock : clothing :: leek : _____

    (A) jewelry   (B) banner   (C) knife   (D) vegetable

11. to go and bring back something : fetch :: to judge harshly : _____

    (A) criticize   (B) vouch   (C) oppose   (D) gesticulate

12. dog : canine :: horse : _____

    (A) porcine   (B) feline   (C) equine   (D) bovine

The Sphinx	scribe	James	Pharaoh
river	mountain	African	pyramids
cuneiform	Mesopotamia	Transylvania	

Study the relationship between the first set of words. Pick one word from the word bank that completes the second pair with this same relationship.

1.	scribe : writer :: _____ : ruler
2.	mountain : land :: _____ : water
3.	peak : mountain :: _____ : valley
4.	Egypt : hieroglyphics :: Mesopotamia : _____
5.	mummy : Egypt :: vampire : _____
6.	mother : Lily :: father : _____
7.	Egypt : hieroglyphics :: _____ : cuneiform
8.	hurricane : storm :: volcano : _____
9.	hieroglyphics : Egypt :: _____ : Mesopotamia
10.	Paris : Eiffel Tower :: Egypt : _____
11.	bank robbers : bank :: tomb raiders : _____
12.	ancient Rome : Caesar :: ancient Egypt : _____
13.	ruler : Pharaoh :: writer : _____
14.	Hanukkah : Hebrew :: Kwanzaa : _____

Study the relationship between the first set of words. Pick the word that completes the second pair with this same relationship.

1. mummy : Egypt :: vampire : _____

   Ⓐ coffin   Ⓑ Pennsylvania   Ⓒ full moon   Ⓓ Transylvania

2. ruler : Pharaoh :: writer : _____

   Ⓐ amulet   Ⓑ scarab   Ⓒ papyrus   Ⓓ scribe

3. peak : mountain :: _____ : valley

   Ⓐ dream   Ⓑ river   Ⓒ ocean   Ⓓ country

4. Paris : Eiffel Tower :: Egypt : _____

   Ⓐ The Great Wall   Ⓑ Big Ben   Ⓒ The Sphinx   Ⓓ Statue of Liberty

5. Colorado : mountains :: _____ : beaches

   Ⓐ South Dakota   Ⓑ Arizona   Ⓒ Oklahoma   Ⓓ Florida

6. Egypt : hieroglyphics :: Mesopotamia : _____

   Ⓐ pharoahs   Ⓑ cuneiform   Ⓒ sanskrit   Ⓓ agriculture

7. hurricane : storm :: volcano : _____

   Ⓐ water   Ⓑ heat   Ⓒ lava   Ⓓ mountain

8. mountain : hill :: lake : _____

   Ⓐ river   Ⓑ pond   Ⓒ ocean   Ⓓ stone

9. bank robbers : bank :: tomb raiders : _____

   Ⓐ Pharaoh   Ⓑ papyrus   Ⓒ Egypt   Ⓓ pyramids

10. scribe : writer :: _____ : ruler

    Ⓐ Osiris   Ⓑ Sphinx   Ⓒ Duke   Ⓓ Pharaoh

11. mountain : land :: _____ : water

    Ⓐ ancient city   Ⓑ douse   Ⓒ river   Ⓓ dream

12. ancient Rome : Caesar :: ancient Egypt : _____

    Ⓐ Sphinx   Ⓑ Duke   Ⓒ Pharaoh   Ⓓ Osiris

vine	speech	promise	quiver
holy	proud	millennium	flee
misery	choices	put together	rude
attract			

Study the relationship between the first set of words. Pick one word from the word bank that completes the second pair with this same relationship.

1.
cover : reveal :: repel : _____

2.
take cover : hide :: run : _____

3.
command : lead :: assemble : _____

4.
oath : promise :: address : _____

5.
brave : afraid :: _____ : ashamed

6.
apples : tree :: grapes : _____

7.
better than all others : superior :: _____ : sacred

8.
to make a decision : decide :: to give your word to someone :

_____

9.
_____ : shake :: divulge : reveal

10.
frescoes : paintings :: options : _____

11.
distraught : upset :: surly : _____

12.
one hundred years : century :: one thousand years : _____

13.
fortune : luck :: misfortune : _____

14.
marquee : sign :: vow : _____

Study the relationship between the first set of words. Pick the word that completes the second pair with this same relationship.

1. surly : grumpy :: meek : _____

    (A) upset   (B) savage   (C) gentle   (D) talkative

2. unkempt : bedraggled :: upset : _____

    (A) flustered   (B) menacing   (C) enthralled   (D) skittish

3. boulevard : road :: yield : _____

    (A) drive   (B) intersection (C) yellow   (D) sign

4. resolution : a determination :: encounter : _____

    (A) an argument   (B) a meeting   (C) a choice   (D) a belief

5. distraught : upset :: surly : _____

    (A) clumsy   (B) rude   (C) devoted   (D) stubborn

6. pledge : promise :: _____ : choose

    (A) dictator   (B) elect   (C) veto   (D) empire

7. _____ : shake :: divulge : reveal

    (A) quiver   (B) turret   (C) tithe   (D) lance

8. a distinctive quality : characteristic :: an ability : _____

    (A) procedure   (B) accent   (C) vocation   (D) talent

9. respect : honor :: worship : _____

    (A) religion   (B) church   (C) faith   (D) praise

10. brave : afraid :: _____ : ashamed

    (A) confused   (B) meek   (C) proud   (D) tomorrow

11. slobber : drool :: whine : _____

    (A) wag   (B) complain   (C) flick   (D) sign

12. school : learn :: church : _____

    (A) worship   (B) teach   (C) heal   (D) love

accolades	swoon	noun
creative	render	assassinated
reputation	freedom	protect
duty	friend	unprecedented
required	luck	

Study the relationship between the first set of words. Pick one word from the word bank that completes the second pair with this same relationship.

1.	to give up : resign :: to cause to be : _____
2.	Richard Nixon : impeached :: Abraham Lincoln : _____
3.	awareness : knowledge :: responsibility : _____
4.	happens regularly : common :: has never happened before : _____
5.	principles and beliefs : philosophy :: opinion of character : _____
6.	_____ : companion :: opponent : rival
7.	_____ : keep safe :: extract : remove
8.	amended : changed :: mandated : _____
9.	allegiance : loyalty :: independence : _____
10.	mathematician : analytical :: artist : _____
11.	achievement : accomplishment :: praise : _____
12.	and : conjunction :: table : _____
13.	walk aimlessly : traipse :: faint : _____
14.	superstition : belief :: fortune : _____

Study the relationship between the first set of words. Pick the word that completes the second pair with this same relationship.

1. to give up : resign :: to cause to be : _____

   Ⓐ simulate   Ⓑ render   Ⓒ interfere   Ⓓ detect

2. _____ : knowledge :: responsibility : duty

   Ⓐ awareness   Ⓑ environment   Ⓒ conservation   Ⓓ action

3. elude : escape :: filch : _____

   Ⓐ give   Ⓑ trick   Ⓒ permit   Ⓓ steal

4. an agreement to stop fighting : _____ :: to win out over other options : prevail

   Ⓐ allowance   Ⓑ crescendo   Ⓒ chaos   Ⓓ truce

5. without giving up : relentlessly :: _____ : deliberately

   Ⓐ accidental   Ⓑ simple   Ⓒ on purpose   Ⓓ simultaneous

6. mandated : required :: traditional : _____

   Ⓐ optional   Ⓑ insulting   Ⓒ customary   Ⓓ correct

7. suspicious : doubtful :: oblivious : _____

   Ⓐ helpful   Ⓑ unaware   Ⓒ hopeful   Ⓓ surprised

8. superstition : belief :: fortune : _____

   Ⓐ chance   Ⓑ luck   Ⓒ mystery   Ⓓ festival

9. furry : hairy :: fury : _____

   Ⓐ duty   Ⓑ responsibility   Ⓒ confusion   Ⓓ anger

10. _____ : luck :: superstition : belief

    Ⓐ fortune   Ⓑ penny   Ⓒ monkey   Ⓓ chance

11. happens regularly : common :: has never happened before : _____

    Ⓐ discriminatory   Ⓑ restrained   Ⓒ unprecedented   Ⓓ galley

12. to fasten : latch :: to direct : _____

    Ⓐ guide   Ⓑ canvas   Ⓒ maintain   Ⓓ anchor

four year term	thin
creative	fairness
integration	Montgomery bus boycott
deserted	citizens
abandon	separate
equality	President

Study the relationship between the first set of words. Pick one word from the word bank that completes the second pair with this same relationship.

1.	discrimination : injustice :: equality : _____
2.	Mohandas Gandhi : civil disobedience :: Rosa Parks : _____
3.	build : construct :: leave : _____
4.	mathematician : analytical :: artist : _____
5.	_____ : abandoned :: inhabited by ghosts : haunted
6.	Senator : six year term :: _____ : four year term
7.	integration : combine] :: segregation : _____
8.	_____ : combining :: segregation : separation
9.	camouflaged : concealed :: abandoned : _____
10.	spindly : _____ :: forlorn : abandoned
11.	Frederick Douglass : freedom :: Martin Luther King, Jr. : _____
12.	senator : six year term :: president : _____
13.	nation : _____ :: Senate : Senators
14.	segregation : separation :: desegregation : _____

Study the relationship between the first set of words. Pick the word that completes the second pair with this same relationship.

1. nation : _____ :: Senate : Senators

   Ⓐ citizens   Ⓑ queen   Ⓒ president   Ⓓ legislature

2. discrimination : injustice :: equality : _____

   Ⓐ protest   Ⓑ fairness   Ⓒ segregation   Ⓓ oppression

3. Montgomery, AL : bus boycott :: Washington DC : _____

   Ⓐ Nobel Peace Prize   Ⓑ March on Washington   Ⓒ Freedom March   Ⓓ segregation

4. Mohandas Gandhi : civil disobedience :: Rosa Parks : _____

   Ⓐ segregation   Ⓑ Montgomery bus boycott   Ⓒ freedom riots   Ⓓ March on Washington

5. camouflaged : concealed :: abandoned : _____

   Ⓐ marred   Ⓑ deserted   Ⓒ enclosed   Ⓓ conceded

6. mathematician : analytical :: artist : _____

   Ⓐ conservative   Ⓑ technical   Ⓒ obscure   Ⓓ creative

7. stymied : hindered :: marooned : _____

   Ⓐ confused   Ⓑ injured   Ⓒ distracted   Ⓓ abandoned

8. build : construct :: leave : _____

   Ⓐ abandon   Ⓑ hide   Ⓒ release   Ⓓ tear down

9. spindly : _____ :: forlorn : abandoned

   Ⓐ filthy   Ⓑ thin   Ⓒ dignified   Ⓓ old

10. Frederick Douglass : freedom :: Martin Luther King, Jr. : _____

    Ⓐ segregation   Ⓑ civil disobedience   Ⓒ equality   Ⓓ racism

11. Frederick Douglass : freedom :: Martin Luther King, Jr. : _____

    Ⓐ equality   Ⓑ civil disobedience   Ⓒ segregation   Ⓓ racism

12. _____ : combining :: segregation : separation

    Ⓐ protest   Ⓑ discrimination   Ⓒ division   Ⓓ integration

Montgomery	March on Washington	gold
peninsula	Memphis, Tennessee	nation
Florida	city	Texas
Arizona	California	islands

Study the relationship between the first set of words. Pick one word from the word bank that completes the second pair with this same relationship.

1. "The Aloha State" : Hawaii :: "The Grand Canyon State" : _____

2. Yellowstone National Park : Wyoming :: Yosemite National Park :

   _____

3. _____ : Key West :: Baja California : Cabo San Lucas

4. Florida : peninsula :: Hawaii : _____

5. California : _____ :: Mexico : silver

6. Colorado : mountains :: _____ : beaches

7. Montgomery, AL : bus boycott :: Washington DC : _____

8. Colorado : state :: Chicago : _____

9. sister : family :: state : _____

10. state : Alabama :: city : _____

11. Hawaii : island :: Florida : _____

12. born : Atlanta, Georgia :: died : _____

13. Hurricane Katrina : Louisiana :: Galveston Hurricane : _____

14. _____ : Alabama :: Memphis : Tennessee

Study the relationship between the first set of words. Pick the word that completes the second pair with this same relationship.

1. Texas : Oklahoma :: _____ : Oregon

   (A) Oregon   (B) California   (C) Kentucky   (D) Mt. Whitney

2. George W. Bush : Texas :: Bill Clinton : _____

   (A) Arkansas   (B) Georgia   (C) Missouri   (D) Alabama

3. March on Washington : Washington DC :: bus boycott : _____

   (A) Montgomery,   (B) Little Rock,   (C) Atlanta,   (D) Memphis,
       Alabama   Arkansas   Georgia   Tennessee

4. California : west :: New York : _____

   (A) south   (B) north   (C) east   (D) city

5. Colorado : state :: Chicago : _____

   (A) man   (B) city   (C) continent   (D) ocean

6. state : Alabama :: city : _____

   (A) town   (B) montgomery   (C) capital   (D) Montgomery

7. Florida : peninsula :: Hawaii : _____

   (A) atoll   (B) coastal   (C) land-locked   (D) islands

8. "The Aloha State" : Hawaii :: "The Grand Canyon State" : _____

   (A) Colorado   (B) New Mexico   (C) Utah   (D) Arizona

9. sister : family :: state : _____

   (A) Delaware   (B) president   (C) nation   (D) city

10. Inuit : Alaska :: Seminole : _____

    (A) Arizona   (B) Florida   (C) South Dakota   (D) Oklahoma

11. _____ : Key West :: Baja California : Cabo San Lucas

    (A) Arizona   (B) Florida   (C) Oklahoma   (D) South Dakota

12. Birmingham : Alabama :: Harlem : _____

    (A) California   (B) New York City   (C) Massachusetts   (D) Georgia

256

Alaska	Greenland
Missouri	Massachusetts
United States of America	New York City
Wyoming	peninsula
Florida	Illinois
Tennessee	grass

Study the relationship between the first set of words. Pick one word from the word bank that completes the second pair with this same relationship.

1. Birmingham : Alabama :: Harlem : _____
2. Montgomery : Alabama :: Memphis : _____
3. Hawaii : island :: Florida : _____
4. Baton Rouge : Louisiana :: Cheyenne : _____
5. Chicago : Illinois :: Boston : _____
6. "The Garden State" : New Jersey :: "The Land of Lincoln" : _____
7. Free State : New York :: Border State : _____
8. _____ : peninsula :: Hawaii : islands
9. Honolulu : Hawaii :: Washington, D.C. : _____
10. James Cook : Hawaii :: Eric the Red : _____
11. Gettysburg : Pennsylvania :: Shiloh : _____
12. desert : sandy :: savannah : _____
13. Carson City : Nevada :: Jefferson City : _____
14. Honolulu : Hawaii :: Juneau : _____

Study the relationship between the first set of words. Pick the word that completes the second pair with this same relationship.

1. New York City : Eastern Standard Time :: Chicago : _____

    (A) Central Standard Time   (B) Illinois   (C) Pacific Standard Time   (D) Mountain Standard Time

2. Free State : New York :: Border State : _____

    (A) Missouri   (B) Georgia   (C) South Carolina   (D) New Hampshire

3. Carson City : Nevada :: Jefferson City : _____

    (A) Missouri   (B) Montana   (C) Nebraska   (D) Illinois

4. Boise : Idaho :: Carson City : _____

    (A) Arizona   (B) Nevada   (C) California   (D) New Mexico

5. Birmingham : Alabama :: Harlem : _____

    (A) Massachusetts   (B) California   (C) Georgia   (D) New York City

6. smallest state : Rhode Island :: largest state : _____

    (A) Idaho   (B) Hawaii   (C) California   (D) Alaska

7. Honolulu : Hawaii :: Washington, D.C. : _____

    (A) Canada   (B) United States of America   (C) New York   (D) Maryland

8. Gettysburg : Pennsylvania :: Shiloh : _____

    (A) Virginia   (B) Missouri   (C) Tennessee   (D) Georgia

9. Hawaii : island :: Florida : _____

    (A) valley   (B) gulf   (C) island   (D) peninsula

10. Montgomery : Alabama :: Memphis : _____

    (A) Arkansas   (B) Georgia   (C) Tennessee   (D) Mississippi

11. "The Garden State" : New Jersey :: "The Land of Lincoln" : _____

    (A) Nebraska   (B) Pennsylvania   (C) Missouri   (D) Illinois

12. James Cook : Hawaii :: Eric the Red : _____

    (A) Antarctica   (B) Greenland   (C) Africa   (D) India

Amazon	Baja California
North Carolina	Tennessee
United States of America	Massachusetts
Louisiana	Texas
Oregon	New York City
California	

Study the relationship between the first set of words. Pick one word from the word bank that completes the second pair with this same relationship.

1.	Montgomery : Alabama :: Memphis : _____
2.	Indianapolis : Indiana :: Salem : _____
3.	Pacific Ocean : Oregon :: Atlantic Ocean : _____
4.	Rio Grande River : Texas :: Mississippi River : _____
5.	Gulf of Mexico : Texas :: Gulf of California : _____
6.	Yellowstone National Park : Wyoming :: Yosemite National Park : _____
7.	Baton Rouge : _____ :: Cheyenne : Wyoming
8.	Birmingham : Alabama :: Harlem : _____
9.	Chicago : Illinois :: Boston : _____
10.	Honolulu : Hawaii :: Washington, D.C. : _____
11.	Egypt : Nile :: Brazil : _____
12.	Texas : Oklahoma :: California : _____
13.	Abraham Lincoln : Illinois :: John F. Kennedy : _____
14.	Hurricane Katrina : Louisiana :: Galveston Hurricane : _____

259

Name _____   **LESSON 255**   Date _____

Study the relationship between the first set of words. Pick the word that completes the second pair with this same relationship.

1. Egypt : Nile :: Brazil : _____

    Ⓐ Amazon   Ⓑ Tiber   Ⓒ Yangtze   Ⓓ Mississippi

2. Gulf of Mexico : Texas :: Gulf of California : _____

    Ⓐ Louisiana   Ⓑ Baja California   Ⓒ Yucatan   Ⓓ Florida

3. Chicago : Illinois :: Boston : _____

    Ⓐ Ohio   Ⓑ Maine   Ⓒ New York   Ⓓ Massachusetts

4. Abraham Lincoln : Illinois :: John F. Kennedy : _____

    Ⓐ New York   Ⓑ Ohio   Ⓒ Massachusetts   Ⓓ California

5. Texas : Oklahoma :: California : _____

    Ⓐ Arkansas   Ⓑ Maine   Ⓒ Oregon   Ⓓ Colorado

6. Yellowstone National Park : Wyoming :: Yosemite National Park : _____

    Ⓐ California   Ⓑ Kentucky   Ⓒ Ohio   Ⓓ Oregon

7. Montgomery : Alabama :: Memphis : _____

    Ⓐ Mississippi   Ⓑ Georgia   Ⓒ Arkansas   Ⓓ Tennessee

8. Baton Rouge : _____ :: Cheyenne : Wyoming

    Ⓐ Wyoming   Ⓑ Louisiana   Ⓒ Ohio   Ⓓ Florida

9. Rio Grande River : Texas :: Mississippi River : _____

    Ⓐ Wyoming   Ⓑ Louisiana   Ⓒ Florida   Ⓓ Ohio

10. Pacific Ocean : Oregon :: Atlantic Ocean : _____

    Ⓐ North Carolina   Ⓑ Texas   Ⓒ Michigan   Ⓓ California

11. Birmingham : Alabama :: Harlem : _____

    Ⓐ New York City   Ⓑ Georgia   Ⓒ Massachusetts   Ⓓ California

12. _____ : TN :: Kentucky : KY

    Ⓐ Mississippi   Ⓑ Virginia   Ⓒ Tennessee   Ⓓ Arkansas

president	Virginia	Alaska
Illinois	Wyoming	Pacific Ocean
Missouri	Mexico City	Massachusetts
Atlantic Ocean	North Carolina	Nevada
Tennessee		

Study the relationship between the first set of words. Pick one word from the word bank that completes the second pair with this same relationship.

1.
   Boise : Idaho :: Carson City : _____

2.
   Honolulu : Hawaii :: Juneau : _____

3.
   Chicago : Illinois :: Boston : _____

4.
   Pacific Ocean : Oregon :: Atlantic Ocean : _____

5.
   Gettysburg : Pennsylvania :: Shiloh : _____

6.
   North Carolina : _____ :: California : Pacific Ocean

7.
   Free State : New York :: Border State : _____

8.
   Carson City : Nevada :: Jefferson City : _____

9.
   North Carolina : Atlantic Ocean :: California : _____

10.
    New Mexico : USA :: Coolidge : _____

11.
    "The Garden State" : New Jersey :: "The Land of Lincoln" : _____

12.
    Pearl Harbor : Hawaii :: Arlington : _____

13.
    New York : New Amsterdam :: _____ : Tenochtitlan

14.
    Baton Rouge : Louisiana :: Cheyenne : _____

Name _____   LESSON 257   Date _____

Study the relationship between the first set of words. Pick the word that completes the second pair with this same relationship.

1. "The Garden State" : New Jersey :: "The Land of Lincoln" : _____

   Ⓐ Illinois   Ⓑ Nebraska   Ⓒ Pennsylvania   Ⓓ Missouri

2. Free State : New York :: Border State : _____

   Ⓐ New Hampshire Ⓑ Missouri   Ⓒ Georgia   Ⓓ South Carolina

3. New Mexico : USA :: Coolidge : _____

   Ⓐ president   Ⓑ state   Ⓒ refrigerator   Ⓓ country

4. North Carolina : Atlantic Ocean :: California : _____

   Ⓐ Indian Ocean   Ⓑ Pacific Ocean   Ⓒ Arctic Ocean   Ⓓ Red Sea

5. Carson City : Nevada :: Jefferson City : _____

   Ⓐ South Carolina Ⓑ Georgia   Ⓒ Montana   Ⓓ Missouri

6. Honolulu : Hawaii :: Washington, D.C. : _____

   Ⓐ Maryland   Ⓑ New York   Ⓒ Canada   Ⓓ United States of America

7. Gettysburg : Pennsylvania :: Shiloh : _____

   Ⓐ Georgia   Ⓑ Tennessee   Ⓒ Virginia   Ⓓ Missouri

8. New York : New Amsterdam :: _____ : Tenochtitlan

   Ⓐ Albuquerque   Ⓑ Baja California Ⓒ Tijuana   Ⓓ Mexico City

9. Baton Rouge : Louisiana :: Cheyenne : _____

   Ⓐ Kansas   Ⓑ Wyoming   Ⓒ Idaho   Ⓓ Nebraska

10. South Dakota : Pierre :: North Dakota : _____

    Ⓐ Ontario   Ⓑ Jean-Luc   Ⓒ Bismarck   Ⓓ borders

11. Abraham Lincoln : Illinois :: John F. Kennedy : _____

    Ⓐ New York   Ⓑ Ohio   Ⓒ California   Ⓓ Massachusetts

12. George W. Bush : Texas :: Bill Clinton : _____

    Ⓐ Missouri   Ⓑ Arkansas   Ⓒ Georgia   Ⓓ Alabama

Louisiana	Massachusetts	Missouri
Pacific Ocean	Florida	Bismarck
Transylvania	Tennessee	Alaska
Lincoln	Illinois	California
Virginia		

Study the relationship between the first set of words. Pick one word from the word bank that completes the second pair with this same relationship.

1.
Rio Grande River : Texas :: Mississippi River : _____

2.
South Dakota : Pierre :: North Dakota : _____

3.
Free State : New York :: Border State : _____

4.
cherry tree : Washington :: honesty : _____

5.
Yellowstone National Park : Wyoming :: Yosemite National Park : _____

6.
smallest state : Rhode Island :: largest state : _____

7.
Pearl Harbor : Hawaii :: Arlington : _____

8.
_____ : Oregon :: Atlantic Ocean : North Carolina

9.
"The Garden State" : New Jersey :: "The Land of Lincoln" : _____

10.
Texas : Oklahoma :: _____ : Oregon

11.
Abraham Lincoln : Illinois :: John F. Kennedy : _____

12.
Gettysburg : Pennsylvania :: Shiloh : _____

13.
mummy : Egypt :: vampire : _____

14.
Inuit : Alaska :: Seminole : _____

Study the relationship between the first set of words. Pick the word that completes the second pair with this same relationship.

1. mummy : Egypt :: vampire : _____

   Ⓐ coffin   Ⓑ Transylvania   Ⓒ full moon   Ⓓ Pennsylvania

2. Inuit : Alaska :: Seminole : _____

   Ⓐ South Dakota   Ⓑ Arizona   Ⓒ Oklahoma   Ⓓ Florida

3. cherry tree : Washington :: honesty : _____

   Ⓐ trustworthy   Ⓑ Lincoln   Ⓒ dishonesty   Ⓓ Oregon

4. Texas : Oklahoma :: _____ : Oregon

   Ⓐ Quebec   Ⓑ Kentucky   Ⓒ Mt. Whitney   Ⓓ California

5. Abraham Lincoln : Illinois :: John F. Kennedy : _____

   Ⓐ Massachusetts   Ⓑ California   Ⓒ Ohio   Ⓓ New York

6. "The Garden State" : New Jersey :: "The Land of Lincoln" : _____

   Ⓐ Nebraska   Ⓑ Missouri   Ⓒ Illinois   Ⓓ Pennsylvania

7. _____ : Oregon :: Atlantic Ocean : North Carolina

   Ⓐ Atlantic Ocean   Ⓑ Red Sea   Ⓒ Pacific Ocean   Ⓓ Southern Ocean

8. Pearl Harbor : Hawaii :: Arlington : _____

   Ⓐ Pennsylvania   Ⓑ Florida   Ⓒ Virginia   Ⓓ New York

9. Yellowstone National Park : Wyoming :: Yosemite National Park : _____

   Ⓐ Kentucky   Ⓑ Oregon   Ⓒ Ohio   Ⓓ California

10. Free State : New York :: Border State : _____

    Ⓐ South Carolina   Ⓑ Georgia   Ⓒ New Hampshire   Ⓓ Missouri

11. South Dakota : Pierre :: North Dakota : _____

    Ⓐ borders   Ⓑ Jean-Luc   Ⓒ Ontario   Ⓓ Bismarck

12. Gettysburg : Pennsylvania :: Shiloh : _____

    Ⓐ Virginia   Ⓑ Missouri   Ⓒ Georgia   Ⓓ Tennessee

Virginia	United States of America
Bismarck	Arizona
country	Florida
Louisiana	Alaska
Oregon	California
Salt Lake City	Tennessee

Study the relationship between the first set of words. Pick one word from the word bank that completes the second pair with this same relationship.

1.
South Dakota : Pierre :: North Dakota : _____

2.
Honolulu : Hawaii :: Juneau : _____

3.
Gettysburg : Pennsylvania :: Shiloh : _____

4.
Inuit : Alaska :: Seminole : _____

5.
Yellowstone National Park : Wyoming :: Yosemite National Park :

_____

6.
Utah : _____ :: Missouri : Jefferson City

7.
Indianapolis : Indiana :: Salem : _____

8.
Rio Grande River : Texas :: Mississippi River : _____

9.
colonies : England :: states : _____

10.
Texas : state :: America : _____

11.
Baton Rouge : _____ :: Cheyenne : Wyoming

12.
Pearl Harbor : Hawaii :: Arlington : _____

13.
Montgomery : Alabama :: Memphis : _____

14.
"The Aloha State" : Hawaii :: "The Grand Canyon State" : _____

Name _____ LESSON 261 Date _____

Study the relationship between the first set of words. Pick the word that completes the second pair with this same relationship.

1. South Dakota : Pierre :: North Dakota : _____

   Ⓐ Ontario   Ⓑ borders   Ⓒ Bismarck   Ⓓ Jean-Luc

2. Gettysburg : Pennsylvania :: Shiloh : _____

   Ⓐ Virginia   Ⓑ Georgia   Ⓒ Missouri   Ⓓ Tennessee

3. Pearl Harbor : Hawaii :: Arlington : _____

   Ⓐ New York   Ⓑ Florida   Ⓒ Virginia   Ⓓ Pennsylvania

4. Mount Rushmore : South Dakota :: Lincoln Memorial : _____

   Ⓐ Washington, DC   Ⓑ Chicago, IL   Ⓒ New York City, NY   Ⓓ Philadelphia, PA

5. Inuit : Alaska :: Seminole : _____

   Ⓐ Florida   Ⓑ Oklahoma   Ⓒ South Dakota   Ⓓ Arizona

6. Gulf of Mexico : _____ :: Gulf of California : Baja California

   Ⓐ Alabama   Ⓑ Florida   Ⓒ Mississippi   Ⓓ Texas

7. Montgomery : Alabama :: Memphis : _____

   Ⓐ Arkansas   Ⓑ Missouri   Ⓒ Tennessee   Ⓓ Virginia

8. _____ : Sacramento :: Utah : Salt Lake City

   Ⓐ Quebec   Ⓑ Ohio   Ⓒ California   Ⓓ Mississippi River

9. colonies : England :: states : _____

   Ⓐ Virginia   Ⓑ United States of America   Ⓒ King George   Ⓓ president

10. Utah : _____ :: Missouri : Jefferson City

    Ⓐ Salt Lake City Ⓑ Moab   Ⓒ Austin   Ⓓ Denver

11. cherry tree : Washington :: honesty : _____

    Ⓐ dishonesty   Ⓑ Lincoln   Ⓒ trustworthy   Ⓓ Oregon

12. Indianapolis : Indiana :: Salem : _____

    Ⓐ Virginia   Ⓑ Oregon   Ⓒ Massachusetts   Ⓓ USA

Study the relationship between the first set of words. Pick the word that completes the second pair with this same relationship.

1. dismal : gloomy :: ample : _____

    A plentiful   **B** impressive   **C** innovative   **D** sturdy

2. stodgy : boring :: garish : _____

    A flashy   **B** courageous   **C** gruesome   **D** impressive

3. national : global :: _____ : celestial

    A astronomical   **B** ethereal   **C** terrestrial   **D** gravitational

4. podium : platform :: spigot : _____

    A knob   **B** rail   **C** faucet   **D** shelf

5. erroneous : mistaken :: imperative : _____

    A required   **B** impressive   **C** honorable   **D** professional

6. something that cannot be seen : invisible :: something that cannot be taken away : _____

    A impressive   **B** irrevocable   **C** untoward   . indeterminable

7. conspire : plot :: consolidate : _____

    A cover   **B** trick   **C** squeeze   **D** combine

8. rostrum : podium :: oration : _____

    A interment   **B** speech   **C** movie   **D** confer

9. supplies : provisions :: pioneers : _____

    A charters   **B** settlers   **C** initiatives   **D** rations

10. deplorable : _____ :: imposing : impressive

    A confusing   **B** terrible   **C** fortunate   **D** great

11. joust : tournament :: peddler : _____

    A merchant   **B** poet   **C** farmer   **D** warrior

12. pioneers : settlers :: annoying animals : _____

    A citizens   **B** varmints   **C** pets   **D** traders

Study the relationship between the first set of words. Pick the word that completes the second pair with this same relationship.

1. national : global :: _____ : celestial

   Ⓐ astronomical   Ⓑ ethereal   Ⓒ terrestrial   Ⓓ gravitational

2. dismal : gloomy :: ample : _____

   Ⓐ plentiful   . innovative   Ⓒ sturdy   Ⓓ impressive

3. deplorable : _____ :: imposing : impressive

   Ⓐ confusing   Ⓑ great   Ⓒ fortunate   Ⓓ terrible

4. something that cannot be seen : invisible :: something that cannot be taken away : _____

   Ⓐ indeterminable   Ⓑ untoward   Ⓒ impressive   Ⓓ irrevocable

5. melody : _____ :: headline : newspaper

   Ⓐ book   Ⓑ minister   Ⓒ bells   Ⓓ song

6. podium : platform :: spigot : _____

   Ⓐ rail   Ⓑ faucet   Ⓒ shelf   Ⓓ knob

7. prestigious : impressive :: ominous : _____

   Ⓐ boring   Ⓑ beautiful   Ⓒ menacing   Ⓓ doubtful

8. supplies : provisions :: pioneers : _____

   Ⓐ settlers   Ⓑ rations   Ⓒ initiatives   Ⓓ charters

9. conspire : plot :: consolidate : _____

   Ⓐ cover   Ⓑ combine   Ⓒ trick   Ⓓ squeeze

10. joust : tournament :: peddler : _____

    Ⓐ merchant   Ⓑ farmer   . warrior   Ⓓ poet

11. pioneers : settlers :: annoying animals : _____

    Ⓐ traders   Ⓑ varmints   Ⓒ pets   Ⓓ citizens

12. mouse : computer :: speaker : _____

    Ⓐ stereo   . podium   Ⓒ platform   Ⓓ kaleidoscope

Name _____   LESSON 264   Date _____

Study the relationship between the first set of words. Pick the word that completes the second pair with this same relationship.

1. conspire : plot :: consolidate : _____

   Ⓐ combine   . cover   Ⓒ trick   . squeeze

2. rostrum : podium :: oration : _____

   Ⓐ movie   Ⓑ interment   Ⓒ confer   Ⓓ speech

3. pioneers : settlers :: annoying animals : _____

   Ⓐ citizens   Ⓑ varmints   Ⓒ pets   Ⓓ traders

4. erroneous : mistaken :: imperative : _____

   Ⓐ impressive   Ⓑ required   Ⓒ professional   Ⓓ honorable

5. podium : platform :: spigot : _____

   Ⓐ rail   Ⓑ knob   Ⓒ shelf   Ⓓ faucet

6. dismal : gloomy :: ample : _____

   Ⓐ plentiful   Ⓑ sturdy   Ⓒ impressive   Ⓓ innovative

7. joust : tournament :: peddler : _____

   Ⓐ warrior   Ⓑ poet   Ⓒ merchant   Ⓓ farmer

8. prestigious : impressive :: ominous : _____

   . doubtful   Ⓑ boring   . beautiful   Ⓓ menacing

9. supplies : provisions :: pioneers : _____

   Ⓐ rations   Ⓑ settlers   Ⓒ charters   Ⓓ initiatives

10. something that cannot be seen : invisible :: something that cannot be taken away : _____

    Ⓐ impressive   Ⓑ irrevocable   Ⓒ untoward   Ⓓ indeterminable

11. melody : _____ :: headline : newspaper

    Ⓐ song   Ⓑ minister   Ⓒ book   Ⓓ bells

12. merciless : cruel :: vile : _____

    Ⓐ repulsive   Ⓑ dangerous   Ⓒ impressive   Ⓓ kind

impressive	newspaper	speech
disappointing	stereo	supplies
crazy	terrestrial	combine
menacing	irrevocable	faucet
required	varmints	

Study the relationship between the first set of words. Pick one word from the word bank that completes the second pair with this same relationship.

1. charmed : lucky :: insane : _____

2. national : global :: _____ : celestial

3. mouse : computer :: speaker : _____

4. _____ : provisions :: pioneers : settlers

5. pioneers : settlers :: annoying animals : _____

6. erroneous : mistaken :: imperative : _____

7. rostrum : podium :: oration : _____

8. conspire : plot :: consolidate : _____

9. inconspicuous : suspicious :: satisfactory : _____

10. prestigious : impressive :: ominous : _____

11. something that cannot be seen : invisible :: something that cannot be taken away :

_____

12. podium : platform :: spigot : _____

13. melody : song :: headline : _____

14. deplorable : terrible :: imposing : _____

terrestrial	stereo	disappointing
varmints	merchant	newspaper
faucet	plentiful	irrevocable
impressive	required	crazy
supplies	menacing	

Study the relationship between the first set of words. Pick one word from the word bank that completes the second pair with this same relationship.

1. inconspicuous : suspicious :: satisfactory : _____

2. melody : song :: headline : _____

3. deplorable : terrible :: imposing : _____

4. something that cannot be seen : invisible :: something that cannot be taken away : _____

5. mouse : computer :: speaker : _____

6. prestigious : impressive :: ominous : _____

7. podium : platform :: spigot : _____

8. charmed : lucky :: insane : _____

9. joust : tournament :: peddler : _____

10. pioneers : settlers :: annoying animals : _____

11. erroneous : mistaken :: imperative : _____

12. _____ : provisions :: pioneers : settlers

13. dismal : gloomy :: ample : _____

14. national : global :: _____ : celestial

menacing	impressive	combine
varmints	irrevocable	faucet
supplies	speech	disappointing
newspaper	required	merchant
crazy	stereo	

Study the relationship between the first set of words. Pick one word from the word bank that completes the second pair with this same relationship.

1.
conspire : plot :: consolidate : _____

2.
inconspicuous : suspicious :: satisfactory : _____

3.
pioneers : settlers :: annoying animals : _____

4.
something that cannot be seen : invisible :: something that cannot be taken away :

_____

5.
deplorable : terrible :: imposing : _____

6.
rostrum : podium :: oration : _____

7.
_____ : provisions :: pioneers : settlers

8.
podium : platform :: spigot : _____

9.
charmed : lucky :: insane : _____

10.   mouse : computer :: speaker : _____

11.
erroneous : mistaken :: imperative : _____

12.
melody : song :: headline : _____

13.
prestigious : impressive :: ominous : _____

14.
joust : tournament :: peddler : _____

Study the relationship between the first set of words. Pick the word that completes the second pair with this same relationship.

1. dental assistant : dentist :: nurse : _____

   (A) doctor   (B) patient   (C) emergency room (D) shot

2. dentist : teeth :: doctor : _____

   . brain   (B) medicine   (C) body   (D) pet

3. Physicians : dermatologist :: Geologists : _____

   (A) zoologist   (B) chemist   (C) volcanologist   (D) anatomist

4. a doctor who treats children : pediatrician :: a doctor who treats people with cancer : _____

   (A) oncologist   (B) cardiologist   (C) neurologist   . surgeon

5. Madre : mother :: padre : _____

   (A) father   (B) doctor   (C) teacher   (D) dentist

6. teeth cleaning : dentist :: haircut : _____

   (A) carpenter   (B) barber   (C) tailor   (D) physician

7. doctor : _____ :: dentist : teeth

   . body   (B) brain   (C) medicine   . pet

8. classroom : teacher :: doctor : _____

   (A) hospital   (B) dentist   (C) patient   (D) nurse

9. broken bone : _____ :: cavity : dentist

   (A) doctor   (B) patient   (C) instructor   (D) farmer

10. glasses : eyes :: braces : _____

   (A) dentist   (B) silver   (C) girls   (D) teeth

Study the relationship between the first set of words. Pick the word that completes the second pair with this same relationship.

1. dental assistant : dentist :: nurse : _____

    doctor   **B** patient   **C** emergency room   **D** shot

2. dentist : teeth :: doctor : _____

    A brain   **B** medicine   **C** body   **D** pet

3. Physicians : dermatologist :: Geologists : _____

    A zoologist   **B** chemist   **C** volcanologist   **D** anatomist

4. a doctor who treats children : pediatrician :: a doctor who treats people with cancer : _____

    A oncologist   **B** cardiologist   **C** neurologist   **D** surgeon

5. madre : mother :: padre : _____

    A father   **B** doctor   **C** teacher   **D** dentist

6. teeth cleaning : dentist :: haircut : _____

    A carpenter   **B** barber   **C** tailor   **D** physician

7. doctor : _____ :: dentist : teeth

    A body   **B** brain   **C** medicine   **D** pet

8. classroom : teacher :: doctor : _____

    A hospital   **B** dentist   **C** patient   **D** nurse

9. broken bone : _____ :: cavity : dentist

    doctor   **B** patient   instructor   **D** farmer

10. glasses : eyes :: braces : _____

    A dentist   **B** silver   **C** girls   **D** teeth

Name _____   LESSON 270   Date _____

Study the relationship between the first set of words. Pick the word that completes the second pair with this same relationship.

1. canine : dog :: cat : _____

    (A) animal   (B) area   (C) feline   (D) ecology

2. Banker : _____ :: Chemist : chemicals

    (A) book   (B) children   (C) home   (D) money

3. goggles : chemicals :: ozone : _____

    (A) ecology   (B) radiation   (C) atmosphere   (D) pollution

4. Physicians : dermatologist :: Geologists : _____

    (A) vulcanologist   (B) anatomist   (C) zoologist   (D) chemist

5. geology : the earth and rocks :: _____ : interactions between organisms and the environment

    (A) ecology   (B) botany   (C) chemistry   (D) biology

6. Johannes Kepler : astronomer :: William Shakespeare : _____

    (A) inventor   (B) explorer   (C) musician   (D) playwright

7. psychology : mind :: ecology : _____

    (A) pollution   (B) science   (C) environment   (D) psychiatry

8. humans : physician :: animals : _____

    (A) veterinarian   (B) equestrian   (C) biologist   (D) mammalian

9. Aristarchus : astronomer :: _____ : philosopher

    (A) Pericles   (B) Socrates   (C) Aristotle   (D) Alexander the Great

10. zoology : animals :: ecology : _____

    (A) environment   (B) plants   (C) space   (D) science

11. paleontologist : fossils :: herpetologist : _____

    . birds   (B) time   (C) humans   (D) reptiles

12. psychology : mind :: ecology : _____

    (A) pollution   (B) environment   (C) science   (D) anatomy

dentist	hospital	barber
volcanologist	father	teeth
body	oncologist	doctor

Study the relationship between the first set of words. Pick one word from the word bank that completes the second pair with this same relationship.

1.	broken bone : _____ :: cavity : dentist
2.	glasses : eyes :: braces : _____
3.	a doctor who treats children : pediatrician :: a doctor who treats people with cancer : _____
4.	dentist : teeth :: doctor : _____
5.	teeth cleaning : dentist :: haircut : _____
6.	dental assistant : dentist :: nurse : _____
7.	Madre : mother :: padre : _____
8.	Physicians : dermatologist :: Geologists : _____
9.	doctor : body :: _____ : teeth
10.	classroom : teacher :: doctor : _____

Select the definition that most nearly defines the given word.

1. **Thoracic Surgeon**
  (A) A specialist in treating heart disorders
  (B) Deals with chest and lung surgery
  (C) Infants doctor
	2. **Neonatologist**
	  (A) Infants doctor
	  (B) Deals with digestive system problems
	  (C) Deals with problems of the elderly

3. **Dentist**
  (A) A doctor who treats people's teeth.
  (B) An eye care professional who is specially trained in a school of optometry
  (C) Kidney doctor
	4. **Cardiologist**
	  (A) One who 'puts you out' for surgery and who monitors the patient's vitals.
	  (B) Deals with mental health
	  (C) Deals with heart diseases

5. **Pediatrician**
  (A) Deals with the problems of brain and nerves
  (B) A specialist in the care of babies.
  (C) Deals with bladder
	6. **Gastrologist**
	  (A) Deals with bone and joint surgery
	  (B) Deals with digestive system problems
	  (C) Medical doctor specializing in children's health

7. **Endocrinologist**
  (A) Cancer doctor
  (B) A specialist in cardiology; a specialist in the structure and function and disorders of the heart.
  (C) Physician who specializes in the diagnosis and treatment of conditions affecting the endocrine system.
	8. **Allergist or Immunologist**
	  (A) Deals with eye problems
	  (B) Diagnoses and treats illnesses and problems related to the immune systems. He treats asthma, allergies, insect bites and stings, etc.
	  (C) doctor who specializes in nervous system diseases

9. **Pathology**
  (A) A doctor who specializes in pregnancy and birth.
  (B) A specialist who administers an anesthetic to a patient before he is treated.
  (C) Scientific and medical study of a disease, its causes, processes and effects,
	10. **Dermatologist**
	  (A) Deals with treatment of arthritis and other diseases of the joints, muscles and bones
	  (B) A doctor who specializes in the physiology and pathology of the skin.
	  (C) Deals with ear, nose and throat surgery

11. **Podiatrist**
  (A) A doctor who cares for the feet.
  (B) Deals with pregnancy and childbirth
  (C) A specialist in cancer disease.
	12. **Psychiatrist**
	  (A) Deals with mental health
	  (B) Foot doctor
	  (C) A specialist in urology.

13. **Obstetrician**
    - (A) A doctor who treats mental, emotional, and behavioral disorders of the mind.
    - (B) A doctor who specializes in pregnancy and birth.
    - (C) One who studies the nature and effects of poisons and their treatment.

14. **Optometrist**
    - (A) Deals with the eyes and eye surgery
    - (B) Deals with the problems of thyroid and other ductless glands
    - (C) A person skilled in testing for defects of vision in order to prescribe corrective glasses.

15. **Toxicologist**
    - (A) A physician specializing in the treatment of burns, breast augmentations, face lifts, etc.
    - (B) Examines regular patients, whole families, sees you for referrals to specialists.
    - (C) One who studies the nature and effects of poisons and their treatment.

16. **Geriatrics Specialist**
    - (A) doctor who specializes in nervous system diseases
    - (B) Deals with problems of the elderly
    - (C) Diagnoses and treats illnesses and problems related to the immune systems. He treats asthma, allergies, insect bites and stings, etc.

17. **Ophthalmologist**
    - (A) Doctor specializing in diagnosing and treating disorder with the skin
    - (B) A physician who specializes in psychiatry.
    - (C) Deals with the eyes and eye surgery

18. **Oncologist**
    - (A) A doctor that studies the urinary system
    - (B) Treats diseases and disorders of the kidneys
    - (C) A specialist in cancer disease.

19. **Nephrologist**
    - (A) A physician specializing in rheumatic diseases.
    - (B) Treats diseases and disorders of the kidneys
    - (C) A specialist in urology.

20. **General Practitioner**
    - (A) Deals with digestive system problems
    - (B) Deals with skin problems
    - (C) Examines regular patients, whole families, sees you for referrals to specialists.

21. **Urologist**
    - (A) A doctor who specializes in pregnancy and birth.
    - (B) Tooth doctor
    - (C) Deals with bladder

22. **Emergency Medicine Doctor**
    - (A) Deals with skin problems
    - (B) - Responds to many medical conditions.
    - (C) The branch of medical science that studies the causes and nature and effects of diseases.

23. **Neurologist**
   A. Deals with problems of the elderly
   B. Deals with the problems of brain and nerves
   C. Deals with bone and joint surgery

24. **Rheumatologist**
   A. A physician specializing in rheumatic diseases.
   B. A doctor who specializes in the physiology and pathology of the skin.
   C. Infants doctor

25. **Anesthesiologist**
   A. Diagnoses and treats illnesses and problems related to sports.
   B. Deals with eye problems
   C. One who 'puts you out' for surgery and who monitors the patient's vitals.

26. **Cosmetic surgeon**
   A. Deals with pregnancy and childbirth
   B. A specialist in cancer disease.
   C. A physician specializing in the treatment of burns, breast augmentations, face lifts, etc.

27. **Orthopedics Specialist**
   A. A doctor that studies the urinary system
   B. The branch of medical science that studies the causes and nature and effects of diseases.
   C. Deals with bone and joint surgery

28. **Sports medicine**
   A. Deals with heart diseases
   B. A physician who specializes in medical and surgical care and treatment of the eyes
   C. Diagnoses and treats illnesses and problems related to sports.

29. **Ecologist**
   A. A biologist who studies the relation between organisms and their environment.
   B. A scientist who studies living organisms.
   C. A scientist who studies the earth.

30. **Biologist**
   A. A person who studies, takes care of and classify animals.
   B. A scientist who studies what substances are made of.
   C. A scientist who studies living organisms.

31. **Geologist**
   A. A scientist who studies the earth.
   B. A physicist who studies astronomy.
   C. Designs and builds body parts and devices.

32. **Zoologist**
   A. A biologist who studies the relation between organisms and their environment.
   B. A scientist who studies what substances are made of.
   C. A specialist in the branch of biology dealing with animals.

33. **Geneticist**
   A. A person who studies, takes care of and classify animals.
   B. A health professional trained in the art of preparing and dispensing drugs.
   C. A biologist who specializes in genetics.

34. **Chemist**
   A. A person who studies, takes care of and classify animals.
   B. A biologist who specializes in genetics.
   C. A scientist who specializes in chemistry.

35. **Paleontologist** (A) A physicist who studies astronomy. (B) A scientist who studies living organisms. (C) A scientist who studies fossils and the past.	36. **Mechanical Engineer** (A) A biologist specializing in the study of plants. (B) Designs and builds body parts and devices. (C) A person responsible for designing, developing, testing, and bringing to production machines and their parts
37. **Botanist** (A) A physicist who studies astronomy. (B) A health professional trained in the art of preparing and dispensing drugs. (C) A biologist specializing in the study of plants.	38. **Biomedical Engineer** (A) Designs and builds body parts and devices. (B) A biologist specializing in the study of plants. (C) A person responsible for designing, developing, testing, and bringing to production machines and their parts

Study the relationship between the first set of words. Pick the word that completes the second pair with this same relationship.

1.   commence : begin :: converge : _____

  Ⓐ correct   Ⓑ end   Ⓒ spread apart   Ⓓ come together

2.   _____ : diving :: ice : curling

  Ⓐ water   Ⓑ blankets   Ⓒ deserts   Ⓓ bullets

3.   line : cast :: _____ : snag

  Ⓐ play   Ⓑ rod   Ⓒ hook   Ⓓ fishing

4.   want : crave :: stop : _____

  Ⓐ start   Ⓑ begin   Ⓒ quit   Ⓓ listen

5.   majestic : grand :: virtuous : _____

  Ⓐ good   Ⓑ confident   Ⓒ gruff   Ⓓ talented

6.   advance : move forward :: protrude : _____

  Ⓐ dive   . stay behind   Ⓒ stick out   Ⓓ circle around

7.   bear : hibernation :: goose : _____

  Ⓐ transition   Ⓑ transportation   Ⓒ migration   Ⓓ globalization

8.   values : beliefs :: virtue : _____

  Ⓐ angry   Ⓑ good   Ⓒ character   Ⓓ immoral

9.   diving : water :: spelunking : _____

  Ⓐ volcanoes   . deserts   Ⓒ caves   Ⓓ sky

10. good : bad :: _____ : horrible

  Ⓐ confused   Ⓑ small   Ⓒ sad   Ⓓ wonderful

11. asleep : awake :: little : _____

  Ⓐ night   Ⓑ pillow   Ⓒ small   Ⓓ big

12. elite : best :: majority : _____

  Ⓐ most   Ⓑ fewest   Ⓒ average   Ⓓ strongest

281

13. _____ : deny :: permit : forbid

 Ⓐ accept Ⓑ return Ⓒ refuse Ⓓ judge

14. milk : cold :: hot chocolate : _____

 Ⓐ good Ⓑ cup Ⓒ hot Ⓓ winter

15. cast : broken bone :: stitches : _____

 Ⓐ cover Ⓑ brown Ⓒ cut Ⓓ bruise

16 advance : move forward :: protrude : _____

 Ⓐ stick out Ⓑ stay behind Ⓒ circle around Ⓓ dive

17. tired : drowsy :: frantic : _____

 Ⓐ awake Ⓑ calm Ⓒ sad Ⓓ worried

18. _____ : excellent :: funny : hilarious

 Ⓐ good Ⓑ talented Ⓒ confident Ⓓ gruff

19. _____ : love :: bad : hate

 Ⓐ talented Ⓑ gruff Ⓒ good Ⓓ confident

20. cut : stitches :: broken bone : _____

 Ⓐ cast Ⓑ bandages Ⓒ skin Ⓓ crutches

21. immigrate : to move to another country :: _____ : to run away

 Ⓐ clue Ⓑ flee Ⓒ track Ⓓ appear

22. commence : begin :: tolerate : _____

 Ⓐ judge Ⓑ end Ⓒ accept Ⓓ charity

23. cave : _____ :: den : wolf

 Ⓐ bear Ⓑ squirrel Ⓒ Chicago Ⓓ dog

24. negotiate : deal :: solicit : _____

 Ⓐ demand Ⓑ release Ⓒ assign Ⓓ ask

25 allow : permit :: forbid : _____

 Ⓐ withdrawal Ⓑ addict Ⓒ ban Ⓓ urge

26	_____ : love :: bad : hate			
	Ⓐ gruff	Ⓑ talented	Ⓒ good	Ⓓ confident

27.	take cover : hide :: _____ : flee			
	Ⓐ sleep	Ⓑ talk	Ⓒ stride	Ⓓ run

28	elite : best :: majority : _____			
	Ⓐ most	Ⓑ strongest	Ⓒ average	Ⓓ fewest

29.	sleepy : tired :: crabby : _____			
	Ⓐ grouchy	Ⓑ kind	Ⓒ awake	Ⓓ sad

30	_____ : excellent :: funny : hilarious			
	Ⓐ confident	Ⓑ gruff	Ⓒ talented	Ⓓ good

31.	forbid : prohibit :: overlook : _____			
	Ⓐ allocate	Ⓑ condone	Ⓒ resign	Ⓓ obscure

32.	tired : drowsy :: frantic : _____			
	Ⓐ worried	Ⓑ sad	Ⓒ calm	Ⓓ awake

33.	tiredness : fatigue :: daydreaming : _____			
	Ⓐ guffaw	Ⓑ reverie	Ⓒ turmoil	Ⓓ ramparts

34.	cast : broken bone :: stitches : _____			
	Ⓐ brown	Ⓑ bruise	Ⓒ cut	Ⓓ cover

35.	wince : flinch :: retort : _____			
	Ⓐ flee	Ⓑ question	Ⓒ reply	Ⓓ trick

36.	backstroke : swimming :: javelin : _____			
	Ⓐ polo	Ⓑ diving	Ⓒ track and field	Ⓓ tennis

Study the relationship between the first set of words. Pick the word that completes the second pair with this same relationship.

1. help : hurt :: live : _____

   (A) die (B) love (C) yell (D) help

2. save : _____ :: hurt : protect

   (A) game (B) achieve (C) champion (D) lose

3. music : hear :: art : _____

   (A) sculpt (B) paint (C) smell (D) see

4. disrespect : honor :: forget : _____

   (A) remember (B) replenish (C) hide (D) control

5. _____ : mold :: corn : grind

   (A) wool (B) clay (C) stone (D) wheat

6. litter : ground :: smog : _____

   (A) air (B) rocks (C) circulatory system (D) lakes

7. balk : refuse :: disclose : _____

   (A) attract (B) forgive (C) hide (D) reveal

8. grateful : thank :: sorry : _____

   (A) insult (B) apologize (C) forgive (D) spoil

9. clutch : hold :: hurl : _____

   (A) connect (B) throw (C) secure (D) drop

10. interested : curious :: addicted : _____

    (A) prepared (B) controlled (C) unable to stop (D) hurt

11. warning : alert :: _____ : forecast

    (A) song (B) prediction (C) good luck charm (D) meteorology

12. bird : flock :: tree : _____

    (A) sparrow   (B) forest   (C) grow   (D) fly

13. damaged : hurt :: ill : _____

    (A) happy   (B) sick   (C) angry   (D) scared

14. donate : give :: grieve : _____

    (A) mourn   (B) forget   (C) forgive   (D) revenge

15. help : hurt :: live : _____

    (A) die   (B) love   (C) help   (D) yell

16. blame : forgive :: insult : _____

    (A) alcove   (B) motif   (C) compliment   (D) bawl

17. pitch : throw :: grab : _____

    (A) toss   (B) hold   (C) jog   (D) take

18. bird : flock :: tree : _____

    (A) fly   (B) forest   (C) grow   (D) sparrow

19. conceal : hide :: mingle : _____

    (A) open   (B) manage   (C) teach   (D) mix

20. settle : _____ :: forgive : pardon

    (A) abandon   (B) oblige   (C) pantomime   (D) compromise

21. ground : fog :: sky : _____

    (A) clouds   (B) wind   (C) snow   (D) weather

22. save : _____ :: hurt : protect

    (A) champion   (B) game   (C) lose   (D) achieve

23. imaginable : foreseeable :: required : _____

    (A) jaded   (B) interim   (C) fateful   (D) mandatory

24. extend : make longer :: postpone : _____

    (A) put off   (B) forget   (C) clean   (D) make shorter

25. sunny : sunburn :: cold : _____

    A shiver   **B** snow   **C** frostbite   **D** winter

26. bird : flock :: tree : _____

    A sparrow   **B** grow   **C** forest   **D** fly

27. coax : persuade :: excuse : _____

    A show   **B** forgive   **C** undo   **D** thank

28. vibration : feel :: _____ : hear

    A click   **B** computer   **C** screen   **D** print

29. fruit : ripen :: flower : _____

    A grow   **B** rain   **C** sprout   **D** bloom

30. tear down : build up :: hurt : _____

    A healed   **B** fall   **C** doctor   **D** broken

31. ground : fog :: sky : _____

    A wind   **B** clouds   **C** weather   **D** snow

32. conceal : hide :: mingle : _____

    A open   **B** manage   **C** teach   **D** mix

33. donate : give :: grieve : _____

    A revenge   **B** forget   **C** forgive   **D** mourn

34. blame : accuse :: confess : _____

    A forgive   **B** trust   **C** admit   **D** allow

35. cake : bake :: hamburgers : _____

    A freeze   **B** grill   **C** boil   **D** roast

36. help : hurt :: live : _____

    A yell   **B** help   **C** love   **D** die

(Answer ID # 0969353)

Study the relationship between the first set of words. Pick the word that completes the second pair with this same relationship.

1.   take charge : lead :: choose : _____

   (A) elect   (B) empire   (C) dictator   (D) veto

2.   assist : aid :: alter : _____

   (A) overcome   (B) discriminate   (C) vision   (D) modify

3.   legible : read :: edible : _____

   (A) wear   (B) hear   (C) eat   (D) know

4.   Labor : relax :: Work : _____

   (A) toil   (B) job   (C) unwind   (D) make

5.   _____ : observe :: apprentice : learn

   (A) coach   (B) referee   (C) spectator   (D) volunteer

6.   _____ : kneel :: teeter : wobble

   (A) jump   (B) squeeze   (C) crouch   (D) smirk

7.   _____ : dark :: white : black

   (A) sleep   (B) light   (C) matches   (D) sound

8.   nice : mean :: honest : _____

   (A) fair   (B) lie   (C) burp   (D) truth

9.   truth : confession :: lie : _____

   (A) perjury   (B) obstruction   (C) innocence   (D) interrogation

10.   _____ : make :: concept : idea

   (A) create   (B) build   (C) dream   (D) perish

11.   leather : stitch :: sweater : _____

   (A) knit   (B) tie   (C) scarf   fold

12.   lay : laid :: lie : _____

   (A) laid   (B) lain   (C) lying   (D) lien

13. lay : laid :: lie : _____

  (A) lien   (B) lying   (C) lain   (D) laid

14. endure : sustain :: overcome : _____

  (A) equalize   (B) dream   (C) triumph   (D) oppress

15. truth : honest :: _____ : dishonest

  (A) vandalize   (B) lie   (C) punch   (D) cheat

16. assist : aid :: alter : _____

  (A) vision   (B) discriminate   (C) modify   (D) overcome

17. endure : sustain :: overcome : _____

  (A) dream   (B) equalize   (C) oppress   (D) triumph

18. _____ : learn :: vacation : relax

  (A) clan   (B) school   (C) apples   (D) herd

19. light : violin :: heavy : _____

  (A) trumpet   (B) piano   (C) guitar   (D) clarinet

20. _____ : dark :: white : black

  (A) sleep   (B) matches   (C) sound   (D) light

21. _____ : make :: concept : idea

  (A) dream   (B) perish   (C) build   (D) create

22. blunder : mistake :: peril : _____

  (A) storage   (B) danger   (C) announcement (D) destiny

23. lose : defeat :: win : _____

  (A) time out   (B) surrender   (C) tie   (D) victory

24. lose : defeat :: win : _____

  (A) war   (B) victory   (C) tie   (D) time out

25. heat : evaporation :: light : _____

  (A) water   (B) steam   (C) darkness   (D) photosynthesis

26. _____ : golf ball :: heavy : bowling ball

(A) light	(B) fly	(C) sleep	(D) darkness

27. truth : honest :: _____ : dishonest

(A) vandalize	(B) cheat	(C) punch	(D) lie

28. lay : laid :: lie : _____

(A) lain	(B) laid	(C) lying	(D) lien

29. isolated : alone :: significant : _____

(A) important	(B) overcome	(C) indulgent	(D) together

30. school : learn :: temple : _____

(A) eat	(B) farm	(C) sleep	(D) worship

31. lose : defeat :: win : _____

(A) victory	(B) tie	(C) time out	(D) battle

32. endure : to bear :: overcome : _____

(A) oppress	(B) equalize	(C) dream	(D) triumph

33. scamper : scurry :: walk : _____

(A) slide	(B) lay	(C) roll	(D) stroll

34. _____ : lie :: ponder : think

(A) enchant	(B) create	(C) celebrate	(D) deceive

35. truth : confession :: lie : _____

(A) innocence	(B) interrogation	(C) obstruction	(D) perjury

36. govern : lead :: elect : _____

(A) nation	(B) choose	(C) Washington, DC	(D) President

(Answer ID # 0629440)

Study the relationship between the first set of words. Pick the word that completes the second pair with this same relationship.

1. jest : joke :: squabble : _____

   (A) argue   (B) hide   (C) sneak   (D) play

2. remove : delete :: store : _____

   (A) tab   (B) save   (C) cut   (D) insert

3. bag : carry :: scale : _____

   (A) pay   (B) move   (C) lift   (D) weigh

4. _____ : turn :: saw : cut

   (A) gasoline   (B) cars   (C) tools   (D) wrench

5. ask : question :: _____ : explain

   (A) say   (B) request   (C) inquire   (D) define

6. compose : write :: plead : _____

   (A) join   (B) pant   (C) mock   (D) beg

7. fragrance : odor :: _____ : shine

   (A) shiny   (B) clan   (C) sheen   (D) dirty

8. _____ : repair :: demolished : rebuild

   (A) controlled   (B) feisty   (C) animated   (D) broken

9. explore : look for :: discover : _____

   . find   (B) cover   (C) seek   (D) hide

10. explore : look for :: discover : _____

    . cover   (B) seek   (C) hide   (D) find

11. burnish : _____ :: glisten : shine

    (A) submit   . polish   (C) increase   (D) draw

12. bookstore : buy :: library : _____

    (A) books   (B) borrow   (C) card   (D) pay

13. helps you see in the dark : flashlight :: helps you pick up dirt when you are sweeping : _____

    (A) dustpan   (B) drill   (C) laundry detergent   (D) saw

14. cajole : coax :: ruminate : _____

    (A) think   (B) prove   (C) discuss   (D) fight

15. scene : seen :: beat : _____

    (A) meat   (B) saw   (C) brow   (D) beet

16. wash : soap :: shave : _____

    (A) shaving cream   (B) conditioner   (C) mirror   (D) shampoo

17. quiver : shake :: mangle : _____

    (A) mix   (B) disfigure   (C) plead   (D) support

18. save : lose :: hurt : _____

    (A) find   (B) protect   (C) lose   (D) hurt

19. pay : cash register :: _____ : dressing room

    (A) unpack   (B) return   (C) shake   (D) try on

20. mend : repair :: _____ : speak

    (A) break   (B) shout   (C) say   (D) overhaul

21. dribble : spill :: _____ : shake

    (A) tithe   (B) turret   (C) lance   (D) quiver

22. jest : joke :: squabble : _____

    (A) hide   (B) sneak   (C) play   (D) argue

23. legible : read :: edible : _____

    (A) hear   (B) rest   (C) quench   (D) eat

24. insist : demand :: escort : _____

    (A) call   (B) plead   (C) accompany   (D) review

25. remove : delete :: store : _____

    Ⓐ tab   Ⓑ cut   Ⓒ insert   Ⓓ save

26. save : lose :: hurt : _____

    Ⓐ lose   Ⓑ protect   Ⓒ hurt   Ⓓ find

27. retrieve : _____ :: save : salvage

    Ⓐ trip   Ⓑ sit   Ⓒ heel   Ⓓ fetch

28. wash : soap :: shave : _____

    Ⓐ mirror   Ⓑ shaving cream   Ⓒ conditioner   Ⓓ shampoo

29. want : _____ :: stop : quit

    Ⓐ habit   Ⓑ crave   Ⓒ drug   Ⓓ zeal

30. comprehend : understand :: contribute : _____

    Ⓐ give   Ⓑ seek   Ⓒ learn   Ⓓ prove

31. broken : repair :: demolished : _____

    Ⓐ tear down   Ⓑ rebuild   Ⓒ renovate   Ⓓ debris

32. missing : lost :: seek : _____

    Ⓐ clue   Ⓑ fight   Ⓒ trail   Ⓓ search

33. to give money in exchange for a good or service : pay :: to have money returned for something that has been paid for : _____

    Ⓐ cost   Ⓑ refund   Ⓒ income   Ⓓ tax

34. pay : cash register :: _____ : dressing room

    Ⓐ return   Ⓑ shake   Ⓒ unpack   Ⓓ try on

35. door : key :: email account : _____

    Ⓐ inbox   Ⓑ password   Ⓒ send   Ⓓ delete

36. sun : _____ :: moon : reflect

    Ⓐ cut   Ⓑ texture   Ⓒ unravel   Ⓓ shine

Name _____   QUIZ 6   Date _____

(Answer ID # 0555055)

Study the relationship between the first set of words. Pick the word that completes the second pair with this same relationship.

1. persist : continue :: reek : _____

   Ⓐ stink   Ⓑ remember   Ⓒ appreciate   Ⓓ disappear

2. smite : strike :: ransack : _____

   Ⓐ punish   Ⓑ chase   Ⓒ help   Ⓓ search

3. mountain : hike :: _____ : swim

   Ⓐ rivers   Ⓑ ocean   Ⓒ waves   Ⓓ sand

4. persist : relent :: rile : _____

   Ⓐ recite   Ⓑ soothe   Ⓒ anger   Ⓓ swell

5. step : stride :: racket : _____

   Ⓐ thicket   Ⓑ clamor   Ⓒ frontier   Ⓓ quiver

6. tether : fasten :: clamber : _____

   Ⓐ climb   Ⓑ disrupt   Ⓒ release   Ⓓ strike

7. _____ : gutter ball :: baseball : strike

   Ⓐ volleyball   Ⓑ bowling   Ⓒ dodge ball   Ⓓ softball

8. _____ : shrink :: get larger : swell

   Ⓐ disappear   Ⓑ get smaller   Ⓒ get louder   Ⓓ stay the same size

9. a group that works together : team :: a storage place : _____

   Ⓐ sweep   Ⓑ cache   Ⓒ tundra   Ⓓ wick

10. tumbleweed : roll :: river : _____

    Ⓐ flow   Ⓑ wilt   Ⓒ break   Ⓓ spread

11. drink : sip :: eat : _____

    Ⓐ swell   Ⓑ growl   Ⓒ nibble   Ⓓ slurp

12. to gather together : cluster :: to clap : _____

| Ⓐ strike | Ⓑ applaud | Ⓒ jeer | Ⓓ huddle |

13. river : flow :: tumbleweed : _____

| Ⓐ break | Ⓑ roll | Ⓒ wilt | Ⓓ spread |

14. hot : sweat :: cold : _____

| Ⓐ fever | Ⓑ itch | Ⓒ shiver | Ⓓ hiccup |

15. sit : stand :: _____ : run

| Ⓐ write | Ⓑ hide | Ⓒ walk | Ⓓ forgive |

16. dirt : hills :: sand : _____

| Ⓐ swells | Ⓑ ditches | Ⓒ drifts | Ⓓ dunes |

17. sweep : broom :: scrub : _____

| Ⓐ clean | Ⓑ sponge | Ⓒ soap | Ⓓ vacuum cleaner |

18. a group that works together : team :: a storage place : _____

| Ⓐ tundra | Ⓑ sweep | Ⓒ cache | Ⓓ wick |

19. step : stride :: racket : _____

| Ⓐ frontier | Ⓑ thicket | Ⓒ quiver | Ⓓ clamor |

20. strike : bowling :: home run : _____

| Ⓐ hockey | Ⓑ golf | Ⓒ tennis | Ⓓ baseball |

21. mountain : hike :: _____ : swim

| Ⓐ ocean | Ⓑ rivers | Ⓒ waves | Ⓓ sand |

22. set clocks ahead for Daylight Savings Time : _____ :: set clocks back for Standard time : fall

| Ⓐ rabbit | Ⓑ seed | Ⓒ May | Ⓓ spring |

23. mimic : imitate :: flatter : _____

| Ⓐ motif | Ⓑ compliment | Ⓒ alcove | Ⓓ sublet |

24. soccer : goal :: football : _____

| Ⓐ strike | Ⓑ touchdown | Ⓒ hole-in-one | Ⓓ home run |

25.	stand : stood :: sit : _____		
	Ⓐ pit	Ⓑ down	Ⓒ sat
26.	hot : sweat :: cold : _____		
	Ⓐ hiccup	Ⓑ shiver	Ⓒ fever	Ⓓ itch
27.	catch : grab :: toss : _____		
	Ⓐ stand	Ⓑ backpack	Ⓒ carry	Ⓓ pitch
28.	tag : running :: "Marco Polo" : _____		
	Ⓐ yelling	Ⓑ spinning	Ⓒ skiing	Ⓓ swimming
29.	listen : ear :: smell : _____		
	Ⓐ hear	. bad	Ⓒ stink	Ⓓ nose
30.	_____ : gutter ball :: baseball : strike		
	Ⓐ volleyball	Ⓑ bowling	Ⓒ dodge ball	Ⓓ softball
31.	arson : setting a fire :: burglary : _____		
	Ⓐ complaining	Ⓑ morals	Ⓒ stealing	Ⓓ running
32.	the distance traveled when taking a long step : stride :: a unit of measurement used by sailors to measure distance : _____		
	Ⓐ breaker	Ⓑ league	Ⓒ pallet	Ⓓ rudder
33.	mountain : hike :: _____ : swim		
	Ⓐ rivers	Ⓑ sand	Ⓒ waves	Ⓓ ocean
34.	flourish : _____ :: perspire : sweat		
	Ⓐ migration	Ⓑ wave	Ⓒ flag	Ⓓ trail
35.	a group that works together : team :: a storage place : _____		
	Ⓐ cache	Ⓑ wick	Ⓒ sweep	Ⓓ tundra
36	sweep : broom :: scrub : _____		
	Ⓐ soap	Ⓑ sponge	Ⓒ vacuum cleaner	Ⓓ clean

(Answer ID # 0777964)

Study the relationship between the first set of words. Pick the word that completes the second pair with this same relationship.

1. put money into a bank : deposit :: take money out of a bank : _____

    Ⓐ withdraw   Ⓑ cash   Ⓒ loan   Ⓓ teller

2. to inspire : motivate :: to lift up : _____

    Ⓐ scope   Ⓑ elevate   Ⓒ aid   Ⓓ tread

3. bike : ride :: ball : _____

    Ⓐ buy   Ⓑ sit   Ⓒ throw   Ⓓ push

4. transfix : _____ :: cogitate : think

    Ⓐ focus   Ⓑ search   Ⓒ fascinate   Ⓓ trick

5. unkempt : bedraggled :: _____ : flustered

    Ⓐ upset   Ⓑ dishonorable   Ⓒ mischievous   Ⓓ rude

6. _____ : fall :: sway : swing

    Ⓐ dull   Ⓑ green   Ⓒ flail   · droop

7. mingle : mix :: weep : _____

    Ⓐ cry   Ⓑ correct   Ⓒ fight   Ⓓ greet

8. addled : confused :: distraught : _____

    Ⓐ upset   Ⓑ rude   Ⓒ dishonorable   Ⓓ mischievous

9. St. : street :: SW : _____

    Ⓐ sidewalk   Ⓑ swings   Ⓒ southwest   Ⓓ swimming pool

10. seafarer : sailing :: merchant : _____

    Ⓐ weaving   Ⓑ writing   Ⓒ cooking   Ⓓ selling

11. to touch gently : caress :: to close tightly : _____

    Ⓐ tread   Ⓑ draft   Ⓒ clench   Ⓓ mount

12. emancipate : free :: secede : _____

    Ⓐ withdraw   Ⓑ enslave   Ⓒ capture   Ⓓ correct

13. _____ : fall :: sway : swing

    (A) droop   (B) flail   (C) green   (D) dull

14. to touch gently : caress :: to close tightly : _____

    (A) clench   (B) tread   (C) draft   (D) mount

15. instruct : _____ :: confess : admit

    (A) change   (B) give   (C) play   (D) teach

16. comprehend : understand :: ponder : _____

    (A) run   (B) prove   (C) think   (D) hold

17. _____ : idea :: urge : desire

    (A) thought   (B) practice   (C) field trip   (D) tattoo

18. upset : calm :: nervous : _____

    (A) angry   (B) worried   (C) relaxed   (D) sad

19. withdraw : secede :: control : _____

    (A) address   (B) unite   (C) indenture   (D) dominate

20. transfix : _____ :: cogitate : think

    (A) search   (B) fascinate   (C) focus   (D) trick

21. to express sorrow with tears : weep :: to express displeasure with words : _____

    (A) quell   (B) sneer   (C) humiliate   (D) complain

22. blade : carving :: loom : _____

    (A) writing   (B) cooking   (C) gardening   (D) weaving

23. unkempt : bedraggled :: _____ : flustered

    (A) rude   (B) dishonorable   (C) mischievous   (D) upset

24. baseball : throw :: basketball : _____

    (A) dribble   (B) kick   (C) slide   (D) push

25. instruct : _____ :: confess : admit

    (A) teach   (B) give   (C) play   (D) change

26.	smile : _____ :: tear : cry			
	(A) laugh	(B) hold	(C) whistle	(D) cry
27.	teach : educate :: beckon : _____			
	(A) process	(B) understand	(C) communicate	(D) summon
28.	tend : care for :: _____ : teach			
	(A) car	(B) leash	(C) train	(D) collar
29.	bike : ride :: ball : _____			
	(A) buy	. push	(C) throw	(D) sit
30.	Instructor : teaches :: Engineer : _____			
	(A) designs	(B) plants	(C) grades	(D) judges
31.	swings : swing back and forth :: monkey bars : _____			
	(A) turn	(B) lift	(C) climb	(D) nuts
32.	_____ : fingerprint :: tire : tread			
	(A) wrist	(B) leg	(C) finger	(D) arm
33.	throw : baseball :: kick : _____			
	(A) door	(B) dog	(C) basketball	(D) soccer ball
34.	addled : confused :: distraught : _____			
	(A) dishonorable	(B) rude	(C) upset	(D) mischievous
35.	withdraw : secede :: control : _____			
	(A) unite	(B) indenture	(C) dominate	(D) address
36.	distraught : _____ :: surly : rude			
	(A) dishonorable	(B) mischievous	(C) upset	(D) rude